INSIDE–OUT
MARKETING

How to Create an Internal
Marketing Strategy

Michael Dunmore

KOGAN
PAGE

First published in 2002

Apart from any fair dealing for the purposes of research or private study, or criticism or review, as permitted under the Copyright, Designs and Patents Act 1988, this publication may only be reproduced, stored or transmitted, in any form or by any means, with the prior permission in writing of the publishers, or in the case of reprographic reproduction in accordance with the terms and licences issued by the CLA. Enquiries concerning reproduction outside these terms should be sent to the publishers at the undermentioned address:

Kogan Page Limited
120 Pentonville Road
London N1 9JN
UK

© Michael Dunmore, 2002

The right of Michael Dunmore to be identified as the author of this work has been asserted by him in accordance with the Copyright, Designs and Patents Act 1988.

British Library Cataloguing in Publication Data

A CIP record for this book is available from the British Library.

ISBN 0 7494 3663 8

Typeset by JS Typesetting Ltd, Wellingborough, Northants
Printed and bound in Great Britain by Biddles Ltd, Guildford and King's Lynn
www.biddles.co.uk

For Sheila, Gordon, Hilary, Caroline and Jamie

Contents

Acknowledgements

There are many people I wish to thank for the help, support and contributions that made it possible for me to write this book, whether directly or indirectly. Firstly, I wish to thank Professor Karin Newman of the Middlesex University Business School for her encouragement and direction, and for providing me with access to information that assisted me in completing the manuscript.

This book includes many references to the writings and presentations of practitioners and academics from a broad range of sources. I trust I have interpreted their writings in an appropriate context. Whilst it is impossible to thank all these people directly, I have attempted to provide full listings of sources of information at the end of each chapter. Any errors or omissions are purely accidental, and for which I apologize unreservedly. In particular, there are two reference sources that provide foundations to almost every chapter of this book. Therefore I wish to express particular gratitude to Professor Richard Lynch of Middlesex University Business School for writing the book *Corporate Strategy* and Valarie Zeithaml and Mary Jo Bitner for *Services Marketing — Integrating customer focus across the firm*. Readers wising to explore further business strategy and service marketing may well find these to be valuable texts.

In addition to drawing upon published information and texts, I have been very fortunate in being provided with the help and encouragement of many people. In particular I wish to thank Trevor Silvester for his enthusiasm and ideas, Alan Calder for his leadership, Peter Warner for sharing his knowledge of the legal sector and Steven Finnemore for his insights into the mobile telephony market.

Lastly, I wish to thank Caroline Kunzler for patiently reorganizing a year of her life so I could complete what follows.

Introduction

AIMS

1. To describe the structure and aim of this book;

2. to introduce internal marketing, internal marketing strategy (IMS) and the components of IMS;

3. to show why IMS is potentially a major driver of business success from the inside out.

BACKGROUND

The approach of this book is to look at some of the strengths that can be built inside an organization on a journey to business success. Looking at a business from the inside out means trying to make sure that what happens inside an organization is integrated and aligned with corporate purpose and corporate strategy. Dangers can be floating at all levels inside an organization just as they can be in the external environment.

When Gerald Ratner of the jewellery retailer Ratners stood up in front of an audience and said his company's products were 'crap', he made a huge hole in the company's bottom line and his career. The media feeding frenzy that followed his comments damaged the reputation of Mr Ratner, the company's share price and public confidence in his company. No wonder that he departed shortly afterwards.

For this book, building strength within an organization means looking at a business from a perspective of the components of internal marketing. IMS can be a critical contributor to achieving and sustaining competitive advantage through its integration with corporate strategy.

THE PURPOSE OF THIS BOOK

The purpose of this book is to provide an understanding of internal marketing and the seven components of IMS. Continuous improvements in organizational performance are fundamental to individual and team progression, and internal marketing can be a major driver of change and enhanced performance. Being able to understand and manage the interrelated aspects of strategy, change, processes, people management and knowledge management is a core management competence in the knowledge-based economy. Also, an understanding of the seven components of IMS provides a greater comprehension of the issues faced by colleagues in a broad range of business disciplines and some of the tools they may use to manage them. Finding solutions to most organizational problems requires people from different teams working together. Developing teams that can work together in a coherent and integrated way towards common goals and outcomes is a foundation to the implementation of a successful IMS.

With the aim of providing an overview of the components of IMS, it is not possible to present an in-depth analysis of theory, strategy and tactics for each component. Whilst HR strategy, for example, is an important aspect of IMS, this book will only concentrate upon the key aspects of HR theory and practice as they relate to IMS. Similarly, this book cannot provide an extensive review of corporate strategy development.

THE STRUCTURE OF THIS BOOK

Each chapter of the book focuses on one of the seven components of IMS, though links are made to other components. The seven components are not mutually exclusive as there are areas of overlap. This emphasizes the importance of an integrated approach to IMS. For example, attempting to define the boundaries and crossovers of internal communication and knowledge management may be of little practical relevance. What is more important is recognizing how these two components and others can be integrated to achieve synergistic improvements in organizational performance. Each chapter is concerned with one of the seven components of IMS:

1. *Vision, mission, values, positioning and personality*
   Corporate vision and its supporting statements provide direct links between business purpose, strategy, values, communications and individual behaviour. A common set of values should crystallize individual behaviour within common goals and frameworks towards the achievement of an organization's purpose.

2. *Corporate strategy*
   Increasingly, organizations consider internal strengths and how these strengths can be leveraged through strategy to achieve sustainable competitive advantage. Concentration upon core competencies and learning processes provides a link between external market forces and activities occurring within organizations.

3. *Processes, service standards and measures*
   Appropriate processes, service standards and measures are critical to the effective delivery of strategy and a brand experience. Calculating gaps between existing and required performance is key to developing a range of actions and measures that link functional, team and individual performance to strategic objectives and performance improvements.

4. *Knowledge management*
   The successful creation, storage, and communication of knowledge are critical success factors for organizations that rely on the 'brainpower' of their employees for innovation, agility and competitive advantage. Effective knowledge management requires that

organizations develop a culture where people contribute to organizational success by volunteering their knowledge, whilst creating systems and environments that encourage the management and communication of appropriate information and knowledge.

5. *Internal communication*
   Successfully communicating business strategy, managing change and motivating people are key foundations to organizational success, providing leadership and internal communication with a strategic role in improving corporate performance.

6. *HR strategy*
   People provide organizational success and it is only by recruiting, developing, rewarding and retaining the right people that an organization can build its reserves of human and intellectual capital. But the right people must also be able to cooperate in cross-functional teams and deliver a brand experience if customers are to have their expectations met.

7. *Integrating internal, interactive and external marketing*
   Organizations should communicate with stakeholder groups using consistent, coherent behaviour and messages to avoid confusion regarding what the company or brand stands for. An integrated approach is therefore required for internal, interactive and external marketing activities to employees, partners, suppliers, customers and other stakeholders.

EXPLORING INTERNAL MARKETING

To put it simply, internal marketing is largely about the things people do within an organization that contribute to the achievement of its purpose. Everybody has an influence upon internal marketing and a part to play in it. The trick is to be working in an organization where it is possible to positively influence the present and future of the organization from the inside – assuming that is how you wish to lead your life and the opportunities are there. The fact that some people do not wish to live in this way is one of the challenges and potential failings of internal marketing. The tough stuff in organizations is always about people and their behaviour, and that includes the people at the very top. Machines and systems are relatively easy to change. Similarly, leaders of some organizations may not wish to engage in a strategy that is largely people-based. For organizations that are exclusively driven by the meeting of monthly or quarterly financial targets, it may be that internal marketing strategy will have little appeal to its leaders. Internal marketing means engaging with an organization's people (the internal marketplace) and its partners (the intermediate marketplace) as a route to improving performance in the external marketplace. This means going beyond seeing people as whipping posts with targets attached to them, to a perception that recognizes the community aspects of organizations and their broader relationships.

The importance of internal marketing

With the growth in significance of the service sector and the knowledge-based economy, internal marketing is increasingly important to organizations. However, the value of IMS is not restricted to organizations that are involved in the marketing of services. Many products have service-related aspects to them and the internal drivers for success in service environments are relevant to organizations that market products. For example, a car dealership sells a product (cars), but the major profit centres will probably be in the parts and servicing areas, which are service-based. Customer experiences with these departments may have a significant impact upon the likelihood of a person repurchasing a car from that dealership.

Also, the importance some organizations appear to attach to their people is reflected in the recent fashion for 'employer branding', where organizations have the aim of implementing policies that attract, develop and retain excellent employees. These organizations are actively marketing themselves as attractive places to work whilst encouraging employees to behave in ways that support business strategy and values. Some employers are trying to be as flexible with their employees as they are with their customers. The overall aim of this strategy is to develop employees who 'live the brand', act as company advocates and ultimately impact positively on corporate profitability. This is based on the view that satisfied employees create satisfied customers who are more loyal and therefore create more profit for the company.

Human resources strategy is an aspect of IMS, but attempting to be an employer of choice involves more than human resource (HR) policies relating to employee recruitment, development and retention. If people actively select roles in organizations where they have choice and the opportunity to grow, learn, challenge and reap rewards from success, then they will require structures, systems, processes, standards and communications that will support them in working at their best. They will also need to be working in a culture that supports employee development and retention. An internal communications manager with the Nokia Corporation described the company as having a hard shell but a soft centre. By this the manager meant that getting a job in Nokia was tough because of the company's stringent recruitment standards, but once you were in, life was good. The organization provided systems, processes, challenges, opportunities and communications that encouraged high performance, but internal checks to ensure people were not pushed too far and suffered as a result.

The challenge of internal marketing

If internal marketing is largely about the things people do in organizations that contribute to their success, and that success is in part determined by organizational culture, then a key aspect of internal marketing strategy will be the creation of an appropriate culture in which internal marketing activities can thrive. This culture will be characterized as one where change is a proactive activity that is wired into an organization's processes and people.

However, it is important to be realistic about the speed and degree of change an organization or its leaders can tolerate, or wish for, and how success might be measured. For large 'bricks and mortar' organizations it might take several years to implement a meaningful 'change programme', depending upon the approach adopted. (And this assumes the marketplace provides the luxury of such a long period of adaptation in response to environmental and competitive change.) Such long periods may mean that by the time a programme has been implemented, market or environmental conditions will have changed versus the original aims of the programme, and so the process commences again. Consequently, it is better to view internal marketing as a voyage rather than a destination. That voyage will be far more comfortable and may involve some sightseeing if internal marketing is wired into organizational culture and strategy rather than something that is done from time to time depending upon the economic cycle or structural change.

Consequently, whilst this book presents examples of how different organizations have tried to manage some or all of the seven components of IMS, it is important to place these examples in the context of a specific organization's problems and a particular organizational culture. IMS does not come in a box as a prescriptive, commodity solution. No two organizations are the same, and what has worked in one organization may not work in another. IMS is a people-based approach to performance improvement and will involve analysis, strategy, teamwork, intuition, patience, experimentation, learning, influencing, lobbying, pragmatism and change if it is to be successful.

Those who will find internal marketing of value

Internal marketing is of relevance to people working in private, non-profit and public sector organizations. The inclusion of the word 'marketing' might suggest IMS is something best left to a marketing department, but IMS should be the concern of everybody in an organization. Peter Drucker described marketing as something so basic it cannot be considered a separate function, and that marketing is about how a business is seen as a final result by its customers.

IMS might be viewed as the application of Drucker's assertion using the resources existing within an organization, with the aim of providing a seamless approach to the way in which people experience that organization. That experience includes physical contact with people, the working environment, business processes and the organization's communications.

Internal marketing draws on thought and practice from many management disciplines including marketing (particularly service marketing theory), customer service, HR, knowledge management (KM), information technology (IT), corporate strategy, operations management and quality management. Therefore internal marketing is not a 'wholly-owned subsidiary' of marketing theory and practice or the exclusive domain of marketers. Internal marketing is an approach to business strategy and performance improvement that relies on the integration of functional strategies across an organization and is therefore of relevance to everybody working in an organization.

A THEORETICAL BACKGROUND TO IMS

The foundations of internal marketing

There is no universally agreed definition of internal marketing and internal marketing is an emergent area of management theory and practice. A review of some of the key literature on the subject of internal marketing over the last two decades or so provides a number of different, but not necessarily conflicting, approaches. These approaches can be viewed as adding different contributions to a growing range of perspectives on internal marketing theory and practice. This evolution of internal marketing can be illustrated through a quick overview of each of the seven components. Each section will be developed in greater depth in later chapters.

Linking people and internal marketing

Some of the earliest contributions to considerations of internal marketing were related to the roles of people in the delivery of services. This is in part linked to a 'growth' in the marketing mix resulting from new contributions to service marketing theory.

The marketing mix

Since the early 1960s, marketers had been using a 'four P' marketing mix of Product, Price, Promotion and Place (distribution channels and the place of sale). Marketers attempt to identify the relative impacts of changes to their Product, Pricing, Promotion and Place on the meeting of objectives, and then develop the optimum approach for delivering their strategy. However, the four Ps approach proved to be limited in its application to the marketing of services. Services involve direct contact between customers and employees as well as processes to support the delivery of that service, and people and processes are not addressed through the four Ps mix.

A further challenge is that unlike products, many services are largely intangible. For example, teaching is an intangible service and is therefore difficult to evaluate immediately. The value or tangibility of the service may only become apparent some time after a teaching session has taken place, such as achieving an increased salary following studying for a MBA. Similarly, buying a ticket for a flight does not 'buy' a seat on an aircraft. The seat is 'consumed' or rented during the flight and then given up when leaving the aircraft. Unlike a product bought in a supermarket, for example, the flight/seat is consumed at the point of delivery, and not taken home and stored in a cupboard or refrigerator for later consumption.

In response to the limitations of the four Ps mix, Booms and Bitner (1981) proposed a seven P marketing mix. The seven Ps service marketing mix included the four Ps, plus People, Physical Evidence and Processes. To return to the example of a flight, People would include people customers came into contact with as a part of their flight experience, including check-in staff, the cabin crew and fellow passengers. Physical Evidence would include the seat on an aircraft, the standard of dress of flight staff and the aircraft environment. Processes include the things that create and deliver a service to a customer at a required level of service quality, such as ensuring the aircraft was fuelled and airworthy for take off, the timely supply of necessary food and drinks, the level of courtesy of flight staff, cleaning the aircraft and so forth.

The seven Ps marketing mix also provided a further important implication. Because the seven Ps mix included considerations of People, Physical Evidence and Processes, it meant that marketers would need to work closely with colleagues in HR, operations, IT, quality and other teams if the required experience was to be delivered to consumers. Therefore marketing is not the 'sole responsibility' of marketers, but an activity involving an entire organization.

The recognition of the importance of people to the delivery of services encouraged greater emphasis on the importance of recruiting, retaining, training and rewarding the right people. Therefore HR strategy is a key component of internal marketing.

Cross-functional working

Gilmore and Carson (1995) provided further bridges between HR, marketing and organizational behaviour by identifying six components of internal marketing, or internal marketing activities:

1. the internal and external marketing interface;

2. the application of the marketing mix to internal customers;

3. the use of marketing training and internal communications methods to engage staff in their role in the organization;

4. the involvement and empowering of employees regarding their relationships with customers;

5. the development of cross-functional participation;

6. the integration of responsibility for internal marketing across functions.

Gilmore and Carson emphasized the need for people to break down their functional silos and work together in developing and implementing internal marketing activities. A further implication is the need to engage staff in their role within the organization. With the importance of people in the delivery of a service experience to customers, it is critical that people behave in ways that are consistent with 'living the brand'. If employee behaviour is not consistent with brand values and service standards, there may be a gap between customer expectations and experiences of the service. Where the service experience does not live up to customer expectations, the customer may be lost to a competitor.

Linking processes, service standards and measures to internal marketing

Early considerations of internal marketing included the views that people should be happy in their jobs if they are to serve their customers effectively and that people within an organization will also act as customers to colleagues. Through this approach, employees are viewed as internal customers and their jobs as internal products. Jobs should therefore be attractive to employees. A further important consideration is that jobs should attract and motivate people to perform whilst meeting the needs of colleagues and the objectives of the organization.

Service quality

Closely linked to views regarding the importance of people to the delivery of services are considerations of internal and external service quality and concepts adopted within total quality management. Zeithaml and Bitner (2000, p 81) describe service quality as: '... a critical component of customer perceptions. In the case of pure services, service quality will be the dominant element in customer's evaluations. In cases where customer service or services are offered in combination with a physical product, service quality may also be very critical in determining customer satisfaction'.

Customer-facing staff require support from colleagues in non-customer-facing roles. The quality of services provided by supporting employees (internal service quality) has an impact upon the quality of service the customer-facing employee is able to provide to customers (external service quality).

From this it follows that if all employees have high levels of customer-consciousness and are service-oriented, higher levels of service quality can be provided by an organization. Building from these considerations of service quality in the early 1980s, a model that linked internal service quality to revenue growth and profitability was presented in 1994.

The Service-Profit Chain

Heskett *et al* presented the Service-Profit Chain in 1994 following a study that showed a positive relationship between internal service quality and increased profits. The Service-Profit Chain identifies a 'chain of events' that stretches from inside the company to its customers. The Chain begins with internal service quality. Put simply this means that if people are providing high levels of internal service quality through their relationships with colleagues, this will improve employee satis-faction, which in turn has a positive effect upon employee loyalty, and so on through the chain to improved profitability.

Internal Service Quality
↓
Employee Satisfaction
↓
Employee Loyalty
↓
External Service Quality
↓
Customer Satisfaction
↓
Customer Loyalty
↓
Revenue Growth and Profitability

Figure 0.1 *The Service-Profit Chain*

James Farrant supports the conclusions of the Service-Profit Chain following a British study:

> *Increasingly links have been established between staff and customer satis-*
> *faction and the bottom line. A recent study by the Institute of Employment*
> *Studies has identified that, in one retail chain, stores where the staff*
> *were more satisfied generated £200,000 more in sales per month than in*
> *other stores. Other research is demonstrating a correlation between*
> *progressive studies in the management of employees, including good*
> *internal communications, and increased organizational performance.*
>
> (Farrant, 2000)

Because of the importance of internal service quality and employee satisfaction to external service quality, revenue growth and profitability, some organizations have made employee satisfaction a key priority. For example, Richard Branson stated the following regarding Virgin:

> *We give top priorities to the interests of our staff; second priority to*
> *those of our customers; third to our shareholders. This is not only a*
> *reflection of the importance of our people, it is also the most positive way*
> *of fitting together these three priorities. Working backwards the interests*
> *of our shareholders depend on high levels of customer satisfaction. . .*
> *which depends on high standards of service from our people, which*
> *depends on happy staff who are proud of the company they work for.*
>
> (Macrae et al, 1996; Ind, 2001)

Measuring service quality

Given the importance of internal and external service quality, it follows that service quality should be measured and improvements made, where necessary, to ensure internal and external customers are provided with the required levels of service quality. 'Gaps' theory provides valuable input to the measurement of service quality, the creation of service standards and the development of strategies to fill gaps between existing and required levels of service quality. The Parasuraman, Zeithaml and Berry (PZB) Gaps Model of Service Quality (1985) is a particularly valuable diagnostic tool for identifying gaps in service quality.

In short, the PZB Model provides a diagnostic approach for identifying where gaps in service quality exist and pointers to the development of strategies to close gaps. These gaps can be related to every component of IMS. Consequently the model provides a diagnostic framework on which to build an effective IMS. By considering service standards and measures in combination with other management tools such as benchmarking and self-assessment, a quantitative approach to IMS can be developed that is directly linked to corporate strategy.

Measuring intellectual capital

With the growing number of organizations relying for their wealth and market value on the knowledge of their employees, the identification, measurement and leveraging of knowledge and intellectual capital is of great importance. For example, Skandia, the financial services company, has developed an approach to the identification and measurement of intellectual capital. Skandia recognizes the importance of its intangible assets and the need to grow them as a source of competitive advantage. These intangible assets include the 'brainpower' of its employees, its ability to innovate, its processes and its relationships with its customers and intermediaries.

Considerations of the 'value' of employees through a broad range of measures, and the management of relationships outside the organization, extend considerations of service quality and other aspects of internal marketing from a process to a strategic level.

Linking internal communication to internal marketing

The importance of developing or enhancing customer-consciousness and a service orientation in employees creates considerations of culture, how the internal market might be communicated with and the messages that might be communicated. Many writers in the 1980s and 1990s considered the application of the marketing mix to the internal marketplace (ie employees), as well as the segmentation of employees into distinct groups, with resulting implications for communications.

Applying the marketing mix within an organization implies that marketing techniques used in external marketing can also be applied to employees. An example would be the use of communication strategy within the internal marketplace. This means considering targeted employees as potential consumers who can be influenced to adopt particular attitudes or behaviours that are considered desirable by other employees (mostly senior managers). It also raises the obvious question as to what happens if employees do not wish to 'buy' the products they are offered in an organization. This is a frequent consideration when employees are faced with revised roles as a result of organizational change.

Marketers use segmentation as a strategic tool by developing marketing strategy and communications based upon targeting defined groups of consumers. Segmentation means breaking down a market into smaller, accessible groups with common, identifiable characteristics. The application of segmentation to internal markets means it is necessary to consider the aims of IMS, who is directing it and at whom. Is a particular objective related to an entire organization, a geographic area, a business unit, a particular department or a particular group of employees? These considerations will also impact the targeting, media, messages, symbols, language and measures used in internal marketing and communications.

Strategic internal communication

Thoughts of messages, language and so forth in relation to internal communication are tactical considerations. However, it is important to consider the importance of internal communications at a strategic level. With the impact of globalization, overcapacity in market segments, increased competitiveness and technological change, organizations have responded to environmental turbulence by adopting a variety of approaches. These approaches have included business process re-engineering, downsizing/delayering, increased employee empowerment and a variety of other programmes that reflect changing fashions in management practice.

One consistent aspect of all of these approaches is the need to create change within an organization. If a company is to follow a new direction or strategy, it is important that employees know what that strategy is, why it is important, what their role is in its implementation, how their performance will be measured and what is in it for them (both logically and emotionally). This lengthy process stretches from the corporate vision to individual comprehension and action. It may also involve stages of communication in which employees contribute to the development of an organization's vision and strategy.

It is also important to place communication in a context that includes behaviour. People absorb communication through the spoken and written word, body language and other cues. Leadership and communication is not simply about stating messages at a presentation or through a corporate video. If the ultimate aim of communication is to change behaviour, then the behaviour of leaders and others is critical in providing examples of desired behaviour.

Therefore internal communication has a strategic role to play within an organization. Sir Martin Sorrell, Chief Executive of WPP Group plc, illustrated the importance of this role in a lecture to the Marketing Society in June 2000. At the time of writing, WPP was the world's largest marketing services group. Sir Martin spoke of three key challenges for CEOs, one of these challenges being internal communications: 'In our view this is critical to focus on, probably more so than external communications. This is possibly a dangerous thing for me to say, given the nature of our business, but I think it is very important to realise. A difficult task facing most CEOs is explaining strategic and structural change – not externally to customers but internally to the people who work in the company'.

Linking knowledge management to internal marketing

Intellectual capital and organizational knowledge are increasingly viewed as key drivers of competitive advantage and wealth. This wealth might be found in learning developed from experience, informal networks, unique processes and technologies, patents and legal contracts and a variety of other sources. As companies develop knowledge, they need to ensure that relevant information and knowledge are made tangible in some form and communicated to relevant people so that further value can be created.

Therefore, in considering information, knowledge and knowledge management as a part of internal marketing, it is possible to identify close links between knowledge management and HR strategy (recruiting, rewarding, retaining, and developing people), internal communications and IT (providing people with access to the information they require to learn, challenge and innovate and the creation of a culture where the volunteering of knowledge is a common occurrence) and service standards and measures (measuring whether its strategy of developing its intellectual and human capital is working).

Linking external and interactive marketing to internal marketing

So far, considerations of communications have been limited to communications occurring within an organization. However, it is important not to see internal communication in isolation from other forms of organizational communication. Ideally, an organization will provide integrated, coherent messages to its employees, customers, end consumers and other stakeholder groups. If there is incongruity in these messages it is possible that people will be confused and corporate or brand reputation may be damaged.

For simplicity we can identify three areas of marketing activity: internal marketing (marketing to employees and service providers/ partners if third parties are also used), interactive marketing (when the customer interacts with the organization) and external marketing (marketing to customers and other stakeholders). These interrelationships are identified through the Services Marketing Triangle, as proposed by Bitner, based upon the work of Gronroos and Kotler (Zeithaml and Bitner, 2000, p 16).

The interdependence of internal, interactive and external marketing can be illustrated through the example of an organization that provides consulting services, with these services provided by some of its employees and associate consultants. The employees and associates can be grouped together as providers. Internal marketing, through the delivery of required levels of internal service quality, provides customer-facing employees and associates with the processes and support required to deliver the required level of service quality to customers. The delivery of services involves interactive marketing through the interactions between customers and providers. Through realistic external communications, the company should shape customer expectations, so their perceptions of service delivery are matched to expectations, or customer expectations exceeded. In simple terms, the company should match its communications with what it delivers. If the company over-promises to customers, then those customers are likely to be disappointed with the service they receive. Similarly, the company must communicate with its providers in a consistent way to avoid disenchantment, which may in turn negatively influence the standard of service provided.

Therefore, the company's internal marketing activity must be consistent and integrated with its external and interactive marketing activities. Failing to achieve this will lead to inconsistent communications and behaviour and undermine the delivery of a consistent brand experience to required level of service quality.

The impact of technology

With the impact of technological change and the growing emphasis placed on customer and supplier relationship management, interactive marketing has become of increased importance. Provider/partner and customer extranets draw relationships closer to the internal marketplace through the supply of information or other value-adding services. In turn, customers and suppliers can be part of new product development processes. Bernard Liautaud, president and CEO of Business Objects, provides this insight to the importance of extranets:

Transparency is in. Barriers are out. Traditionally, a company's means of doing business were fiercely guarded. The company would endeavour to insulate its processes from the scrutiny of its business customers to prevent those customers from uncovering a piece of intelligence that might be used to negotiate a better price. Or worse, the information might prompt the customer to take its business to a competitor.

The Internet is forcing this to change. B2B e-commerce is rewriting those old rules. Companies are being forced to become more transparent as customers and business partners become more demanding and have more information at their disposal to negotiate optimal contracts. More and more, we are seeing companies using e-business intelligence over extranets to provide that transparency. Just as they empowered their employees with information, they are now extending their information democracies by placing information embassies within the borders of their customers (providing customer care extranets) or suppliers and partners (providing supply chain extranets).

(Liautaud and Hammon, 2000)

This blurring of the parameters of internal, intermediate and external markets illustrates the importance of integrating internal, interactive and external marketing and relationship management.

Internal relationship management

The importance of relationship management was emphasized by Varey and Lewis who carried out a review of literature on the subject of internal marketing. Their conclusions included that internal marketing should be viewed as internal relationship management. They also stated that an internal customer relationship management system has a number of key features:

▌ *The 'voice' of the customer is incorporated into product/service decisions.*

▌ *Customer commitment is earned in a 'social' contract.*

▌ *There is an open exchange of ideas for mutual gain.*

▌ *Employees develop a greater identification with the corporation (just as the supplying corporation must become more customer-oriented).*

▌ *Customers are involved in product design, production and service.*

▮ *There is a close partnership between suppliers and customers.*

▮ *Customers are viewed as individual people and so are 'value' providers.*

▮ *There is a continuous interaction and dialogue between suppliers and customers.*

▮ *There is a focus on discovering, creating, arousing and responding to customer needs.*

▮ *Relationships are viewed as enterprise assets.*

▮ *There is a systematic collection and dissemination of customer information (detailing and negotiating requirements, expectations, needs, attitudes and satisfaction).*

▮ *Communications in the internal market are targeted through segmentation analysis.*

(Varey and Lewis, 1999, p 941)

This list of key features illustrates how internal marketing must be linked with an understanding of the external environment and relationships. This approach based upon internal relationship management also means that internal marketing cannot be seen purely from a perspective of economic transactions, but that considerations of social systems, communications, knowledge and learning will also be of importance.

Linking corporate strategy to internal marketing

Organizations have a broad range of tools they can use to help select the strategy they decide to pursue. With the increased need to act swiftly and perhaps globally in the implementation of strategy, some traditional models of strategy development have become less popular as they have tended to be prescriptive. For fast-moving marketplaces, such as online services or mobile telecommunications, a more emergent approach may be required, with a blurring of strategy development, implementation and amendment, as changes occur in the market and experiential learning takes place.

In addition to emergent approaches to strategy development and implementation, recent developments in strategic thought have also shown an increasing focus upon factors, existing within organizations, that can lead to the creation of sustainable competitive advantage. This is not to say that these internal strengths are not viewed in relation to customer needs and a changing environment, but that considerations of knowledge and intellectual capital can be foundations to strategy development.

If a learning-based approach to strategy development is adopted, then all or a large number of people within an organization will contribute to the development of its strategy. This requires extensive vertical and horizontal communication, and knowledge sharing must be fundamental to that organization's culture. Creating such a culture requires internal marketing and the integration of HR, marketing, IT, operations, quality management, finance and other functional strategies. Varey (1995, p 45) summarizes the broad implications of internal marketing with: 'Internal marketing encourages the view that marketing is a process which involves the whole firm as the means by which a match is continuously maintained between its offerings and its targeted customers' needs'.

Internal marketing can therefore provide a pivotal contribution in creating the internal conditions that can drive corporate strategy and sustainable competitive advantage. Also, internal marketing can support strategy through an integrated approach to the internal drivers that are critical to the successful implementation of corporate strategy.

Linking vision, mission, values, positioning and personality to internal marketing

Whilst business strategy and tactical planning identify specific activities that require implementation for an organization to meet its goals, strategy requires a link to a vision of where a company is going and a context to that strategy.

Considerations of vision, mission and values provide a link between an organization's purpose and the desired culture of that organization. Culture, in a nutshell, is about how people behave. And marketing is ultimately about one thing: influencing behaviour. Internal marketing has a key role in shaping culture through influencing behaviour in directions that are compatible with an organization's vision and purpose. Achieving behavioural change requires, in part, belief in a vision and purpose by an organization's people that crystallizes statements of intent into tangible action and outcomes. The importance of linking an organization's vision and culture to the behaviour of every member of that organization is demonstrated in this quotation from Ind:

> *Engaging employees with the organisation's overall purpose is vital if organisations are to use the full intellectual capital at their disposal. Often commentators write about organisations as abstract constructs and talk about value creation in terms of financial measures. What this ignores is that organisations are collections of people joined together in pursuit of a common cause, and it is people who create value. In top-down, command-and-control organisations the abstract view often prevails and HR professionals bemoan the difficulties of persuading senior managers that nurturing people is important.*
>
> *Largely this is because executives see the creation of intellectual capital as their preserve. They generate the ideas, create knowledge and then impart their wisdom to others to implement. Even when these organisations have employee suggestion schemes, quality circles and other forms of employee involvement, passing judgement on the input and refining ideas is seen as a top-level activity.*
>
> *This separation of thinking from doing survives because it is familiar and unthreatening. It relies on a militaristic model – which even the military now sees as outdated – that stresses hierarchy and the power of status. Overall it does not require the wide dissemination of purpose and values because management has control.*
>
> *(Ind, 2001)*

Defining internal marketing

There are many interpretations of internal marketing though, as stated earlier, there is no 'official' definition. Some of these definitions are provided below. By placing them in chronological order, it is possible to see how views of what internal marketing is concerned with have broadened since the late 1970s:

> *1980 – . . . internal marketing means applying the philosophy and practices of marketing to people who serve the external customers so that (1) the best possible people can be employed and retained and (2) they will do their best possible work.*
>
> *(Authors unknown, 1993, The Foundations of Internal Marketing, paper presented at EMAC Conference, p 150)*

1981 – . . . *the objective of internal marketing is to get motivated and customer-conscious personnel.*

(Gronroos, 1981)

1984 – . . . *viewing employees as internal customers, viewing jobs as internal products that satisfy the needs and wants of these internal customers while addressing the objectives of the organization.*

(Berry, 1984)

1990 – *Internal marketing is a process of encouraging employees to accept changes in company philosophy or policy.*

(Reardon and Enis, 1990)

1991 – *Internal marketing is attracting, developing, motivating and retaining qualified employees through job-products that satisfy their needs. Internal marketing is the philosophy of treating employees as customers. . . and it is the strategy of shaping job-products to fit human needs.*

(Berry and Parasuraman, 1991)

1991 – . . . *an important activity in developing a customer-focused organization. . . Fundamental aims of internal marketing are to develop internal and external customer awareness and remove functional barriers to organizational effectiveness.*

(Christopher, Payne and Ballantyne, 1991)

1993 – *Internal marketing is the set of activities aimed at establishing and improving internal exchange processes, for the purpose of achieving the organizational and/or departmental goals as efficiently and effectively as possible.*

(Authors unknown, 1993, The Foundations of Internal Marketing, paper presented at EMAC Conference, p 151)

1993 – . . . *we suggest that internal marketing involves a planned effort to overcome organisational resistance to change and to align, motivate and integrate employees towards the effective implementation of corporate and functional strategies.*

(Rafiq and Ahmed, 1993)

1995 – Internal marketing is a process and mechanism for ensuring effective responsiveness to environmental changes, flexibility for adopting newly designed administrative arrangements efficiently, and continuous improvement in performance. Internal marketing can assist the organization to match its responses to environmental change and to enhance its capacity continuously.

(Varey, 1995, p 52)

1995 – Internal marketing is any form of marketing within an organisation which focuses staff attention on the internal activities that need to be changed in order to enhance external market place performance.

(Ballantyne, Christopher and Payne, 1995)

1997 – Internal marketing is a relationship development process in which staff autonomy and know-how combine to create and circulate new organisational knowledge that will challenge internal activities which need to be changed to enhance quality in marketplace relationships.

(Ballantyne, 1997)

1998 – . . . those activities that improve internal communications and customer-consciousness among employees, and the link between these activities and external marketplace performance.

(Hogg, Carter and Dunne, 1998)

1999 – . . . a goal-oriented social process, and a conceptual system for continually creating rapid strategic organisational change in response to the macro-environment (society) and the micro-environment (the community which constitutes the organisation).

(Varey and Lewis, 1999, p 937)

2000 – My experience of internal marketing comes down to this. It is a strategy for developing relationships between staff across internal organisational boundaries. This is done so that staff autonomy and know-how combine in opening up knowledge generating processes and challenge any internal activities that need to be changed. The purpose of this activity is to enhance the quality of external marketing relationships.

(Ballantyne, 2000)

A further definition

For this book, the definition of internal marketing that will be adopted is that internal marketing is concerned with the resources and activities occurring within an organization that influence the nature of its culture and competitiveness as a route to achieving its purpose.

The reason this definition does not include reference to particular activities such as internal communication or KM is because the number of 'components' of internal marketing has increased over the last two decades and we can assume that this will continue to occur as management theory and practice evolve. It is doubtful whether knowledge management, for example, was even on the business strategy radar of most organizations in 1981. IMS is an emergent area of strategy, suggesting a flexible approach is needed.

Time is included as an aspect of the definition through reference to an organization's purpose. The need to consider future competitiveness should be fundamental to business strategy. Therefore, IMS should be forward-looking and relate to what is happening in the environment outside of the organization. This has implications for the monitoring and prediction of market activity and the ability of an organization to structure itself in creating and anticipating change.

KEY LEARNING POINTS

1. Internal marketing is an emergent area of management theory and practice. There is no universally agreed definition of internal marketing. Differing approaches can be seen as adding contributions to a growing range of perspectives on internal marketing theory and practice. Service marketing theory and concepts of service quality are particularly important foundations to IMS, which in turn emphasizes the importance of people in creating sustainable competitive advantage for organizations.

2. Internal marketing draws upon theory and practice from a broad range of business disciplines including marketing, customer service, corporate strategy, operations management, quality management, HR, KM and IT.

3. The definition of internal marketing adopted in this book is that internal marketing is concerned with the activities and resources occurring within an organization that influence the nature of its culture and competitiveness as a route to achieving its purpose.

4. Seven components of internal marketing have been identified. These components are not mutually exclusive but provide areas of overlap, emphasizing the importance of an integrated approach to IMS:

   - vision, mission, values, positioning and personality;

   - corporate strategy;

   - processes, service standards and measures;

   - knowledge management;

   - internal communication;

   - HR strategy;

   - integrating internal, interactive and external marketing.

5. Internal marketing does not come in a box as a prescriptive or commodity solution to unique organizational issues. It is best viewed as a recipe of ingredients that should be selected, measured and mixed in the appropriate quantities to maximize their impact upon organizational culture, competitiveness and the achievement of corporate purpose.

6. With the level of change and turbulence existing in many markets, IMS should be viewed as a voyage towards achieving and sustaining competitive advantage with many interesting ports along the way, rather than a destination in itself.

7. Internal marketing activities should be integrated with interactive and external marketing activities to provide a consistent and coherent series of communications and behaviours inside and outside an organization.

SOURCES

Dunne, P and Barnes, J (2000) A Relationships and Value-Creation View, in *Internal Marketing – Directions for management*, ed R Varey and B Lewis, pp 192–220, Routledge, London

Edvinsson, L and Malone, M (1997) *Intellectual Capital*, Piatkus, London

Ewing, M, Caruana, A and Rivers, G (1997) [accessed 24 December 2000] *An Internal Marketing Approach to Public Sector Management: The marketing and human resources interface* [Online] http://www.cbs.curtin.edu.au/MKT/RESEARCH/9713.html

Foreman, S and Money, A (1995) Internal Marketing: Concepts, measurement and application, *Journal of Marketing Management*, **11**, pp 755–68

Hays, R (1996) The Strategic Power of Internal Service Excellence, *Business Horizons*, **39** (4), pp 15–20

Ind, N (1997) *The Corporate Brand*, Macmillan Business, London

Lings, I and Brooks, R (1998) Implementing and Measuring the Effectiveness of Internal Marketing, *Journal of Marketing Management*, **14**, pp 325–51

Lings, I (1999) Balancing Internal and External Market Orientations, *Journal of Marketing Management*, **15**, pp 239–63

Lynch, R (2000) *Corporate Strategy*, Prentice Hall, Harlow

Mitchell, S and Hayes, M (1999) Internal Marketing: The ultimate relationship?, *Journal of Targeting, Measurement and Analysis for Marketing*, **7** (3), pp 245–60

Zeithaml, A and Bitner, M J (2000) *Services Marketing – Integrating customer focus across the firm*, McGraw-Hill

REFERENCES

Ballantyne, D, Christopher, M, and Payne, A (1995) Improving the Quality Of Services Marketing: Service (re)design is the critical link, *Journal of Marketing Management*, **2**, pp 7–24

Ballantyne, D (1997) Internal Networks for Internal Marketing, *Journal of Marketing Management*, **13**, p 354

Ballantyne, D (2000) The Strengths And Weaknesses of Internal Marketing, in *Internal Marketing – Directions for management*, ed J Varey and B Lewis, p 43, Routledge, London

Berry, L (1984) The Employee As Customer, in *Services Marketing*, ed C Lovelock, p 272, Kent Publishing, Boston

Berry, L and Parasuraman, A (1991) *Marketing Services: Competing through quality*, p 151, The Free Press, New York

Booms, B and Bitner, M J (1981) Marketing Strategies and Organisational Structures for Service Firms, in *Marketing of Services*, ed J Donnely and W George, pp 47–51, American Marketing Association, Chicago

Christopher, M, Payne, A and Ballantyne, D (1991) *Relationship Marketing: Bringing quality, customer service and marketing together*, Butterworth Heinemann, Oxford

Farrant, J (2000) *Internal Communications*, p 2, Hawksmere, London

Gilmore, A and Carson, D (1995) Managing and Marketing to Internal Customers, in *Understanding Services Management*, ed W Glynn and J Barnes, pp 295–321, John Wiley and Sons, Chichester

Gronroos, C (1981) Internal Marketing – an integral part of marketing theory, in *Marketing of Services*, ed J Donnelly and W George, p 237, American Marketing Association Proceedings Series

Heskett *et al* (1994) Putting the Service-Profit Chain to Work, *Harvard Business Review*, **72** (March–April) pp 164–74

Hogg, G, Carter, S and Dunne, A (1998) Investing In People: Internal marketing and corporate culture, *Journal of Marketing Management*, **14**, p 880

Ind, N (2001) Living the Brand – Why organisations need purpose and values, *Market Leader*, **15** (Winter), p 34, The Marketing Society, London

Liautaud, B and Hammond, M (2001) *e-Business Intelligence*, p 195, McGraw-Hill, New York

Macrae *et al* (1996) An Invitation From MELNET 96 to Contribute to The 'Brand Learning Organisation', *The Journal of Brand Management*, **3** (4), p 232

Parasuraman, A, Zeithaml, V and Berry, L (1985) A Conceptual Model of Service Quality and its Implications for Future Research, *Journal of Marketing*, **49** (Fall), pp 41–50

Rafiq, M and Ahmed, P (1993) The Scope of Internal Marketing: Defining the boundary between marketing and human resource management, *Journal of Marketing Management*, **9**, p 222

Reardon, K and Enis, B (1990) Establishing a Companywide Customer Orientation Through Persuasive Internal Marketing, *Management Communication Quarterly*, **3** (3), p 376

Sorrell, M (2000) Three Critical Challenges Facing CEOs, *Market Leader*, **10** (Autumn), p 20, The Marketing Society, London

Varey, R (1995) A Model of Internal Marketing for Building and Sustaining Competitive Service Advantage, *Journal of Marketing Management*, **11**, pp 45, 52

Varey, R and Lewis, B (1999) A Broadened Conception of Internal Marketing, *European Journal of Marketing*, **33** (9/10), pp 937, 941

Zeithaml, A and Bitner, M J (2000) *Services Marketing – Integrating customer focus across the firm*, McGraw-Hill, pp 16, 81

1

Vision, mission, values, positioning and personality

AIMS

1. To identify the importance of corporate vision, mission, values, positioning and personality in relation to sustainable competitive advantage;

2. to show the importance of linking corporate vision and supporting statements with the brand experience through employee behaviour and communications.

INTRODUCTION

The popularity of developing organizational statements about vision, mission and values can be linked to the knowledge paradigm and recent contributions to corporate strategy, including the work of Kay, Hamel, Prahalad, and Senge. Effectively communicating an organization's vision, mission and values provides leaders, marketers and HR specialists with some of their greatest challenges. Aligning attitudes and behaviour with a new vision can take several years to accomplish if substantial cultural change is required.

The importance of creating and communicating an organization's vision, mission, values and personality is well illustrated by organizations such as The Body Shop and Pret A Manger. There is a passion about The Body Shop and Pret A Manger that provides a wholly integrated approach to branding and behaviour which, in turn, give customers a particular brand experience. The strength of these organizations comes from internal drivers that ultimately impact their competitive advantage and brand reputation. For these companies, there are consistent values in their culture, products and people that are supported by processes and communications to deliver the brand experience.

Developing a corporate vision and the supporting statements has one key purpose: to direct an organization towards the achievement of competitive advantage. These statements should give strategic shape to an organization, providing a navigation aid and motivation for people regarding strategy development and implementation. Corporate vision, mission and values should indicate 'where we're going', 'why it's important' and 'how we do things around here'. These statements should also indicate how a particular organization is different from its competitors. The organization's competitive advantage should be communicated in these statements (and made real through performance) so that all stakeholders can identify why a particular organization is different to and better than its competitors.

For some organizations the development of a vision and supporting statements has occurred more as a fashion accessory than a clearly defined process with specific outcomes in terms of change and competitive advantage. Because the development of vision statements and so forth has been fashionable in recent years, it is possible to imagine the conversations in some boardrooms that are along the lines of 'well, we'd better have one too, or else it'll seem as if we're behind the times'.

Corporate vision

In the following quotation Kakabadse identifies the importance of creating a corporate vision:

> *Vision gives leaders and their companies a sense of direction and purpose, enabling them to allocate resources well, to develop and grow. It unites all the disparate elements of a company – such as products, pricing and*

brand – and helps to formulate an overall strategy. It implies continuity – a future for both the entity and its employees – and, if communicated effectively, gives staff clear goals. This encourages effort and achievement.

Equally importantly, vision gives firms a competitive edge and enables them to succeed in a fast-changing marketplace in which international boundaries have broken down and the Internet has completely altered the way many firms do business – enabling a one-man band to compete with a global corporation.

(Kakabadse, 2001)

Kakabadse, in the same work, also states the importance of vision in relation to culture, and therefore behaviour:

To create effective visioning through team-working, organisations must develop a culture that is built on trust and rewards creativity and diversity. Team members must develop a collective sense of responsibility and direction. Effective visioning requires a willingness to consider all the options and to share information needed to develop them. It also demands that staff commit to a plan of action that is in the best interests of the organisation, even if this may result in unwelcome changes.

Poorly developed vision and mission statements can be viewed as general statements that provide little benefit and appear as dogma or poor quality PR. They typically follow a style of: 'We will be the best at. . . by delivering our customers world-class standards of. . . and provide an above-average return on investment to our shareholders whilst supporting the development of our employees'. This generic style of vision statement provides little in the way of orienting strategic direction or creating a motivating force for employees because it does not have credibility or an emotional driver.

Developing a corporate vision is not just for the sake of including a few lines of copy in the annual report or posters on the employee kitchen noticeboard. It is naïve to assume that printing a few words will suddenly lead to remarkable changes in individual and corporate performance. It is an insult to employees to expect that simply having a gaggle of directors cooped up in a hotel for a couple of days and returning to the office with the corporate equivalent of the Ten Commandments will have any meaningful impact. A dog is not just for Christmas and a corporate vision is not just for a quick fix.

Positioning and personality

Much has been written about the importance of organizations developing and communicating corporate vision, mission and values. In this book, consideration will also be given to positioning and brand or corporate personality. The reason for this is that whilst written statements of visions and so forth provide a navigation aid for people, by extending these considerations to positioning and brand personality more detailed and effective guidance for behaviour and communications can be given. Therefore, the view being presented here is that the communication of brand or corporate positioning and personality will provide greater support to internal communication and understanding of strategic intent.

It is also important to consider whether it is a corporate brand or a product/service brand that is under consideration. For example, the Volkswagen Group includes the VW, Audi, SEAT and Skoda brands, with each brand promoted as a separate and competing entity. Beneath these brands are models of cars that will be promoted within the brand structure for that particular business unit. Consequently, developing a vision and supporting statements for each brand is a different proposition to the development of any corporate statements for the Group.

Corporate statements

To start at the top, the development of a corporate vision, mission and so forth can be viewed as the beginning of a strategy development process. The vision and mission provide a context to the development and communication of strategy. The following definitions illustrate the interrelatedness of a vision and its supporting statements:

▌ vision – what an organization or brand aims to achieve in the future;

▌ mission – the organization or brand purpose;

▌ values – how the mission is accomplished;

▌ positioning – where an organization or brand is positioned in the marketplace and how it is differentiated versus competitors;

▌ personality – how values are translated into personality traits and communicated through behaviour and written communications.

The vision, mission and values statements of an organization (Kendric Ash) are provided in the case study below to illustrate how these statements provide a context to strategy development and implementation, behaviour and communication.

_____

Kendric Ash

Kendric Ash is a company that provides consulting services to private, public and non-profit organizations, with the aim of improving organizational performance.

The Kendric Ash vision
'To be globally recognised as a world-class strategic partner adding value through continuous innovation and competitive performance improvement'. This vision statement identifies that the organization has strong growth ambitions. Located in the United Kingdom, and servicing clients within that country, Kendric Ash must grow outside its current national marketplace to achieve its vision.

The Kendric Ash mission
'To be a stakeholder delivering continuous, competitive performance improvement to our customers through trusted partnership and best of breed services'. The mission provides a context to the organization's approach to its relationships with customers through the use of 'stakeholder' and 'trusted partnership'. The outcome of these ongoing relationships will be demonstrated through continuous competitive performance improvements. In addition to providing potential customers with an idea of how Kendric Ash works and what it seeks to achieve, the mission also provides employees with the realization that their work must support the maintenance of relationships based upon continuous improvement and world-class services. This in turn has implications for the organization's recruitment, retention and development processes.

The Kendric Ash main proposition

▌ *to be a trusted partner;*

▌ *involved in the identification and improvement of key business metrics from the start through to contract management whether of insourced, outsourced or multisourced services;*

▌ *seeking to understand and share our customers' values and key business objectives;*

▌ *ensuring continuous innovation and performance improvement;*

▮ *demonstrating significant added value not just contract management;*

▮ *utilising the Business Excellence Model;*

▮ *a long-term stakeholder in our customers' business paid on success measured by improvements in league table position/key business metrics.*

Few organizations state a 'main proposition' as a part of their corporate statements. The proposition set out by Kendric Ash indicates to potential and existing customers how the organization approaches relationships and the improvement of organizational performance, and how those improvements might be measured and rewarded. The vision, mission and main proposition provide a picture of what it is like to work with and for Kendric Ash, and this is further defined by the organization's core values.

The Kendric Ash core values

▮ *'be proud of Kendric Ash – it is our company' [ie all employees are shareholders];*

▮ *delight customers by exceeding expectations;*

▮ *win – only the best is good enough;*

▮ *respect individuals;*

▮ *act with integrity – deliver promises;*

▮ *succeed through teamwork and have fun;*

▮ *be socially responsible.*

There is an advertising campaign running in the United Kingdom at the time of writing for a range of home maintenance products that help protect garden fences and other domestic constructions from weathering. The advertisement stresses that the products do exactly what it says on the tin. This is a simple and direct message: the product says it will protect your woodwork; use it and that is what will happen.

The statements from the Kendric Ash case study have a similar function and directness. The statements provide an indication of what the people at Kendric Ash do, how they do it and what you can expect if they work with you, or if you work for them. These simple and direct statements also provide a structure for decision-making, behaviour and communication that integrates external, interactive and internal marketing. Kendric Ash sounds like a challenging and interesting place to work – where it delivers measurable results, through considerate people, and where you get to be a shareholder if you're good enough to get hired. Having provided an example of a vision statement and its supporting components, these components will be reviewed in greater depth.

Vision and mission

A vision should provide a clear identification of where an organization is going so that people know the general direction of the organization and their work. The vision should provide a common picture for the people within an organization as to where the organization is heading and connect them to it, linking the external environment to internal resources. However, simply putting a new vision statement in front of employees and expecting them to suddenly change their behaviour is clearly an unrealistic expectation. Further variables and influences are also involved.

There are no definite rules about how to develop or write a vision or the supporting statements. Some organizations develop vision and value statements, not bothering with a mission statement, as the vision and mission effectively become rolled into one. Johnson & Johnson, have a lengthy written credo that provides employees with guidance regarding company values and behaviour.

The Johnson & Johnson credo

The Johnson & Johnson Credo is as follows:

> We believe our first responsibility is to the doctors, nurses and patients, to mothers and all others who use our products and services. In meeting their needs everything we do must be of high quality. We must constantly strive to reduce our costs in order to maintain reasonable prices. Customers' orders must be serviced promptly and accurately. Our suppliers and distributors must have an opportunity to make a fair profit.
>
> We are responsible to our employees, the men and women who work with us throughout the world. Everyone must be considered as an individual. We must respect their dignity and recognize their merit. They must have a sense of security in their jobs. Compensation must be fair and adequate, and working conditions clean, orderly and safe. Employees must feel free to make suggestions and complaints. There must be equal opportunity for employment, development and advancement for those

qualified. We must provide competent management, and their actions must be just and ethical.

We are responsible to the communities in which we live and work and to the world community as well. We must be good citizens – support good works and charities and bear our fair share of taxes. We must encourage civic improvements and better health and education. We must maintain in good order the property we are privileged to use, protecting the environment and natural resources.

Our final responsibility is to our stockholders. Business must make a sound profit. We must experiment with new ideas. Research must be carried on, innovative programs developed and mistakes paid for. New equipment must be purchased, new facilities provided and new products launched. Reserves must be created to provide for adverse times. When we operate according to these principles, the stockholders should realize a fair return.

Approaches to vision and mission development

There is no prescribed route to the development of a vision and supporting statements. What is important is developing clear statements that will guide people to working towards the same goals in a consistent way. For example, Komatsu developed a very simple vision for its employees: 'To encircle Caterpillar'. This call to arms makes it very clear as to what the people at Komatsu should have been doing in their work, and how, at the end of each day, they could calculate their contribution to that vision.

Vision and mission statements that are too specific may prove limiting when developing strategy and, as a result, an organization may fail to exploit potential new opportunities or adapt to a changing environment. Further considerations include whether a vision or mission will realistically provide meaning for all employees, particularly those carrying out relatively simple tasks, how employees might react if managers and executives act in ways that are inconsistent with the statements and if people are not provided with adequate resources to meet the expectations provided in the statements. Given these potential banana skins, Bartkus, Glassman and McAfee conclude that:

We believe the purpose of a mission statement should be to communicate a description of the firm that allows current and prospective employees, suppliers, investors and customers to determine whether they want to be involved with it. The statement should be nothing more than a communication device that realistically reflects what managers, directors, and owners believe the firm is, and where it is likely to be headed. . .

> _Mission statements have been sold to companies on the basis that they can accomplish many objectives – focus managerial efforts, provide decision-making criteria, motivate employees to work harder. However, companies have other mechanisms for accomplishing these tasks that are far more effective than a mission statement. Most firms would be better off if they narrowed the purpose of the mission statement to that of realistically communicating product and market objectives to stakeholders. The best mission statements simply define the company's business and suggest a future goal._

> _(Bartkus, Glassman and McAfee, 2000)_

This approach could be considered as limiting, and what Bartkus _et al_ are proposing could be interpreted as a positioning statement. Positioning statements will be referred to later in this chapter. Also, Bartkus _et al_ make no reference to value statements, which form an important link between vision, mission, strategy and internal marketing. It is important to consider vision in its broadest sense, and to consider that a vision should stimulate innovation and the creation of competitive advantage.

However, developing vision and supporting statements is not a guarantee of future success. The following brief reference to Lego and a case study in the next chapter illustrate that the development of a vision and supporting statements is not enough, if viewed purely as a process, to improve business performance. The development of appropriate strategy linked to a vision and supporting statements is also a critical factor. Similarly, vision statements, whilst identifying an aspiration, should be rooted in achievable reality. If they are not, then it is logical to conclude that flawed strategy and disappointed stakeholders may be created.

Lego – rebuilding a brand

Lego produces toys for young children and, in expanding from this core product, has created branded ranges of clothing and accessories as well as theme parks. Using external suppliers, Lego gained an assessment of its image in the minds of stakeholders. The assessment identified that Lego had a very strong image, leading to the conclusion that the organization should see itself as a leader in creativity and learning rather than simply in terms of its products. The company's image was distilled to these words or values: imagination, invention, togetherness, learning and fun. The company also decided that it needed to develop a vision that was more closely aligned to its stakeholder image.

Following research with employees and external stakeholders the company adopted the vision that it would become the strongest brand among families with children by 2005. This was obviously a challenging vision to realize given the strength and resources of such brands and companies as Disney and McDonalds. Arguably, this was an unrealistic vision for a privately owned company faced with these and many other high-profile competitors.

To support its newly adopted vision and image, Lego implemented a programme of cultural change that included workshops, in which employees shared their aspirations for the company and themselves, as a route to aligning vision, image and culture. In addition, restructuring occurred.

Lego will be returned to in the next chapter through a further case study that is more closely related to the strategy adopted by Lego in the face of significant market change. In this case study, the Lego vision is criticized as being too broad, lacking a clear direction, and steering Lego towards an inappropriate strategy.

Values

Values act as guiding principles to the way people working for a company behave and should, therefore, indicate the desired organizational culture. If employees are to be able to recall values and use them for reference and direction, then it is reasonable to assume that the values should be easy to remember, actionable and motivating. If accepting the view that people can remember five plus or minus two things, a conclusion is that more than seven values becomes too much for most people to remember, and that three values are more likely to be remembered by the majority of people in a population.

In an article published in 2000, Begley and Boyd describe the importance of values in relation to HR policies and culture. In flatter organizations where speed of action is of increasing importance, values as drivers of behaviour are potentially of great relevance. Where people have greater individual responsibility and little time to consume volumes of written policies, values provide a guiding framework for organizational culture and behaviour. In describing the issues faced by HR executives in several Fortune 500 companies, the authors state:

Not only was each company wrestling with the same problem, but each had come to a similar situation. In the end, they all determined that the corporate culture needed to create a fabric for employee behaviour. They realized as well that values serve as hallmarks of corporate culture. A core set of values conducive to corporate success should constitute a foundational element of the desired culture. Other components, such as corporate norms, stories and symbols, should reflect these core values.

(Begley and Boyd, 2000)

The authors also identify three key links to assess in the value-based culture approach:

1. Are the key values of the company clearly articulated?

2. Are these values instrumental to a success-driven corporate culture?

3. Do the company's HR policies reflect and enhance a corporate value-based culture?

Values therefore provide a framework for expected behaviour as well as an indicator of corporate culture. For employers that wish to attract and retain particular types of individuals, especially in a tight labour market with skills shortages, the promoting of values can be an important influence upon recruiting potential employees and retaining them. For example, the Getty Images Web site provides the following details for potential recruits:

Life at Getty Images – our culture and values

Getty Images is the global market-leader providing visual content to the media, design, advertising and editorial industries. When you join Getty Images you don't just get a job. You get a way of life. So what is it really like to work at Getty? Well, life at Getty Images is underpinned by our values set. They determine everything we do, and how we do it. Join Getty Images, and you'll share our passion for these values.

Innovation

We're global market leaders. We create the future. We innovate to stay at the leading edge. We're using the Net to revolutionize this industry, and the way we work with our customers. When you join Getty Images, you'll work with people who greet new ways of working with enthusiasm, not fear. You'll work with colleagues who refuse to accept that there are limitations to what our business can do – and to where their careers can go.

Openness

Revolution and change are not for those with closed minds. We're always open to new ideas and new ways of working. We respect diverse views and never assume that what worked yesterday will work tomorrow. Or even today.

Bold and audacious thinking

We're at the very forefront of our industry. We're leading the way. We're the one to watch. We change the very rules of our industry through bold and audacious actions, decisions and innovations.

Agility

Our success is driven by our ability to move fast, anticipate our customers' changing business needs and respond rapidly to competitive market changes. Even before they happen. The digital environment is hugely exciting but it is also largely uncharted territory – our people regard ambiguity and uncertainty as an essential part of an adventure rather than a nightmare! If you are not highly resilient to change, then Getty is not the place for you.

Integrity

Without exception, all of our business relationships and practices are built on a foundation of trust. We absolutely believe in fair, truthful and constructive communication.

Fun

What is the point of working somewhere if you can't have fun whilst doing it? Our working environment is characterized by good humour and a 'can do' attitude. So you can see that life at Getty Images is about constantly looking forward: always looking to the future. Always looking for new ways of doing things. Better, faster, different. Yet we remain cool, calm and contemporary. We remain focused and we expect and get results.

The Getty Images Web site also provides case studies of some of its employees; identifying why people joined the organization, how their careers have progressed and why Getty Images is their employer of choice. The message is simple: these values drive our business, if you like to live your life like this, come talk to us.

Getty Images is fortunate in that it is a relatively new business, though it has acquired a number of existing image libraries and absorbed them within its corporate brand structure. For new businesses, 'setting up shop' provides a clean sheet for the development of its values. Where an organization recognizes that due to environmental change it must change its values or 'create' them as part of a change programme, then a more challenging set of circumstances is provided.

A further interesting aspect regarding the Getty Images statement of its culture and values is the language used to communicate its messages. The tone of voice adopted implies youthful enthusiasm, coupled with a direct, relaxed, non-hierarchical, dynamic style. The language used reinforces the overall messages and brand identity, which in turn reinforces the organization's values. This is an important point in relation to positioning and brand personality.

Positioning

Positioning is a strategic marketing tool and might be described as the 'marketing envelope'. That envelope provides the context for a brand's marketing mix by addressing what it is that a particular brand stands for. For example, Rolls Royce is positioned within a niche in the overall market for cars. It is positioned as a luxury car brand, and its products and communications must be in unison to ensure its brand values and brand personality are communicated so as to encourage people to think of the brand in a particular way. Similarly, this brand position must be reflected in the behaviours and communications of people making, selling and servicing these cars.

Consequently, positioning acts as an important directional device for communications and behaviour by providing a framework that links internal, interactive and external marketing and acting as an envelope to support the creation of a coherent, integrated marketing mix. From a consumer's perspective, positioning concerns how a brand is perceived in the mind of an individual consumer. To refer back to the earlier example of Rolls Royce, a person might perceive Rolls Royce cars as more than just luxury cars. The Rolls Royce name may bring to mind images of heritage, luxurious travel, opulence, wealth, social prestige, high-quality engineering, the sleekness of the Lalique 'Spirit of Ecstasy' figure on the radiator, a history of design and quality, a clock whose tick is louder than the car's engine, and so forth. All of these perceptions and relative perceptions of competitor products will influence how individuals perceive the Rolls Royce brand, and consequently how it is positioned within their mental constructs.

For individuals, a corporate brand or service/product brand's perceived identity will therefore be comprised of tangible and intangible elements. This perceived position will have been built from relatively easily discernable aspects such as price, design and the sales environment, as well as less tangible things that may well be created through personal experience, the views of people whose opinions we value and advertising. Understanding these elements is of great importance for internal marketing. Where people are critical to delivering a brand experience, this experience must relate to corporate or brand positioning. Any negative divergence between expectations and performance will undermine the brand.

If people working in an organization are to live the brand, they must understand the tangible and intangible aspects of that brand and how they can reinforce the positive values and benefits that form the brand in terms of the marketplace and the minds of customers. Behaviour must therefore reflect positioning, and, if people are to behave and communicate in a way that is consistent with a corporate or brand position, then that positioning must be communicated to them in a way that will create the desired attitudes and behaviours.

For brands, a positioning statement will vary by approach, market category and a variety of other market variables. In their book *Advertising Communications and Promotion Management*, Rossiter and Percy (1998) provide specific approaches to the development of positioning statements. But typically, a positioning statement will take the form of:

1. To (the target audience);

2. (name of the brand) is the brand of (category need);

3. that offers (brand benefit or benefits).

To provide an illustration of a positioning statement that conforms to this format, this is a made up positioning statement for Ferrari cars: 'To conspicuous, wealthy males aged 30–45 Ferrari is the ultimate sports car brand because of performance, styling and its Formula One racing pedigree'. However, more complex positioning statements can be developed that provide stronger direction for communications, as can be identified within the following short case study for PLATO Learning Inc.

PLATO Learning

PLATO Learning develops and markets educational software and learning systems. The company is a provider of e-learning resources and solutions to the education sector in the United States and several other countries.

When he was appointed as CEO in 2000, John Murray immediately set about developing vision and supporting statements with colleagues. Murray believed that providing a clear sense of the company's future direction would be a fundamental part of achieving the step change in performance he wished the company to accomplish. The PLATO Learning vision was agreed as:

PLATO Learning creates technology-based learning environments that give: Teachers the capacity to personalize instruction for every learner on demand, anytime, anywhere; Communities the confidence their students are fully engaged in real learning, with accountability, measurable performance, and real results, and; Students the excitement of learning, motivation for personal growth, and the necessary foundation on which to build a productive life and good citizenship.

To support the vision and define the company's purpose and the contribution the organization wished to make to society, a mission statement was created: 'To ensure the success of all learners throughout their lifetimes'.

As a route to developing a culture that would support the vision and mission, company values were also developed based around accountability, trust and mutual respect, hard work, honesty/integrity and consistency/fairness. The company also developed five overarching goals that were to be used for measuring the organization's progress against its mission. PLATO Learning uses the overarching goals as the touchstones for its business planning. The objectives and activities contained in annual business plans are all geared to the achievement of the goals, providing a concentration of attention and resources to achieving the company's purpose. This includes the company's approach to acquisitions, with considerations for acquisitions focused on the achievement of the goals, mission and vision. The goals also direct internal communication messages and activities.

As a part of its greater market focus, the company also developed a proposition that was aligned with its goals and sales and marketing strategies. The company's positioning statement incorporates this proposition, providing a framework for internal, interactive and external communications messages. The positioning statement therefore provides further granularity by translating the overarching goals into what it is that provides the company with competitive advantage. The positioning statement also provides all employees with a concise statement as to how the company is focusing its communication efforts and messages:

To organizations providing education and learning that wish to achieve measurable improvements in learner performance and cost savings through technology-based learning environments, PLATO Learning is a leading brand providing improved performance through integrated solutions that link standards-based aligned curricula, courseware and administrative tools to improved results in the home, workplace and community.

PLATO Learning's customers will benefit from increased efficiency showing as measurable reductions in costs and savings in time, plus increased effectiveness showing as measurable improvements in learner achievement on standards tests and a reduction in the number of learners who fail to graduate, plus an extension of the 'learning day'.

The advertising and communications for PLATO Learning should emphasize cost and time saving and how these savings could be reallocated for other initiatives, and must mention PLATO Learning's expertise in the delivery of improvements in results-based education and learning in the home, workplace and community, supported by integrated courseware and administrative systems that are aligned to standards-based curricula.

Concise Positioning Statement: 'The comprehensive, core curriculum company whose products get real results'.

Brand personality

The PLATO Learning comprehensive positioning statement provides a link between the brand strategy and its communications. However, further definition of a brand's communications can be achieved through the development of a brand personality document. This document should align brand positioning with a personality. In turn, this personality should be aligned with the brand's visual identity. If brand communications are to be aligned with positioning, then it is necessary to understand the brand's 'personality' so that people connected with the brand can behave and communicate in ways that support the brand values, positioning and personality traits.

Similarly to positioning statements, brand personality descriptions are not generally included when organizations publish vision or mission statements. However, statements of brand personality are of great importance to marketers. Brand identity documents will generally include a list of personality traits that will relate to the brand values. The traits serve to identify how the brand should be communicated through behaviour and communications, including tone of voice and design. For example, a youth-oriented brand would wish to communicate through language, imagery and behaviour that are relevant to the targeted young people. The brand personality is essentially the brand's body language and spoken voice.

With the need to integrate internal, interactive and external marketing and the implications for 'living the brand', considerations of brand personality are of great importance in supporting the delivery of a consistent brand experience. What this also suggests is that a statement of brand personality and tone of voice should be consistent with key internal communication messages. For example, the Nokia Corporation stresses 'Connecting People'. This is reflected in its values and communications with internal and external audiences. A further example of the link between values, brand personality and communications is provided in the following case study of One 2 One (Clarke *et al*, 2000).

One 2 One

One 2 One (now a part of T-Mobile), the UK mobile telephone network has three brand values (though at the time of writing a new brand identity was in development following T-Mobile's acquisition of One 2 One):

1. connectivity – demonstrating an understanding of the real personal emotional benefit that communication gives customers, rather than discussing the technology that facilitates this communication;

2. enabling – helping customers to make the right choices for themselves by providing consumers with the tools to make informed choices;

3. closeness – the emotional benefit for consumers of providing the One 2 One service by enabling customers to get close to the things that matter to them.

The core values and personality of One 2 One are reflected in the brand name. The name encompasses connectivity and enabling and closeness. Closeness is a key value for One 2 One, not only because it is the core benefit sought by consumers, but also because One 2 One believes that it is through communication that the brand can achieve closeness with its customers. The company also believes this closeness can be achieved through communication that is people-centred, informal and uses a conversational tone of voice to develop rapport with customers. If this rapport is not established, an emotional relationship with the brand will not be developed. This value of closeness provides a very important consideration for internal marketing within One 2 One, as it will relate to the organization's internal and external communications as well as its customer service processes and recruitment policies.

From considerations of brand values and communication, the One 2 One brand personality was developed to guide employees in their interactions with customers, and similarly for the organization's advertising communications, which focus upon closeness. This theme of closeness is supported by the value of enabling through the One 2 One Web site with the use of a virtual customer service representative called Yasmin. One 2 One was one of the earliest users of virtual assistants on the Internet. The One 2 One brand personality is to come to life through these personality traits:

What the brand is	*What the brand is not*
informal	matey
insightful	banal
warm	sentimental
passionate	uncommitted
straightforward	simplistic

From the words that identified the One 2 One brand personality traits, a range of guidelines were provided for employees regarding behaviour and communications. These guidelines illustrate how the use of language is important in delivering the brand personality and values. The overall aim was to give people the tools to deliver the desired brand experience for One 2 One as a route to customer acquisition and retention.

Conclusions

The development of vision and supporting statements provides a context for the development of an organization's objectives and strategy. (The relationship between vision, mission and strategy development will be explored further in the next chapter.) Furthermore, in a time of turbulent change and flatter or virtual organizations where the concept of a 'job for life' is unlikely to be relevant, and where cross-functional team working is a necessity, such guiding principles provide a framework for desired behaviour and communications.

With the need to align internal, interactive and external marketing, it is also important to bring corporate statements to an operational level. Whether referring to a corporate brand or a product/service brand, corporate or brand strategy must be related to values, positioning and personality that support the delivery of the brand experience through consistent behaviour and communications. These elements must also be developed with the intent that the process will support the creation and sustaining of competitive advantage. There is no point in creating these statements if they do not relate to the needs and desires of the external, intermediate and internal marketplaces.

THEORIES, MODELS AND PERSPECTIVES

Lipton – vision and performance

Links between corporate vision creation and implementation and corporate performance have been identified. In an article published in 1996, Lipton stated that:

> *When I analysed more than thirty independent international studies that used organizational vision as a central variable, my conclusion was clear: managers who develop and communicate a vision skilfully can make a profound organizational impact. Sound data now support the intuitive appeal of visions. Concrete performance measures such as profit, return on shareholder equity, employee turnover, and rate of new product development improve when visions are used as strategic tools to manage organizational cultures.*

Lipton also identified five ways in which a vision can provide benefits to an organization:

1. by enhancing a wide range of performance measures;

2. by promoting change;

3. by providing the basis for a strategic plan;

4. by motivating individuals and facilitating the recruitment of talent;

5. by helping to keep decision-making in context.

Lipton concluded that the vision statements of the most effective organizations included three elements: the mission or purpose, a strategy for achieving the purpose and an indication of the culture that would be required to achieve the mission and its related strategy. Lipton also identified considerations for each of these areas:

Mission

▌ What business(es) are we in?

▌ What is our fundamental purpose or reason for being?

▌ What types of products or services do we make or provide?

▌ How do we define the customers we serve?

▌ For whose benefit are all our efforts?

▌ What unique value do we bring our customers?

▌ Are we confident that this mission is distinct and unique from any other organization that may provide a similar product or service?

▌ Are we describing what we do or why we do it?

Strategy

▌ What is the basic approach to achieving the mission?

▌ What is the distinct competence or competitive advantage that will characterize our organizational or departmental success?

Culture

▌ What are (or should be) the hallmarks of our culture and leadership style?

▌ How do (or should) we treat each other and how should we work together?

▌ What do we believe about ourselves?

▌ What do we stand for?

▌ What values do we hold dear?

▌ What characterizes an effective employee?

▌ In what ways is our organization a great place to work?

A cross-referencing between the Kendric Ash statements and these components illustrate a close relationship between the approach adopted by Kendric Ash and Lipton's framework.

Hatch and Schultz – vision and image

Hatch and Schultz (2001) propose that an organization's vision must be aligned with its culture and image if it is to develop a strong corporate brand. Hatch and Schultz developed 'The Corporate Branding Tool Kit', which is used to identify three interrelated gaps. In very basic terms, identifying each of these gaps involves asking the following questions:

The vision-culture gap

▌ Does your company practice the values it promotes?

▌ Does your company's vision inspire all its subcultures?

▌ Are your vision and culture differentiated from those of your competitors?

The image-culture gap

▌ What images do stakeholders associate with your company?

▌ In what ways do your employees and stakeholders interact?

▌ Do your employees care what stakeholders think of the company?

The image-vision gap

▌ Who are your stakeholders?

▌ What do your stakeholders want from your company?

▌ Are you effectively communicating your vision to your stakeholders?

This approach was adopted by Lego when it recognized a new strategy was necessary for the company. Some of the implications of adopting this approach will be explored in the next chapter.

Smith – developing a vision

There are many ways that an organization can go about developing its vision and supporting elements. They range from consultation with a broad range of stakeholders (as with the Lego example), to senior management developing its statement and then informing its people of how the organization will be directed.

The approach adopted will in part be led by the culture of the organization and in part by environmental factors. For organizations facing the need for radical and fast change, including mergers and acquisitions, the only available route may be 'tell'. Where time, environment and culture allow it, a more inclusive approach may be more likely to achieve participation and buy-in from people. Given that a key reason for developing a vision and supporting elements is to galvanize people into directed action, we can assume that the more people take ownership of the type of organization they work in and its goals, the more likely they are to work towards those goals.

Five stages in the shared vision process

Smith (1998) has identified five approaches to the development of an organizational vision, where the approach adopted will be influenced by the level of people's involvement in the process and the level of an organization's dependency upon leaders to provide the future direction of the organization. The five possible approaches are: telling, selling, testing, consulting and co-creating. These approaches can be viewed as points along a continuum.

Telling would be characterized where there is minimum involvement by employees and where there is strong direction setting by leaders. Co-creating would represent high levels of active involvement by people in an organization, with little direction provided by leaders. Smith states: 'In this picture of the five stages, the further to the left, the more the organization depends on a strong leader to "tell" everyone what the shared vision should be. The further to the right, the more leadership, direction-setting and learning capacity of the organization as a whole must have. Here, the boss is less "the person with the answers", and more the convener of a robust process'.

Organizations will have varying audiences in terms of their stakeholders and will wish to have a variety of relationships with these stakeholders. Where organizations wish to ensure a close 'fit' between their vision and supporting elements and perspectives of the stakeholders, then stakeholder views should be considered as a part of a shared vision process. These kinds of considerations would be particularly relevant for organizations where social and/or environmental issues have a strong influence on the organization's activities. A democratic and involving approach could have potential further benefits in terms of a positive influence on the organization's reputation.

For example, Shell, following the damage to its corporate reputation as a result of the Brent Spar and Nigeria crises, carried out a review of its values and activities. Shell deliberately attempted to engage key stakeholders, including environmental groups and other non-governmental organizations, in a dialogue regarding sustainable energies and whether Shell's values reflected how a global corporation should be viewed in the early 21st century. For global or multinational companies, considerations of culture will be of great potential influence upon developing a shared vision and supporting elements. A vision and its related elements will need to galvanize people in all locations and not contain wording that might cause offence in any cultures.

Dearlove and Coomber – values

Dearlove and Coomber conducted research into the impact of business values on business performance. They cite companies such as GE, Disney, Sony and Merck as organizations that have consistently outperformed their competitors, concluding this is because these companies have an explicitly stated set of values or guiding principles: 'which drive the business, and which take priority over short-term profit maximization'. From their own research, the authors conclude the following regarding values and corporate performance:

It is difficult to prove a direct link, but our research suggests that values-driven businesses enjoy important advantages over other organizations in a number of areas, including:

▌ _staff recruitment, development and retention;_

▌ _motivation, and achieving alignment between organizational and individual goals;_

▌ _change management;_

▌ _crisis management._

We believe that companies can improve their business performance by:

▋ *distilling their core values (core values cannot be created but must be 'discovered'), and communicating them to employees;*

▋ *strengthening the link between the values and aspirations of individuals and those of the organization, using mutual interest to engage the talents and commitment of workers;*

▋ *using values as the cultural glue to 'connect' employees and support a social community based on shared goals.*

(Dearlove and Coomber, 1999)

The authors also provide these important comments:

What emerged most clearly from our investigations, however, was that values are no quick fix. Nor are they a magic charm against the vagaries of the business world. Defining a set of principles is just the beginning. To get the benefits, an organization has to live and breathe its values. It is necessary to make the connection between what the employee and the organization are trying to achieve. That requires the translation of the organization's values into something individuals can put into practice during their everyday working lives.

The successful values-driven businesses we examined do not try to achieve an exact match between organizational and individual values. 'Values clones' is not the aim. Rather, it is to use values to establish common ground as a platform to support a more effective organizational culture.

(Dearlove and Coomber, 1999)

KEY LEARNING POINTS

1. The development of statements regarding corporate vision, mission, values, positioning and personality should be developed with the aim of using these statements to crystallize behaviour that is directed to achieving sustainable competitive advantage. These statements should provide shape and context for strategy development, implementation, behaviour and communications.

2. There are no 'rules' regarding the approach an organization may take in creating vision and supporting statements, or which statements may or may not be developed. The level of involvement of the people within an organization in the creation of a vision will be determined by a variety of factors, including culture, external influences and size. Arguably, however, the more people contribute to the creation of a vision, the more likely they are to work towards it.

3. Vision – what an organization or brand aims to achieve in the future.

4. Mission – the organization or brand purpose.

5. Values – how the mission is accomplished.

6. Positioning – where an organization or brand is positioned in the marketplace and how it is differentiated versus competitors.

7. Personality – how values are translated into personality traits and communicated through behaviour and written communications.

SOURCES

Lynch, R (2000) _Corporate Strategy_, Prentice Hall, Harlow
Ries, A and Trout J (1986) _Positioning: The battle for your mind_, McGraw Hill
Rossiter, J and Percy, L (1998) _Advertising Communications and Promotion Management_, McGraw-Hill

Web sites

http://www.gettylife.com/lifemain.htm [accessed 1 May 2001]
http://www.kendricash.com/cultmain.htm [accessed 1 May 2001]

REFERENCES

Bartkus, B, Glassman, M and McAfee, B (2000) Mission Statements: Are they smoke and mirrors?, _Business Horizons_ (November–December), pp 23–28

Begley, T and Boyd, D (2000) Articulating Corporate Values Through Human Resource Policies, *Business Horizons* (July–August), pp 8–12

Clarke, A *et al* (2000) One 2 One's E-Strategy, MA Marketing Management Programme (Strategic Marketing), Middlesex University Business School

Dearlove, D and Coomber S (1999) *Heart and Soul – A study of the impact of corporate and individual values on business*, Blessing/White

Hatch, M and Schultz, M (2001) Are the Strategic Stars Aligned for Your Corporate Brand?, *Harvard Business Review* (February), pp 128–34

Kakabadse, A (2001) What Is Vision? Sheer Inspiration – The UK's 100 most visionary companies, *Management Today*, p 4

Lipton, M (1996) Demystifying the Development of an Organizational Vision, *Sloan Management Review* (Summer), pp 83–92

Rossiter, J and Percy, L (1998) Advertising Communications and Promotion Management, McGraw-Hill, p 141

Smith, B (1998) Building Shared Vision: How to begin, in *The Fifth Discipline Fieldbook*, eds P Senge *et al*, pp 312–26, Nicholas Brealey Publishing, London

2

Corporate strategy

AIMS

1. To identify the interrelated foundations of corporate strategy and IMS;

2. to illustrate how strategy selection and implementation are influenced by an organization's internal resources.

INTRODUCTION

Recent perspectives on corporate strategy have included an increased 'internal emphasis' through considerations of an organization's core competencies and distinctive capabilities in relation to the marketplace and other aspects of the external environment. These approaches look to an organization's inner strengths and emphasize the desirability of developing these competencies and capabilities as a route to sustainable competitive advantage.

Many organizations are discovering that success is closely related to the concentration of their strategy on particular sectors, niches, processes or capabilities. For example, if the creation of innovative products or superior service delivery are considered to be critical factors for success in a marketplace, organizations will need to develop a culture, work-force, processes, knowledge and systems that will realize these factors.

It is therefore possible to develop direct links between sustainable competitive advantage, corporate strategy and internal marketing. The reciprocal relationship between business strategy and internal resources means that the selection of a particular corporate or brand strategy will have a direct impact on the IMS adopted by an organization. Strategy selection and implementation provides a link between vision and functional strategies, with internal marketing having a key role in the integration of these functional strategies.

The following case studies illustrate how corporate strategy has an impact upon the activities of people working in organizations, and why it is important to consider the internal resources of an organization when developing corporate strategy. The cases also introduce a broad range of issues that must be considered when developing an IMS. These issues include whether organizations that are driven exclusively by financial targets can realistically develop internal positioning as employers of choice, the challenges for IMS when a disconnect occurs between aspects of its external and internal marketing and the negative outcomes of developing strategies that are not related to an organization's internal capabilities.

Barclays Group – banking on a BIG brand

Chief Executive Matthew Barrett introduced value-based management at Barclays, the UK-based banking and financial services organization, in 1999. The aim of the approach was to encourage employees to be more focused in the way they grew their business units and the related products and services, with an overall objective of doubling shareholder value within four years. In an article published in *Marketing* (Simms, 2001) Barrett stated: 'Strategic development is becoming sharper as businesses tailor their strategies more closely to market and competitive conditions, to our own strengths and competencies and with a close eye on best-in-breed specialists in each category. Gone are the days of one-size-fits-all strategies'.

Creating the desired level of growth required significant change within the company, and Barclays Group began the implementation of a major change programme in 2000. It was anticipated that the programme would take four years to implement fully within the organization. A review of this programme and the strategy development that underpinned it illustrates many of the links between corporate and internal marketing strategy.

Barclays wished to be positioned as a leading global player within the banking sector and recognized that its brand strategy should reflect this ambition. The company also recognized that if it were to respond to a changing marketplace, its people and organizational architecture would also need to change, as would the Barclays' corporate identity.

The organization's vision was developed as: 'To be the powerful enabler enhancing our customers' lives and businesses'. The organization's brand strategy to support this vision is built upon four brand strengths, or distinctive capabilities, through which the Group believed competitive advantage would be achieved:

1. International stature – we are a world-class organization that our clients trust and rely on to fulfil their aspirations around the world.

2. Accessible expertise – we deliver the right solutions, to the right people, at the right time, in a way that they want.

3. Individual recognition – we treat people as individuals, respecting the lifetime value of our relationships and responding to their changing needs.

4. Progressive – we use our expertise and understanding of our clients' needs to deliver relevant innovations and new ways of doing things.

The brand strategy was underpinned through a brand personality that was to represent a 'powerful enabler':

▌ human;

▌ passionate;

▌ experienced;

▌ intelligent;

▌ powerful.

To support the organization's vision as being a powerful enabler, a new corporate visual identity was implemented. Also, an external communications campaign was launched using the word 'BIG' to emphasize the powerful, global intent of the Group, whilst providing a message that was meant to be emotionally aspirational for customers.

Internally, the company needed to communicate its vision and brand strategy, and develop the behaviours amongst its employees that would deliver them. An 'employer of choice' programme was developed that provided links between desired employee and customer experiences of the organization. (The underlying model for this is the Service-Profit Chain [see Chapter 1].), and links can also be identified to the Employee-Customer-Profit Chain at Sears, which will be described in the next chapter.) The aim was to provide 'a great people experience' (for employees) that would lead to 'a great customer experience'. For example, the programme identified that for a customer to experience the Barclays brand as 'passionate', this would be enabled by employees who are inspired and committed in their work and in their interactions with other employees. The links between employee behaviour and the brand personality within the Barclays programme are:

A great people experience	A great customer experience
challenged and supported	human
inspired and committed	passionate
capable and creative	experienced
credible and resourceful	intelligent
trusted and informed	powerful

The four brand strengths were also related to the employer of choice programme through four principles:

Brand strength	Employer of choice principle
international stature	valuing diversity
progressive	driving to be the best
individual recognition	promoting individual responsibility
accessible expertise	building capacity

Creating change within Barclays required an extensive programme with four key areas of activity targeted at different segments of Barclays' employees:

1. leadership – transforming leadership behaviour and competencies to support the desired employee and customer experiences;

2. HR policy and practice – activities to embed the programme through inductions, education and training and appraisals;

3. communications – encouraging 'living the brand' through workshops, presentations and communications activity;

4. feedback and evaluation – measuring the impact of the programme through focus groups, surveys and management information related to individual events, issues and key components of the brand strategy.

Implementing a programme of this scale is obviously a major exercise involving tens of thousands of employees. Not surprisingly there were challenges in the early stages of its implementation. For example, some senior managers who had participated in workshops were energized by the employer of choice programme and wished to behave in 'the new way', but when returning to their workplace became frustrated by colleagues who had not been exposed to the programme and resisted its principles. As a result, additional support was provided for these managers to maintain their enthusiasm for programme implementation.

Other difficulties with the programme included its initial development, which was a marketing-driven initiative. Initial involvement was not sought from internal communications or HR teams, resulting in a six-month delay in progressing the programme whilst these other teams became engaged in it. This emphasizes the need to develop cross-functional teams in the development and implementation of internal marketing activities.

Barclays also faced challenges due to its external advertising campaign that promoted Barclays as a big bank. Some customers interpreted the campaign message as indicating that as they were 'small' customers, Barclays would not wish to have them as customers. Also, whilst the 'Big' campaign was running, Barclays announced it would be closing a significant number of branches in the United Kingdom and making approximately 7,000 people redundant. Some commentators interpreted these communications as providing dissonance between Barclays' external communications and behaviour. Why would a big bank be reducing its branch network? An article published in the *The Economist* (March, 2001), provided these comments:

> *On average, branches and their staff account for about half of the costs of a typical retail bank. Bankers at one stage hoped that they might be able to persuade their customers to do business through the Internet, allowing branches to be shut down. But customers have since made it clear that while they want the convenience of Internet banking, they also insist on branches. A public-relations disaster at Barclays Bank, which closed 171 British branches on a single day last year, has made others very wary of trying something similar.*

In competitive response, NatWest launched an advertising campaign with the aim of attracting unhappy Barclays' customers. The key message of this campaign was that NatWest was supporting rather than reducing its branch network and providing new approaches to banking that provided distinct benefits to its customers.

The 'Big' campaign was underpinned by a message that being Big meant Barclay's could make things happen. Big translated into resources, ability, expertise, sophistication, understanding, confidence, empowerment and security. The 'Big' message combines the four brand strengths that Barclays wished to develop by illustrating to customers that Barclays was providing access to a broad range of financial services through a variety of channels, including the Internet. It was therefore empowering its customers. As one of the advertisements states: 'You know what this means, don't you? – We're all bank managers now'.

This campaign therefore had strong implications for Barclays' IMS, as it is in part encouraging customers to self-serve over the Internet as a way of self-empowering their interactions with Barclays. A key consideration here is that transactions conducted on the Internet occur at a fraction of the cost of similar transactions conducted at branches. This in turn has obvious impact upon internal processes, the relative value-add of services provided by high street branches, communications and employee recruitment, training and development. If Barclays' customers really are being empowered as bank managers, then what does this mean for staff currently performing this role and those aspiring to that position?

Therefore, some Barclays customers could have interpreted this campaign as acting against two of the brand strengths or distinctive capabilities: accessible expertise and individual recognition, and similarly for the personality traits of human and passionate. Arguably, some employees may have perceived similar contradictions in terms of communications messages and corporate behaviour. However, Barclays' business strategy also clearly prioritizes bottom-line performance, including the profitability of its branch operations and individual customers. The Group appears prepared to weather adverse public relations and the loss of some customers in anticipation of its strategy producing overall improvements in profitability.

As a footnote to this case study, in April 2001 Barclays announced it would be extending the opening hours of some of its UK branches. This policy meant the bank would be recruiting approximately 2,000 new employees. Sadly, when Barclays reduced the size of its branch network it made 7,000 people redundant, at great personal and financial cost and with the loss of centuries of accumulated knowledge. In August 2001, an article published in the *Financial Mail on Sunday* (Oldfield, 2001) reported on research conducted by MORI Financial Services Corporate Image, stating:

> *The research tracks issues such as reputations for treating customers fairly, satisfaction with service, and value for money. It is used internally to assess how the public and customers perceive the banks. Barclays flounders at the bottom of the league tables. The research shows that:*

> ▌ *Only a fifth of customers believe the bank offers value for money, a 6 per cent fall on the November count.*

> ▌ *Less than half of its customers said the bank has a reputation for treating customers fairly.*

> ▌ *Barclays had the lowest number of customers satisfied with its service.*

> ▌ *Customers' faith in the Barclays brand had fallen.*

The article also identified that the research was published just as Barclays had announced a 16 per cent rise in half-year profits to £1.6 billion.

London Communications Agency – the metropolitan line

The benefits of developing strategy through considering and integrating opportunities in the external environment and internal strengths are as applicable to small as they are to large organizations. A small company that developed its strategy through this integrative approach is London Communications Agency (LCA). LCA is a communications agency that is focused upon delivering strategic communications consulting on issues that relate to London.

The two founders of the agency have backgrounds in communications and related areas of marketing covering the private, non-profit and public sectors. Prior to commencing LCA, their work had been largely focused upon London-specific strategic issues such as inward investment, property, transportation and skills development.

With the creation of a regional government for London and recognizing that London was a large marketplace with its own strategic and communication issues, the founders decided to commence LCA as a niche, strategic communications agency. In doing so, they were able to initiate the first agency of its type in London.

LCA took its well-developed knowledge of London's strategic and communications issues, a range of relationships developed in the private, non-profit and public sectors within London, and matched these with a gap in the marketplace for highly focused strategic consultancy. As a result, LCA has an expanding portfolio of clients in a broad range of sectors.

As the agency expands its network of clients it reinforces the prime benefit of its market position. By increasing its knowledge of London-related issues through new projects, this in turn creates referrals for strategic consulting from new clients.

Lego – bricks and clicks?

The Lego brand has a tremendous heritage, and building from a foundation of interlocking bricks, the product range has become increasingly sophisticated and innovative. In addition, the Lego brand has been stretched to include Legoland parks, software and clothing and accessories. This expansion might suggest the company is on a winning streak through a strategy based upon stretching the Lego brand from 'bricks' to a broad range of child-oriented products and services. Unfortunately, this is not entirely the situation.

Following a profit of £45 million in 1999 on a turnover of £860 million, in March 2001 Lego announced it made a loss of approximately £90 million in 2000. As a result the company made 500 workers redundant and closed some of its factories. In an article entitled 'A Brick Too Far' published in *Marketing Week* (Benady, 2001), David Benady describes this dramatic change in fortune as resulting from a lack of focus upon its core business:

> *Critics of the company's strategy say executives have lost sight of why kids and parents love the multi-coloured plastic building blocks. Instead of revelling in the brand values of Lego – it is a creative way to teach children physical manipulation and hand-to-eye skills and is also fun – management is diluting the brand with a thousand extensions, marketing partnerships and licensing deals. This confuses children and their parents, many of whom grew up with the Lego brand.*

Lego has been faced with a number of serious challenges. The patent on its bricks ran out in 1981, leading to the production of ranges of similar products by new competitors. The growth in popularity of video and computer games averted expenditure from construction to electronic toys. Changing trends within the youth market have reduced the age groups to which Lego has appeal.

In response to these challenges, Lego has expanded into the production of wristwatches and books, and a broad variety of licensing activities. Benady continues: 'The shelves of toy shops are buckling under the weight of all these new takes on the Lego brand. There are branded clothes and bags and Lego even plans to produce television programmes for families and children. Its aim of becoming the world's top family brand is just the sort of bold mission statement that senior executives love – the sort that is so broad as to indicate a lack of clear direction'.

Lego's Chief Executive Officer's response to the unfavourable results was to state the company would refocus on its core business, yet he also announced it would be developing licensing relationships with Disney and Harry Potter, leading to criticism from Benady that it was in fact diluting its values and brand still further:

> But Lego's push into technology markets puts it into contention with the iconoclasm of PlayStation or the older teenage pop image of mobile phones – a battle that will be hard to win.
>
> Still, many parents would prefer their children to play with Lego rather than sit in front of the television or a computer game – it is a constructive toy rather than a destructive one like many PlayStation games. Some are surprised that Lego is launching a television station. 'Leave it to the professionals', says one observer. The brand risks losing its position as the creative, constructive alternative to watching the television and the more decadent end of the video games market.

This brief overview of some of Lego's activities illustrates the importance of concentration when developing strategy. Lego attempted to increase revenue through a range of brand extensions that took its attention away from its core product and values by producing products such as watches and books that were outside its core competencies. These activities will now be licensed to other manufacturers.

As noted in the previous chapter, Lego followed a process for developing a vision and a set of values, with that vision being: 'To be known as the strongest brand in the world among families with children by 2005'. This was considered a realistic vision based upon the Lego Company being among the 10 most famous brands among families with children. However, given the strength of Disney and other almost ubiquitous brands among these families, a more realistic view might be that Lego has set itself up for failure, and in turn adopted an unrealistic strategy that would lead to the disenchantment of employees. A press release published on the Lego Web site in November 2000 provides these comments:

> After the considerable growth in 1999, we, in Top Management, over-estimated sales and our optimism resulted in too many cost-demanding initiatives being initiated. In

order to reach our ambitious goal in 2005 more quickly, we were perhaps more driven by the wish for quantitative growth than for qualitative and healthy growth. Therefore, costs increased greatly in a year when sales were very disappointing. A large estimated surplus was turned into a loss!

A further conclusion from this brief review of Lego's activities might be that simply developing a vision and set of values for a company is of limited value if these statements are not related to a realistic evaluation of an organization's competencies and the external environment. Whilst Lego went through a programme of change based upon its newly developed value set, it might have been more successful if management energy and attention had been concentrated on its internal competencies and processes as a route to improving its financial and market position.

THEORIES, MODELS AND PERSPECTIVES

Lynch (2000) defines corporate strategy as: '. . . the linking process between the management of the organization's internal resources and its external relationships with its customers, suppliers, competitors and the economic and social environment in which it exists'. A key aspect of this definition is the inclusion of an organization's internal resources as being a critical factor within corporate strategy and the importance of linking these resources to external relationships and the environment.

Resource-based approaches to strategy development include considerations of the competencies existing within an organization as input to strategy development, and how concentration on the development of these inner strengths can contribute to sustainable competitive advantage. As a general statement, the more an organization looks to internal strengths and the involvement of its people as drivers of its strategy, the greater the importance of IMS. However, these internal resources must be placed in context with the organization's vision, mission and values and the external and competitive environments.

Ohmae – key factors for success

Considerations of key factors for success provide a link between industry-based and resource-based approaches to strategy development. Ohmae (1983) proposes identifying industry-specific key factors for success that will influence an organization's strategy. Ohmae describes key factors for success as the resources, skills and attributes of the organizations in an industry that are essential to deliver success in the marketplace, and proposes three main areas for analysis: customers, competitors and corporation.

Ohmae's approach provides interesting input to approaches to strategy development. However, identifying key factors for success within an industry may not prove wholly adequate for strategy development. Competitive advantage requires differentiation between competitors through unique activities that provide superior performance in areas that are highly valued by customers. Developing the skills and competencies that can generate this differentiation requires a deeper look within the organization, and considerations of internal resources. The development of these resources will almost certainly require the support of an IMS.

The resource-based view

Depending upon the way in which an organization develops its strategy, the resource-based view can be seen as either an alternative or complementary approach to the industry-based perspective to strategic analysis and development. Supporters of this approach believe it is better to develop strategy by considering the organization's unique or exceptional resources.

Kay – distinctive capabilities

Kay (1993) proposes that sustainable competitive advantage can be developed through three distinctive capabilities – architecture, reputation and innovative ability:

▌ architecture – resources resulting from the network of relationships that exist within and around an organization;

▌ reputation – an organization's ability to communicate favourable information about itself to its customers;

■ innovative ability – where an organization develops innovative products and services as a route to achieving sustainable competitive advantage.

An article published in *The Economist* (April, 2001) regarding the longevity or otherwise of companies, included reference to the thoughts of Kay (and how distinctive capabilities must be continuously managed if they are to provide competitive advantage), as well as the findings of research by David Garvin of the Harvard Business School:

> *Mr Garvin, who is doing a five-year study of the management of ten global giants, sees two main routes to durability. One is 'active reinvention', such as GE's ability deliberately to adapt. The other is 'organic adaptation': 3M, founded in 1902, has survived by edging sideways from abrasives and adhesives into new markets. Looking at the crop of companies that have soared to the top in the past decade or so, he singles out Dell Computers as possibly having sufficiently flexible and transferable supply-chain management to be tomorrow's 3M.*
>
> *Reinvention and adaptability are not the whole story, however. John Kay, a British economist, points to the importance of competitive advantage. Market power, of the sort conveyed by licences or regulation, tends to erode over time. Technological innovation brings transitory gains, unless a company understands how to reinvest to widen its base, as Glaxo has done. But brands and reputation, if managed properly, can also prove remarkably durable. Yet 'it is possible to screw up', admits Mr Kay. 'My students cannot believe that Hilton was once a generic term for a very good hotel'. GE is an extraordinary example of a company whose strength lies in its ability to pick and train the best managerial talent. For most of the 20th century, GE had a succession of chief executives just as admired as Jack Welch.*

Examples of organizations that show links to these distinctive capabilities include The Dow Chemical Company, the Co-operative Bank and Sony. Each of the strategies adopted by these companies has implications for the type of culture required to sustain the strategy and consequently for internal marketing strategy.

Dow Chemical

Dow Chemical has developed an intellectual asset management process that allows the management of its intellectual assets such as trademarks, trade secrets, disclosures of inventions and key technical know-how. The aim of this process is to improve the organization's exploitation of its intellectual assets. Basically, units within the organization register details of their intellectual assets on a database. Businesses within the company have access to the database and strategies are developed to lever further value from existing intellectual assets, whilst taking into account competitive threats and existing strategic gaps in intellectual assets (Bukowitz and Williams, 2000). Dow Chemical's management of its intellectual property assets has also been used as a route to reducing costs. In 1994 the company began an audit of these assets and achieved $50 million in savings in taxes and maintenance fees related to patents that were no longer considered necessary to the company, and that were donated to universities and non-profit organizations (Rivette and Kline, 2000).

The Co-operative Bank

The Co-operative Bank published its first ethical policy a decade ago, and in doing so the bank was distinctively repositioned. The bank believes a third of all its new customers join because of its ethical stance. The core proposition of the bank is that it will not lend money or offer financial services to companies that are considered to be involved in unethical practices. These practices include human rights abuses, the arms trade and animal testing. This market positioning provides the organization with many opportunities to communicate favourable information to its customers and other publics to reinforce its ethical stance and reputation. These communications include consultation exercises with its customers to understand the changing views of customers as to what they consider to be unethical practices (Treanor, 2001).

Sony

Sony follows a strategy of constant innovation through new product introductions and frequent changes to existing products to achieve competitive advantage. The results of this strategy are illustrated by comparing the number of product introductions from Sony between 1980 and 1989 with those of competitors. During this period, Sony introduced over 170 models, more than double that of Aiwa and over four times the level of Toshiba (Baker and Hart, 1999).

Hamel and Prahalad – core competencies

A further resource-based approach developed by Hamel and Prahalad (1994) concerns an organization's core competencies. Core competencies involve the integration of skills, knowledge and technology with the aim of creating competitive advantage. Hamel and Prahalad identify three key areas of core competencies:

1. Customer value – the organization's skills must have a real impact upon the way customers view the organization, so they perceive it as having a differential advantage in its area of specialization.

2. Competitor differentiation – the core skills must be unique versus those of competitors.

3. Extendable – the core skills must be extendable beyond the currently available products and services to provide for the creation of new products and services in the future.

Identifying core competencies may prove a difficult activity or process. In an article published in 1997, Coyne *et al* identified the challenges managers face in identifying and developing core competencies. The authors believe it is necessary to define competencies in a precise manner if the concept is to be fully exploited, and to avoid broad generalizations, such as 'marketing' or 'service'. To this end, the authors provide the following definition: 'A core competence is a combination of complementary skills and knowledge bases embedded in a group or team that results in the ability to execute one or more critical processes to a world-class standard'. From this the authors defined two categories of core competencies: insight/foresight competencies that enable a company to discover or learn facts or patterns that create first-mover advantages; and frontline execution competencies, where a company has a unique ability to consistently deliver products and services that are nearly equal in quality to products and services that would be produced by the best craftsperson under ideal circumstances. As a route to evaluating core competencies and their potential strategic value, the authors propose a process of questioning in the following areas:

1. Are our skills truly superior?

2. How sustainable is the superiority?

3. How much value can the competence generate in comparison to other economic levers?

4. Is the competence integral to our value proposition?

If the result of this questioning is that a company does not possess a core competence, then a further consideration is whether a competence or competencies can be developed within a meaningful time frame. The authors propose three potential routes: 'There seem to be three distinct routes to developing a core competence: *evolution*, where a company attempts to build a skill at the same time as the individuals involved perform their usual jobs; *incubation*, where a separate group is formed to focus exclusively on the chosen competence; and *acquisition*, where one company purchases another to obtain the skills it seeks'.

Coyne *et al* also state that companies that have been able to create core competencies appear to have followed consistent principles where the competence steers the power structure of the company, so the source of the skill is the driver of decision-making in the company. For example, if clothing designers hold the key skills existing within a designer clothing brand, the designers should be able to exert a dominant influence on the decision-making within the company. And secondly, where the core competence strategy is selected by the CEO, with the CEO selecting only one, or possibly two competencies to develop at any time.

As a cautionary note, Coyne *et al* conclude: 'A small number of firms already have a core competence. These fortunate few can devote their energies to sustaining and enhancing it. For most, however, the task is different. They must stop proclaiming that they have a competence, get serious about defining it, test to see if it would be valuable, and then set about developing it. If they do not, they will continue to see mirages and perish in the sand'.

The human-resource-based view

Resource-based views of strategy development emphasize the importance of the development of unique core skills, innovation and internal relationships. At a fundamental level these factors can be considered HR-related as they rely upon people behaving in particular ways to accomplish them successfully. (But this could be said of any strategy, regardless of its title.) This creates direct links between the resource-based and HR-based approaches to strategy development. However, a catalyst is required for people to devote their working time to the creation of competitive advantage through their individual and team-based actions. Putting aside fear and bullying, this catalyst might be described as culture. Creating a culture that is founded upon passion, flexibility, innovation, communication and knowledge sharing could be considered fundamental for organizations that wish to compete effectively in a fast-moving, global marketplace. The fact that some organizations are unable to motivate their people to this level of performance suggests these organizations are not paying sufficient attention to the internal strategies that encourage and enable improved performance from their people.

The human-resource-based view of strategy development focuses upon an organization's people, culture and structure and the relationship of these factors to change. Supporters of this view place HR-related considerations at the core of strategy development, rather than thinking of them as something to be considered once strategy formulation has taken place. A foundation to this book is that people, culture and change are key components of business success – if aligned in an appropriate manner. Achieving that alignment in relation to corporate purpose is what internal marketing strategy should be focused upon.

The European Foundation Quality Management (EFQM) Model

A further approach to strategy development is provided through the Business Excellence or EFQM Model. Stated simply, the model is based upon the assumption that: 'Excellent results with respect to *Performance*, *Customers*, *People* and *Society* are achieved through *Leadership* driving *Policy and Strategy*, *People*, *Partnerships and Resources*, and *Processes*' (British Quality Foundation). From the model, leadership, people, policy and strategy, partnerships and resources and processes are identified as enablers that achieve results in terms of people, customers, society and key performance indicators.

For organizations (or business units) adopting the model as a route to improving performance, it is necessary to carry out a self-assessment. This means reviewing the organization's activities as they relate to each of the components of the model. The assessment provides a review of strengths and weaknesses that are used to create an action plan for improving performance. A comparison of the components of internal marketing strategy with those of the model shows the seven components are considered within parts of The Excellence Model.

A key consideration for organizations that pursue The Excellence Model approach is whether it provides the optimum approach for the development of strategy. A self-assessment is a resource-intensive activity, but it has the advantage of drawing in people from across an organization to carry out the assessment and contribute to the action planning process. This can also provide an opportunity for people to learn about areas of an organization in which they have little knowledge or contact and to promote the development of integrated functional strategies. The self-assessment process can therefore be used to develop organizational knowledge, encourage teamworking, improve internal communication and create company ambassadors.

Ethical and social considerations

An aspect of the EFQM model is the inclusion of considerations relating to society. As noted earlier, the Co-operative Bank has adopted ethical considerations as core to its proposition. Increasingly, an organization's reputation and identity, and ultimately its profitability, will be related to its relationship with society. An article published in *The Times* (Golzen, 2001), stated that a report from the Ashridge Centre for Business and Society identified 36 per cent of Fortune 500 companies had decided not to proceed with proposed investment projects because of ethical or environmental concerns. The article also included this quotation from a speech given by Michael Porter: 'In a more socially and environmentally aware world, corporate responsibility in these spheres will itself be a source of competitive advantage'.

Mary Goodyear (2001) has incorporated considerations of corporate citizenship within a model of the development of international marketing. This model proposes a marketing hierarchy, where the top level (Stage 6) is cause-related marketing. Cause-related marketing occurs where an organization and a charity are involved in a mutually-beneficial, long-term relationship and, as a result of this relationship, a consumer uses a company to effect social change:

> *What will Stage Six be? It has already started. It assumes a consumer who is cynical, knowledgeable and often 'brand weary', more or less saturated with all the goods they need. It assumes a market place that is highly competitive and a media arena that is hopelessly cluttered and intrusive.*
>
> *It also recognizes that in the West at least, well-fed citizens are increasingly aware of overarching problems such as Third World poverty, environmental degradation or challenges of biodiversity. It also recognizes*

that while governments are shrinking and having fewer funds to allocate to solving problems, the power of the private sector is growing. So why shouldn't corporations use their resources for the common good?

Recent research seems to confirm this. David Grayson at the Global Public Affairs Institute Conference in October 2000 reported on a survey amongst 25,000 consumers conducted in 23 countries, which reflects the changing role for corporations. Where 1% (in the UK) felt that the business of a business is to make profit, pay taxes, provide jobs and obey the laws, 39% wanted companies to set higher ethical standards and build a better society for all.

At the same time as consumers are beginning to expect more from big business, so corporations, in an increasingly competitive environment, are struggling to find new branding opportunities.

Goodyear does not extend her analysis to an organization's internal marketplace. However, if the social or community-relevant aspects of an organization's behaviour become of increasing importance, we can hypothesize that such a move will also impact its internal marketing. If an organization wishes to be an employer of choice in a social environment where people place greater emphasis upon ethical behaviour, then people will increasingly consider these aspects when deciding whether they wish to work for an organization. In addition, we can hypothesize that organizations behaving in ways that are considered to be socially unacceptable by existing employees will face the possibility of internal disruption as segments of the internal marketplace protest against the activities occurring in the external environment.

In the quotation above, Goodyear identifies consumers who are cynical, knowledgeable and often brand weary. This description could no doubt be adopted by large numbers of employees within organizations and their attitude towards their employers.

KEY LEARNING POINTS

1. Corporate strategy involves linking an organization's internal resources and external relationships with its economic and social environment.

2. The development of corporate strategy must be placed in the context of an organization's vision, mission, objectives and values.

3. The aim of corporate strategy is to develop and sustain competitive advantage.

4. The level of turbulence and speed of change within many marketplaces means that emergent rather than prescriptive approaches to strategy development and implementation may be required, placing greater emphasis upon experimentation and learning-based strategies as a route to competitive advantage.

5. Recent approaches to strategy development have placed a particular emphasis upon the internal strengths of organizations as drivers of strategy development and sources of competitive advantage.

6. A greater focus upon internal strengths may lead to organizations taking a more focused approach to strategy development and implementation, with concentration upon opportunities that result from the exploitation of core competencies and distinctive capabilities.

7. The greater the importance placed upon people in contributing to an organization's competitive advantage, the greater the importance of internal marketing strategy in integrating functional strategies, developing people, skills and competencies and organizational learning.

SOURCES

Birchall, D and Tovstiga, G (1999) The Strategic Potential of a Firm's Knowledge Portfolio, *Journal of General Management*, **25** (1), Autumn, pp 1–16

Crabb, S (2000) Handy and Porter Rally the Faithful, *People Management*, 9 November, pp 9–11

Hedberg, A (2001) Lego Picks Rainey Kelly for £60m Global Business, *Marketing Week*, **13** December, p 10

Lynch, R (2000) *Corporate Strategy*, Prentice Hall, Harlow

Tait, A (2000) Barclays Brand Values, Barclays Group, Conference presentation, Communicating Corporate Vision and Values, Conference Partnership, London, October

Web sites

http://www.barclays.co.uk [accessed 9 May 2001, 7 September 2001]
http://www.economist.com [accessed 4 May 2001]
http://www.lego.com [accessed 7 September 2001]
http://www.oise.om.ca/~bwillard/ideaslo.htm [accessed 6 November 1998]

REFERENCES

Baker, M and Hart, S (1999) *Product Strategy and Management*, Prentice Hall Europe, Hemel Hempstead, pp 118–19

Benady, D (2001) A Brick Too Far, *Marketing Week*, March 15, pp 26–29

British Quality Foundation, *The Excellence Model*, Promotional literature

Bukowitz, W and Williams, R (2000) *The Knowledge Management Field-book*, pp 234–36, Prentice Hall, Harlow

Coyne, K, Hall, S and Clifford, P (1997) Is Your Core Competence a Mirage?, *The McKinsey Quarterly*, **1**, pp 40–54

Golzen, G (2001) The Moral High Ground, *The Times*, London, May 17

Goodyear, M (2001) Marketing Evolves from Selling to Citizenship, *Market Leader* (Spring), pp 30–36, The Marketing Society

Hamel, G and Prahalad, C (1994) *Competing for the Future*, Harvard Business School Press, Boston

Kay, J (1993) *Foundations of Corporate Success*, Oxford University Press

Lynch, R (2000) *Corporate Strategy*, p 8, Prentice Hall, Harlow

Ohmae, K (1983) *The Mind of the Strategist*, Penguin, New York

Oldfield, C (2001) Barclays Slammed by its Customers, *Financial Mail on Sunday*, August 5

Rivette, K and Kline, D (2000) Discovering New Value in Intellectual Property, *Harvard Business Review* (January–February), pp 54–66

Simms, J (2001) Marketing for Value, *Marketing*, 28 June, pp 34–35

The Economist, anonymous (2001) Retail Banking – Beautifying branches, March 24, p 113

The Economist, anonymous (2001) Corporate Durability – A talent for longevity, April 14, pp 75–78

Treanor, J (2001) Power to the People in Co-op Bank's Ethical Poll, *The Guardian*, London, April 17

3

Processes, service standards and measures

AIMS

1. To identify the importance of service standards, measures and processes in contributing to organizational success;

2. to illustrate the importance of Gap analysis and measures of service quality to internal marketing and customer satisfaction.

INTRODUCTION

You can only get to where you want to go if you already know where you are. For businesses it is obvious to state that if performance is to be improved, it is necessary to know your present performance levels. If you decide where you want to go you can create strategies to fill the gaps in performance. However, it is customers who will largely determine where you need to go. Therefore, as a business, knowing where to go involves knowing about customer needs, customer perceptions and their priorities. Getting there is about delivering an experience or experiences that are desired by the customer.

Perhaps not surprisingly, therefore, performance measurement is of fundamental importance to organizations that wish to achieve and sustain competitive advantage. Given that competitive advantage is derived from the management of internal and external factors, it is obvious that identifying and measuring the key drivers of the creation of competitive advantage are critical to the effective implementation of any strategy.

There is an old saying that goes: what gets measured gets managed. This suggests that what gets measured within an organization should be related to behaviour. With finite resources, it is of great importance that key business drivers are identified and activity is focused on those drivers. Since processes operate across an organization and not in vertical stacks, it is also important that measures are integrated to ensure that the activities of teams are supportive rather than conflicting.

Customer drivers

Measuring what happens in a business is a critical step in aligning internal activities with business objectives and responding to external factors. If what is happening inside a business is not measured, it is not possible to recognize or achieve success. Similarly, if what is important to measure is not identified, it will be impossible to focus behaviour on the key drivers to success in the marketplace. It is these kinds of considerations that lead organizations to consider how they measure not only the profitability of their customers and consequently where they will focus their resources, but how this focus will be interpreted as behaviour within an organization.

New economy – new measures

Measurement is very much on the management agenda for a variety of reasons. If businesses are to leverage increasing amounts of value from their resources, then those resources need to be measured to identify their value-adding contributions. Measurement is also a hot topic because of the changing nature of the economy and the evaluation of organizational capital. Traditionally, companies were valued on the basis of capital as identified in annual accounts. However, as economies have become increasingly service- and knowledge-based rather than manufacturing-based, the evaluations of companies have not been adequately explained through traditional financial measures alone. For many organizations, valuation through their share price is several times their 'book' value. If these 'intangible' aspects have greater value than the measurable assets that are manifested through conventional accounting practices, then it makes sense to identify what those intangibles are and to leverage them.

Knowledge-based organizations have much of their wealth lodged in a variety of places including the minds of their people, relationships, brands, processes and patents. This presents the obvious problem of how do you identify, measure and leverage these intangibles to create greater value? The importance of intangibles in relation to company valuation is identified in this quotation from Newman (2001): 'From a firm's perspective we are in an age in which management is increasingly about "intangibles". In 1988 Interbrand found that intangibles accounted for 56 per cent of the market capitalization of the FTSE 100. By 1998 this had risen to 71 per cent. Companies with strong brands no longer look at their tangible assets'.

With the increased awareness of the importance of brands, quality, people, innovation, processes, systems, relationships and customer satisfaction to corporate value, it is logical that organizations have looked to other measures beyond the purely financial to evaluate performance. From the Service-Profit Chain it is possible to develop a link between internal service quality and market performance. Therefore it makes sense for organizations, and particularly service-based companies, to identify, measure and manage the key internal drivers that contribute to competitive advantage. Measuring things for the sake of it just leads to a waste of resources and attention.

The importance of service quality measures

Increased competition, globalization, technological advances and structural change within economies have all encouraged new approaches to measuring performance. Management approaches such as total quality management, benchmarking, business process re-engineering and knowledge management have stimulated a greater awareness of measures and their link to performance improvement that go beyond purely financial considerations.

This chapter will therefore focus on some of the commonly used approaches to measurement that relate to internal marketing. As a result, much of the emphasis of this chapter is placed upon service quality measurement. The reason for this is that considerations of service quality and service marketing provide key theoretical underpinnings to internal marketing and, beyond that, to the foundations of customer relationship management. Also, considerations of service quality link directly to the Service-Profit Chain, which builds a crucial relationship between considerations of internal and external performance. For organizations that do perceive internal resources as fundamental drivers to corporate performance, then an understanding of service quality is as important to the body corporate as breathing.

Service quality

No doubt you have a favourite restaurant that you like to visit repeatedly or a preference for flying with a particular airline. This overall preference is probably based upon a number of different components that together build your overall perception of that airline or restaurant as being 'the best'. This preferred service might also provide a benchmark for when you evaluate similar services.

From the restaurant owner's perspective, your experience could be broken down into a series of process steps or moments of truth. Each moment of truth is a point of contact between yourself and the restaurant. For example, how you were greeted at the door, how your coat was taken, how you were shown to your table and the manner in which the restaurant's employees address you. The owner will also wish to ensure that the environment reflects the style of the restaurant, so the physical evidence is aligned with its positioning. If it is an expensive restaurant, then the table linen should 'feel right' and tables should be sufficiently distanced from others so that other guests do not have a negative impact upon your experience. Therefore the restaurant owner will need to identify, in minute detail, how to deliver the desired experience through the restaurant's environment, people and processes. His team has to 'live the brand', and to do this, the team members need to know what that means in very precise terms of behaviour and related standards. The restaurant owner will also need to ensure that his or her team is committed to delivering the required level of quality, meaning that the right kind of culture must be created that encourages high levels of quality and employee satisfaction.

Therefore, like any business, a restaurant is about bringing together a range of activities to create an experience or a product that meets the expectations of the consumer or purchaser. To constantly and reliably deliver that experience or product requires processes and people, and sustaining competitive advantage in those processes requires setting service standards and measuring performance over time. If the restaurant owner knows what the key priorities and values of the restaurant's customers are, then the owner will be able to develop and deliver the desired experience to customers by focusing on the contacts that are of particular importance to customers.

If the restaurant experience currently falls short of customer expectations, then the owner needs to calculate the gaps between current and required performance and develop strategies to fill them. But having closed those gaps, the process of measurement must continue. People's expectations are being raised all the time and new restaurants will open, providing competition and opportunities for diners to go elsewhere. The restaurant owner will therefore need to know about how performance compares with that of competitors and benchmark performance against those competitors to ensure superiority of delivery. The restaurant owner will also wish to know how changes in processes impact overall financial status, to provide direct links between what happens in the restaurant and kitchen and the restaurant's profitability. In fact, the analysis will need to consider factors occurring before ingredients arrive in the kitchen, such as the quality of those ingredients and the timeliness of their delivery or selection.

As a way of illustrating what can happen when organizations fail to understand the importance of service quality and the underpinning of standards and processes, the following short case provides a sad, but real, example.

Higher education – low standards

This case provides insights into a range of issues as a way of illustrating why it is important to measure service quality. The organization on which the case is based must remain anonymous, for reasons that will become obvious. The organization provided highly specialized education and charged a premium versus competing institutions. This premium was charged because of a perception within the organization that it provided superior service and facilities compared with competitors and a superior physical location – at the centre of the business sector to which its courses related.

A review of some of the organization's core processes shows that its supposed 'superior' position was founded on a myth. This was in part because in many key areas of its operations the organization lacked meaningful processes, and in part because the senior managers within the organization had not acted on student criticisms of the educational experience. Consequently, in the few areas where the measuring of performance occurred, the results and implications of these measures were not turned into meaningful actions for improvement.

Campus facilities were not compatible with the supposed positioning of the organization, with students complaining about catering standards and the eating environment, a lack of space in the library as well as inadequate supplies of books and computers. These factors contributed to a questioning from some students as to the value for money provided by the organization. A conclusion that might be reached is that the organization had over-stretched its resources by enrolling too many students and, as a result, was unable to provide adequate capacity to meet student requirements.

For staff, morale was generally perceived as low, in part because they worked in a highly politicized environment where appraisal procedures were not adequately communicated or implemented. Also, the organization had experienced difficulties in filling some key positions. The low morale was cascaded to the general treatment of students and the way in which they were communicated with.

Some members of the teaching staff displayed undesirable behaviour, such as delivering lectures whilst drunk, and students described some lecturers' comments as offensive. Training and development for many members of the teaching staff was so poor that they were unable to operate presentation aids. For some courses, lecturers were unsure as to exactly what they should have been teaching.

This brief look at an education institution illustrates what can happen when a number of key considerations are ignored, including market positioning. This organization failed to recognize that its customers were just that: paying customers. Student satisfaction levels were, understandably, low and from this we can anticipate that they would not recommend the institution to prospective students. Personal referrals are frequently the most important source of new business for a service-based organization, and therefore service quality and customer satisfaction simply cannot be ignored if a business is to survive and grow.

A lack of processes, service standards and measures meant the organization was not taking adequate steps to ensure that students were being provided with required standards of teaching, facilities and resources. This shows what can happen when a failure to develop meaningful processes, standards and measures occurs. However, poor service quality issues can be addressed as a route towards achieving competitive advantage, as illustrated in the case of Focus Quality Services.

Focus Quality Services – investors in processes and standards

Focus Quality Services (FQS) was in a similar position to the organization in the education institution in that it was failing to deliver required standards of service quality, but FQS took a proactive route to dealing with the issues it faced.

FQS was an unusual hybrid in that it was a wholly owned subsidiary of a quasi-governmental body. (See the case study of Focus Central London in Chapter 5 on internal communication to see how FQS was related to government policy.) This unusual situation meant that whilst FQS's remit was to deliver services that supported government policy, it was run along private sector lines. The company was dedicated to the promotion and delivery of training and development services to support large organizations that wished to achieve the Investors in People (IiP) standard. IiP is a UK government-sponsored initiative with the aim of encouraging organizations to implement business planning and related processes that align the development and training of people with business objectives. Organizations that commit to achieving the standard undergo assessments of their performance against the standard, and implement processes and procedures to close any gaps.

For FQS, the company was in the situation of facing very challenging IiP targets, but without a track record that suggested the targets could be met without significant change. In response, a business process re-engineering project was implemented, with process changes geared to meeting customer requirements.

Supported by consultants, a project team drawn from across the organization was created. The team identified the key processes it would prioritize for re-engineering, and then set about mapping the steps that made up the key processes. In parallel to this work, a research study was undertaken to identify the priorities and values of a sample of FQS's customers. This enabled FQS to understand exactly what its customers prioritized in terms of how they wanted services delivered. The research study also established benchmarks for the current level of service provided by FQS to its customers across a range of measures.

With processes mapped, and quantitative measures allocated to process steps including transaction volumes and costs, it was possible to identify which steps in processes were value adding or necessary to sustain a process, or simply non-value adding.

From the process maps, service contact maps were developed. This meant identifying every point of contact (or moment of truth) between the company and a customer whether through personal contact or the receipt of promotional literature or an invoice. These contact points were listed in a typical sequence of events. Using research with customers, each point of contact was evaluated across each of the five components of service quality: tangibility; empathy; responsiveness; reliability and assurance.

The next step in the project was to create a revised service blueprint that identified new ways of promoting and delivering services. Each revised step was considered in relation to the results of the research that identified customer priorities and the research that identified customer evaluations of process steps against the five components of service quality. From this analysis, a blueprint was developed that described in very precise terms how the services would be promoted and delivered at every point of contact. A further aim of this section of the project was to identify which contact points could be eliminated from the chain of contacts to improve efficiency and the customer experience.

Customers then evaluated the revised blueprint, with agreement achieved upon a service blueprint that described 'the ideal customer experience'. Following agreement of the blueprint, process changes were implemented along with supporting changes to information systems that were critical to delivering the 'blueprint experience'. Processes were also put in place to support customer relationship management and service recovery in the event of customers becoming dissatisfied at any point in the delivery of services.

Complementary activities included the implementation of training programmes for customer and non-customer facing staff to ensure that desired levels of service could be delivered. Guidance on behaviour and communication was provided through the creation of a document that described how people within the organization would behave, dress and communicate with customers. Also, metrics were developed for key aspects of the new processes so that individual, team and corporate performance could be measured.

By adopting the revised blueprints, FQS eliminated many non value-adding steps in its processes, releasing resources that could be focused on improving customer relationships and increasing income. The company's processes were then validated to ISO 9001 standard. The project also created substantial annualized cost savings. Research showed that customer recommendation levels were increased from very low levels to 85 per cent within one year following the implementation of the new blueprint.

Prior to the introduction of revised processes, FQS knew little of how its customers evaluated its service quality, which activities were value-adding or which parts of its loose structure of processes were or were not being delivered. Through mapping, calculation and research, FQS made step change in the quality of its service delivery and in its achievements, becoming the leader in its sector.

Benchmarking

In the example of FQS, the company identified through its customer research the standards required by customers in relation to service quality and the standards provided by companies delivering similar services. This information provided benchmarks for service standards, and research activities were developed for providing an ongoing monitoring of competitor performance.

Benchmarking is an activity that has been adopted by many organizations as an enabler of continuous improvements in performance and the transfer of best practice. Benchmarking has foundations in total quality management and in turn the 'world-class' school of management thought. Being 'world-class' was a particularly popular corporate consideration during the 1970s and 1980s, and was built on the belief that by benchmarking performance against other organizations, a company could develop superior positioning by doing things better.

An obvious attraction of this approach is that it provides a link between the critical success factors within a sector and the performance levels a company would set itself to achieve. These levels would change over time, but they could be linked to internal processes, measures and behaviours. In very simple terms, benchmarking supports the identification of gaps in performance and subsequent closure strategies.

Many benchmarking 'clubs' exist, as do surveys of particular sectors that allow participants to evaluate their performance against that of other companies. For example, the Financial Services Special Interest Group (FiSSInG) provides members with benchmarking opportunities across a range of services, with a particular emphasis on HR-related benchmarking. FiSSInG defines benchmarking as: '. . . a continuous, systematic process for comparing performance of organizations, functions, processes or economics, policies or sectors of business against the "best in class", aiming to match and exceed those performance levels. Benchmarking enables us to identify and improve key business processes, avoid trial and error, reduce development costs and time to implement, and improve performance, service and market share' (FiSSIng, 2000).

Benchmarking has been adopted by many organizations within the public, non-profit and private sectors, and is encouraged through the EFQM Excellence Model. In promoting its own benchmarking service for investment banks, MIB Partners plc provides these statistics in its promotional material on the adoption of benchmarking:

❙ Sixty-seven per cent of firms use benchmarking.

❙ Eighty-two per cent of benchmarking programmes are regarded as successful.

❙ Seventy-seven per cent of benchmark users consider benchmarking as an integral part of managing performance improvement.

❙ Eighty-four per cent of benchmark users consider benchmarking as an essential staff motivator.

❙ Seventy-nine per cent of benchmark users consider benchmarking as able to provide an early warning sign of competitive disadvantage.

However, whilst benchmarking provides a route for evaluating performance, effective strategies are required to achieve gap closures. Benchmarking is not a strategy in itself, as identified by Nattermann (2000), who has highlighted some of the potential negative impacts of benchmarking.

Follow the leader

Fundamental to Nattermann's argument is the view that benchmarking is an operational and not a strategic tool. He presents a view of marketplaces as collections of businesses where companies are attracted by high margins, and where these companies copy the market leader through adherence to benchmarking. Put simply, Nattermann's view is that if you match your activities to those of the market leader, then you become like them, crowding out the same area of the market and reducing margins through increasing competitive activity. This is how Nattermann describes the situation: '. . . they all want to occupy the point on the strategic landscape that their most successful competitor has staked out. Soon other competitors can be seen herding, lemming-like, around that best practice company's product, pricing, and channel strategies. Products and services become increasingly commoditized, and margins tumble as more and more companies compete for smaller segments of customers and industry resources'.

Nattermann recognizes the important role of benchmarking as a tool for increasing a company's performance – for example, the gains made by the US automobile industry by adopting Japanese manufacturing techniques – but illustrates how competitors in the German wireless telecommunications market reduced industry margins by approximately 50 per cent between 1993 and 1998 by 'herding' around a similar point on the strategic landscape.

An obvious conclusion of this analysis is that companies need to find well-differentiated positions in a market, such as the entry strategy of The Body Shop into 'open space' within the cosmetics sector. But as with the marketplace The Body Shop now faces, companies must constantly seek new propositions to sustain differentiation and competitive advantage. Therefore, whilst benchmarking can be an important tool for improving corporate performance, it should be placed in the context of the overall objective of achieving sustainable competitive advantage.

Nattermann does not explore the implications of his views in relation to the internal marketplace, but it follows logically that simply developing performance benchmarks for internal service quality against those of competitors may not lead to meaningful, long-term relative improvements in performance. What is needed is the creation of innovative differentiators that are valued by employees and customers and that contribute to sustainable competitive advantage. Where differentiation through innovation is a key factor for success, a culture that encourages innovation is clearly required.

Sears – chain of events

In the introduction to this book, reference was made to the Service-Profit Chain, and the links that provided a relationship between employee satisfaction and corporate profitability, through internal and external service quality. In an article published in 1998 in the *Harvard Business Review*, Rucci et al (1998, p 75–97) wrote the 'Employee-Customer-Profit Chain At Sears'. Similarly to the Service-Profit Chain, Sears identified direct, quantifiable links between employee attitudes and corporate performance.

The authors identified how Sears, Roebuck and Company created great change in its performance and how the organization developed a model that linked employee attitudes to customer satisfaction and financial performance. This model relates to so-named Total Performance Indicators (TPIs), that, according to the article, show us:

> . . . *how well we are doing with customers, employees, and investors. We understand the several layers of factors that drive employee attitudes, and we know how employee attitudes affect employee retention, how employee retention affects the drivers of customer satisfaction, how customer satisfaction affects financials, and a great deal more. We have also calculated the lag time between a change in any of those metrics and a corresponding change in financial performance, so that we can see a shift in, say, employee attitudes, we know not only how but also when it will affect results. Our TPIs make the employee-customer-profit chain operational because we manage the company on the basis of these indicators, with remarkably positive results.*

From this, it might appear that Sears had discovered the managerial Crown Jewels. And in a way, it had. It is a remarkable achievement for an organization to be able to identify and quantify the complex chain of attitudes and behaviours that link employee and customer satisfaction and financial performance and, by implication, measure the value of its internal communication and HR strategies. But to assume that the 'Sears model' can be cloned for every business would be an oversimplification. The Crown Jewels that are zealously guarded within the Tower of London are for the exclusive use of one family and have been collected over a long period of time. And this family does not appear to wish to hire them out for bar mitzvahs and high school graduations. But even if it did, and you took a crown out of its box, you might find that it did not fit. And so it is for the Employee-Customer-Profit Chain at Sears: it may not fit any other company. However, the processes adopted by Sears, leading to the identification of the Employee-Customer-Profit Chain, provide an opportunity for other organizations to learn and consider whether developing a similar type of model would not only contribute to competitive advantage, but bring about a change in their attitudes and approaches to internal and external marketplaces.

Developing its model took Sears several years of extraordinarily hard work and determination. The company developed objectives and measures that were linked to three categories: Sears' employees, its stores and its investors. These categories were simply identified as: a compelling place to work; a compelling place to shop and a compelling place to invest.

Through analysis of historic data and new research, including employee surveys, Sears was able to identify the key dimensions that linked employee satisfaction to employee loyalty and employee attitude to customers. At a very basic level, the model identifies that a five-unit increase in employee attitude creates a 1.3 unit increase in customer impression that leads to a 0.5 per cent increase in revenue growth.

The model not only provides a predictive role for customer impression and revenue following employee attitude surveys, but it also has applications for the skills and attitudes that are evaluated when Sears hires new staff and develops existing people, as well as broader aspects of its HR and communications strategies. Employee rewards, for example, are related to TPIs.

The Sears case study provides an illustration of where measures of employee attitudes have been directly linked to business performance. With the importance of employees to customer satisfaction and corporate performance, it is not surprising that forms of performance measurement have developed that encompass a range of considerations that go beyond the purely financial. One such approach is the Balanced Scorecard.

The Balanced Scorecard

As identified in the Sears case, the company developed a variety of measures that might be described as a performance scorecard. In developing its TPIs, Sears decided: '. . . we wanted to go well beyond the usual balanced scorecard, commonly just a set of untested assumptions, and nail down the drivers of future financial performance with statistical rigor' (Rucci *et al*, 1998, p 89).

Describing the Balanced Scorecard as 'just a set of untested assumptions' would no doubt create a response from Kaplan and Norton (1996), who introduced the concept of the Balanced Scorecard in their book of the same name. In commenting upon the relevance of the Balanced Scorecard to internal communication, Clutterbuck (2001) states:

> *Like so many management concepts, the balanced scorecard is mainly a clever repackaging of ideas that have been around for a long time – in this case, since at least the early 1970s. That's not to disparage their usefulness – they help to focus top management's attention on areas it wouldn't otherwise consider. But when the fad goes out of vogue, as they all do eventually, the good practices associated with it tend to fall into disuse. There are therefore considerable dangers to tying communication practice too closely to the balanced scorecard.*

Whilst the Balanced Scorecard is not without its critics, if I have interpreted Clutterbuck's comments correctly, he is in part saying: don't throw the baby out with the bathwater.

The Balanced Scorecard provides links between organizational vision and strategy and four key performance areas through related objectives, measures, targets and initiatives. Kaplan and Norton (1996) provide the following reasons as to why they believe new approaches to measurement are required and why they believe the Balanced Scorecard is of particular relevance:

> *The collision between the irresistible force to build long-range competitive capabilities and the immovable object of the historic-cost financial accounting model has created a new synthesis: the Balanced Scorecard. The Balanced Scorecard retains traditional financial measures. But financial measures tell the story of past events, an adequate story for industrial age companies for which investments in long-term capabilities and customer relationships were not critical for success. These financial measures are inadequate, however, for guiding and evaluating the journey that information age companies must make to create future value through investment in customers, suppliers, employees, processes, technology, and innovation.*
>
> *The Balanced Scorecard complements financial measures of past performance with measures of the drivers of future performance. The objectives and measures of the scorecard are derived from an organization's vision and strategy. The objectives and measures view organizational performance from four perspectives: financial, customer, internal business process, and learning and growth.*

The authors also identify how the Balanced Scorecard acts as a strategic framework for action through a cycle of learning and the alignment of vision, strategy, objectives, communication and feedback. In very simple terms, an organization adopting the Balanced Scorecard approach will identify the key drivers to performance within each of the key areas and measures for those drivers. The measures are then related to initiatives and objectives that can be cascaded across and down the organization.

In their writings, Kaplan and Norton provide many examples of organizations that have benefited through the adoption of the Balanced Scorecard as an enabler of improved business performance, whilst agreeing that it is obviously important for a company to select the right measures for its scorecard. As a route to linking internal and external marketing strategy, the Balanced Scorecard is a very attractive tool. By creating direct relationships between an organization's vision, strategy, internal processes, learning and growth, customers and financial performance, key aspects of internal marketing strategy can be aligned with corporate strategy.

Actually carrying out this kind of change as a route to integrating functional strategies is obviously a great challenge, and will no doubt generate the typical responses when fiefdoms, cultures and processes are considered to be under attack. But what is obvious is that the Balanced Scorecard is not about simply imposing a new set of measures on an organization. It is also about following through and creating cultural change as a part of a route to aligning the internal and external marketplaces and differing stakeholder needs. The authors provide an example of one insurance company that built its strategic management system based upon the Balanced Scorecard within a 30-month period, from clarifying the vision through to the linking of employee objectives and rewards to the Scorecard (Kaplan and Norton, 1996, in the *Harvard Business Review*).

People satisfaction

Measuring internal service quality and employee satisfaction is a key consideration in internal marketing. For organizations that do measure these factors and their constituent elements, and then act upon the results, there are clear benefits, as identified in the Sears case above. Key considerations are whether the elements being measured are of importance and whether the results of questionnaires lead to actionable items. If it is not possible to relate responses to questions on a questionnaire to behaviour, then they will prove to be of little value. Some organizations display a cynical approach to employee satisfaction questionnaires, such as failing to publish the results, changing a large number of questions each time a questionnaire is distributed so that comparative analysis becomes impossible or simply stopping doing them because the results are anticipated to be so bad.

Identifying what needs to be measured, and consequently the questions to ask, will depend upon the correct identification of key drivers of performance and their relative importance. At Sears, for example, a part of the process that led to the development of the Employee-Customer-Profit Chain included gathering 80,000 employee surveys. The group carrying out this work identified six core values that employees felt strongly about: honesty, integrity, respect for the individual, teamwork, trust and customer focus. Further analysis found that responses to 10 questions and statements in particular had a higher impact upon employee behaviour and subsequently on customer satisfaction. The first six of these related to attitude about the job, with the following four related to attitude about the company (Rucci *et al*, 1998):

1. I like the kind of work I do.

2. My work gives me a sense of accomplishment.

3. I am proud to say I work at Sears.

4. How does the amount of work you are expected to do influence your overall attitude about your job?

5. How do your physical working conditions influence your overall attitude about your job?

6. How does the way you are treated by those who supervise you influence your overall attitude about your job?

7. I feel good about the future of the company.

8. Sears is making the changes necessary to compete effectively.

9. I understand our business strategy.

10. Do you see a connection between the work you do and the company's strategic objectives?

Fuzzy logic

Making a link between answers to 'soft' questions and 'hard' numbers about business performance may require extensive investment in research and statistical analysis. Sears has obviously managed to make those links. MORI has conducted research to assist companies identify which measures on employee satisfaction surveys are key to focus upon by identifying links between certain measures and business performance (Brown, 2001).

However, making the links between perceptions of internal and external service quality and performance is necessary if companies are to improve service quality, and in turn improve employee and customer satisfaction and retention. Service quality is a route to competitive advantage. By understanding perceptions of service quality and developing appropriate measures it becomes more likely that organizations will be able to turn the 'soft' perceptions of consumers and employees into the 'hard' facts of business performance. That understanding may well be achieved through an understanding of moments of truth where customer and organization interact and the brand experience is created.

In his book *Customer Relationship Management – Making hard decisions with soft numbers*, Anton (1996) describes how customer-perceived value measurements can be linked to internal process metrics and performance measures. He also provides examples of what he describes as 'Fuzzy Logic': the logic that links customer perceptions to service quality. These are a small sample of his Fuzzy Logics:

Customer satisfaction is a state of mind in which his or her needs, wants, and expectations throughout the product/service life have been met or exceeded, resulting in repurchase and loyalty.

You cannot improve externally what you don't measure internally.

Where possible, you should ensure that the internal metrics that you select are behaviourally anchored.

Let the customer define the outcome of each of your company's processes.

In today's business world, to retain customers you cannot look at it as if you were selling a product, instead, you are providing customer-perceived quality.

Anton also provides this nugget in the introduction to his book: 'A recent survey completed by Purdue University researchers showed that 87 per cent of the Fortune 500 companies surveyed had the words "customer relationships" or "customer satisfaction" in their corporate mission statement, yet only 18 per cent had implemented a method for measuring this elusive asset'.

THEORIES, MODELS AND PERSPECTIVES

The Parasuraman, Zeithaml and Berry (PZB) Gaps Model of Service Quality (1985)

The earlier FQS case study provided reference to the importance of customer expectations in shaping a customer's evaluation (or perception) of the services provided by a company. A key foundation to the Gaps approach to service quality is that expectations and perceptions of services affect customer satisfaction. If a gap exists between expectations and perceptions (for example where expected service quality exceeds perceived [ie experienced] service quality), the customer will be dissatisfied. A goal of an organization should be to close this 'gap' between expectations and perceptions.

Considerations of service quality provide the foundation to the Gaps approach to service marketing. A critical point to understand in relation to this is that the perception of quality is held in the mind of the consumer. It is not appropriate for the service provider to believe it can set the level of service quality based on its assumptions about consumer perceptions. The PZB Gaps Model (as outlined in Zeithaml and Bitner, 2000) identifies four key areas for the diagnosis of gaps in service quality:

▮ Gap 1 – The Expectations Gap – not knowing what customers expect;

▮ Gap 2 – The Design and Specifications Gap – not selecting the right service designs and standards;

▮ Gap 3 – The Service Delivery Gap – not delivering to service standards;

▮ Gap 4 – The Communication Gap – not matching performance to promises.

Gap 1 – The Expectations Gap

This gap relates to the difference between customer expectations of service quality and a company's understanding of those expectations. The gap can arise from poor focus in four main areas: market research; upward communication; customer relationships and service recovery.

Gap 2 – The Design and Specifications Gap

Gap 2 can arise through poor service design and a lack of customer-defined standards for processes. This emphasizes the need to understand customer perceptions so that service designs and standards are set at levels that reflect customer requirements. This gap will include considerations of the environment in which the service is delivered.

Gap 3 – The Service Delivery Gap

Gap 3 might be described as the 'people gap'. Not delivering agreed service standards can be caused through employees not meeting the required standards due to a range of HR-related issues including recruitment, inappropriate support and reward systems and a lack of empowerment and teamwork. Gap 3 is frequently the most difficult gap to close.

Intermediaries can also have an adverse impact on service quality for a variety of reasons including channel conflict, poor central quality control and issues regarding costs and rewards. This is why franchisers will generally have strict quality standards and monitoring processes to ensure franchisees deliver services to the required quality standards.

Customers too have impact upon service quality. If they are unaware of the role they are expected to play in service delivery (for example, preparatory work in advance of attending a training course), they are more likely to find fault with the service. Similarly, customers will expect to receive goods and services when they want them (for example, the provision of 'just in time' training to meet immediate learning requirements), and not have to wait due to poor capacity management.

Gap 4 – The Communication Gap

Gap 4 can arise through a lack of integration and consistency in internal and external communications and through over-promising in communications and personal selling. If a customer is promised specific product or service features and benefits that are not delivered, there is clearly a difference between promise and performance

The PZB Gaps Model provides a comprehensive diagnostic approach to evaluating the quality of an organization's service delivery that builds upon the elements of the service marketing mix. However, further consideration of service quality introduces routes to evaluating customer expectations and perceptions of services.

Measuring service quality

Related to the PZB Gaps Model is the recognition that customers do not perceive service quality as a one-dimensional concept. Five dimensions of assessment for service quality have been identified. Sometimes customers will use all of the dimensions to determine service quality perceptions, and at other times any possible permutation of the dimensions. The five dimensions of service quality, as identified by Parasuraman, Zeithaml and Berry are:

1. Reliability – performing the promised service dependably and accurately. Reliability has strong implications for brand perceptions due to the importance of producing the 'brand experience' consistently on repeated occasions.

2. Responsiveness – helping customers and providing prompt service.

3. Assurance – employees' knowledge and courtesy and their ability to inspire trust and confidence in the customer. This dimension is likely to be particularly important for services where customers perceive purchases as involving high risk and/or where they feel uncertain about their ability to evaluate outcomes.

4. Empathy – the caring, individualized attention provided by employees to customers, whether face-to-face, by telephone, letter or online.

5. Tangibles – the appearance of an organization's physical facilities, equipment, people and published materials.

The five dimensions of service quality in relation to service delivery can be measured through the SERVQUAL instrument or questionnaire, where the gaps between customer perceptions and expectations of service quality can be measured and related to the five dimensions. The SERVQUAL approach is still used in research relating to service quality, as are adaptations of it. Typically, 21 questions are used to evaluate perceptions of a service across the five dimensions with a further nine questions relating to customer expectations. Comparing perceptions with expectations allows gaps in service quality to be identified.

Criticisms have been made of the SERVQUAL instrument, with some contributors proposing it is only necessary to measure perceptions, leading to the generation of the SERVPERV instrument for measuring customer perceptions of a service. In the FQS case provided earlier in this chapter, the SERVQUAL instrument was not used to evaluate customer expectations or experiences. An alternative approach was adopted by asking customers to provide their perceptions of each moment of truth between the company and the customer. These comments were then broken down to identify FQS's performance in terms of each component of service quality.

Measuring internal service quality

From studies carried out in large Swedish service companies, Edvarsson, Larsson and Setterlind (1997), used factor analysis to identify five key dimensions for the measurement of employees' perceptions of internal service quality. The approach to measuring internal service quality was inspired by the SERVQUAL approach, but with the instrument adapted for the collection of data from employees rather than customers. The five key dimensions that emerged were:

1. public image – physical facilities, equipment, employee appearance, printed materials;

2. reliability – honouring commitments, solving problems, doing things initially;

3. responsiveness – effective communication, prompt response, service orientation, willingness to accommodate;

4. confidence in relationships – atmosphere of trust, comfortable interpersonal relations, relationship kindness, respect and belief in the competence of co-workers;

5. sensitivity and empathy – sincere concern, personal attentiveness, caring and responsiveness to needs.

Within their paper, the authors published the questionnaire used for their study. Also, the authors concluded:

First, internal service quality is based on work conditions characterised by neither too much nor too little stress. An optimal stress level, when it comes to workload for instance, is achieved not when employees feel at ease in their jobs or have little to do, but rather when they feel that they have freedom to decide the pace and organisation of their work. Second, organising for quality – leadership at all levels in the organisation appears to be crucial for success. Our data indicate that top management as well as supervisors should give employees targets to work towards and should be able to initiate and carry out changes and create work conditions so that employees do not need to worry about job security. Third, important assignments and interesting and stimulating work combined with reasonable pay is crucial for service quality.

Edvinsson and Malone – intellectual capital

As noted in the introduction to this chapter, the market capitalizations of many companies are greater than the asset value as shown through their annual report and accounts. This difference in value is therefore an 'intangible asset' that might be comprised of a number of different elements including perceptions of brand value (though calculations of brand value may be included in some company accounts), goodwill and the company's intellectual capital.

In recognizing the difference between its 'book' and 'market' values, Skandia, the financial services company, published the world's first Intellectual Capital Report to augment its annual report and accounts in 1995. (Though a comment in an article published in *The Economist*, May 2001, states the company's 'efforts in this direction seem to have petered out after 1999, when its most recent supplement was published'.)

Skandia's 'hidden' value was identified as 'intellectual capital', and a model was developed to demonstrate how the company's intellectual capital was assessed. Furthermore, recognizing the importance of intellectual capital to its future growth, survival and competitive advantage, Skandia developed not only an approach to measuring intellectual capital, but also strategies to ensure it was developing its intellectual capital in the desired way.

There are no 'formal' (ie universally agreed) approaches for measuring intellectual capital in the way that accounting practice has developed. However, in their book *Intellectual Capital*, Edvinsson and Malone (1997) provide a strong argument for why it is important to measure intellectual capital, and then go on to describe the 'Skandia Model'. They make this comment: '. . . this lack of common practices for disclosing and visualizing Intellectual Capital hurts all stakeholders and investors. They, too, can miss a subtle change in tenor or the loss of a key knowledge-carrying employee that signals the coming eclipse of a corporate star. And more often, they simply don't spot until the last minute the private new start-up that is about to change the world' (p 7).

Later on in the same work (p 11), Edvinsson and Malone state that intellectual capital = human capital + structural capital, and define human and structural capital as:

1. **Human capital.** *The combined knowledge, skill, innovativeness, and ability of the company's individual employees to meet the tasks at hand. It also includes the company's values, culture, and philosophy. Human capital cannot be owned by the company.*

2. **Structural capital.** *The hardware, software, databases, organizational structures, patents, trademarks, and everything else of organizational capability that supports those employees', productivity – in a word, everything left at the office when the employees go home. Structural capital also includes customer capital, the relationships developed with key customers. Unlike human capital, structural capital can be owned and thereby traded.*

The Skandia market value scheme

These considerations were expanded to provide the Skandia Market Value Scheme, a model of the contributors to Skandia's market value. Commencing with market value, as noted above, the market value of an organization is composed of its financial capital (tangible assets) and intellectual capital (intangible assets). The intellectual capital can be segmented by human capital and structural capital, as noted above.

Structural capital is comprised of customer capital (a valuation of customer relationships) and organizational capital (the systems and philosophy that speed knowledge flows within the organization and to external channels). Organizational capital is segmented by innovation capital (the ability of an organization to continually renew itself and the results of innovation such as trademarks and patents as well as the skills used in bringing new products and services to market with speed) and process capital (the work processes and employee programmes that enhance the delivery or manufacture of new services and products).

The Skandia navigator

Skandia also developed a strategic model for the management of its overall market value that takes into account the components of the

Skandia Market Value Scheme. This model is known as the Skandia Navigator, where the focus is upon five areas: finance, customers, people, process and renewal and development. There are clearly links here between this model and a Balanced Scorecard approach.

From its model, Skandia developed a range of measures that were considered to provide an evaluation of the organization across these key aspects of its operations, and ultimately, a measure of its total intellectual capital. These measures provide a variety of benchmarks for the organization's performance over time.

Through the Navigator, Skandia has developed a model where the organization believes it has identified the key drivers to its future success, recognizing that its success will be based upon its people focusing their activities on those drivers. In turn, it has recognized that by making the 'intangible' 'tangible' through the use of measures, it will be better placed to leverage the components of its intellectual capital to sustain competitive advantage. This in turn means that any organization following a similar approach will require a culture, values and leadership that support intellectual capital growth. This kind of organization might be described as a 'learning organization'. Considerations of learning organizations and related aspects of intellectual capital and knowledge management provide a link to the next chapter.

KEY LEARNING POINTS

1. Performance measurement is of fundamental importance to organizations that wish to achieve and sustain competitive advantage.

2. Performance improvements can only be achieved by calculating current performance, identifying desired performance and measuring progress against quantifiable objectives.

3. Performance measurement should be focused upon the key drivers of organizational performance and link behaviour occurring within an organization with impact in the external marketplace.

4. Changes occurring in the global economy have stimulated approaches to performance measurement that are much broader than the purely financial, to include considerations of intellectual capital, customer satisfaction, employee satisfaction, processes and supplier performance.

5. Empirical research has established strong links between internal and external service quality and profitability, with the result that some organizations are placing great emphasis upon employee satisfaction as a route to improving financial performance.

6. Measures of service quality are of great importance as a diagnostic route to closing gaps between customer expectations and perceptions. The use of gaps models, such as the PZB Gaps Model, provides for a diagnosis and prescription for gaps closure that will involve considerations of processes, internal service quality standards and measures.

7. Processes generally operate laterally within an organization, rather than in vertical silos. As a result, improvements in internal and external service quality will require the effective integration of functional strategies and cross-departmental activities.

SOURCES

Kaplan, S and Norton, D (1996) *The Balanced Scorecard*, Harvard Business School Press, Boston

Viele, T, Dale, B and Williams, R (2000) ISO 9000 Series and Excellence Models: Fad to fashion to fit, *Journal of General Management*, **25** (3), pp 50–66

Zeithaml, V and Bitner, M J (2000) *Services Marketing – Integrating customer focus across the firm*, McGraw-Hill

REFERENCES

Anton, J (1996) *Customer Relationship Management – Making hard decisions with soft numbers*, Prentice Hall, Upper Saddle River, New Jersey

Brown, A (2001) *Getting The Best Value From Your Communications Research*, MORI, Conference presentation, Next Generation Communication Strategies, IQPC Conference, February, London

Clutterbuck, D (2001) Talking Point – How relevant is the 'balanced scorecard' approach to internal communication?, *Internal Communication*, **62** (February), p 5

Edvarsson, B, Larsson, G and Setterlind, S (1997) Internal Service Quality and the Psychosocial Environment: An empirical analysis of conceptual interrelatedness, *The Services Industries Journal*, **17** (April), pp 252–63

Edvinsson, L and Malone, M (1997) *Intellectual Capital*, Piatkus, London, pp 7, 11

Financial Services Special Interest Group (2000) Introduction, *Benchmarking Club Members Manual*, FiSSInG, Bournemouth, p 1

Kaplan, S and Norton, D (1996) *The Balanced Scorecard*, Harvard Business School Press, Boston, p 8

Kaplan, S and Norton, D (1996) Using the Balanced Scorecard as a Strategic Management System, *Harvard Business Review* (January–February), pp 75–85

MIB Partners plc, *GAUGE™ Benchmark – Cost benchmark analysis for investment banks*, Promotional literature, p 5

Nattermann, P (2000) Best Practice ≠ Best Strategy, *The McKinsey Quarterly*, **2**, pp 22–31

Newman, K (2001) *The Sorcerer's Apprentice? Alchemy, seduction and confusion in modern marketing*, Marketing and Service Quality Research Centre, Middlesex University Business School

Rucci, A, Kirn, S and Quinn, R (1998) The Employee-Customer-Profit Chain At Sears, *Harvard Business Review* (January–February), pp 75–97

The Economist, anonymous (2001) Touchy Feely, 19 May, p 102

Zeithaml, V and Bitner, M J (2000) *Services Marketing – Integrating customer focus across the firm*, McGraw-Hill

4

Knowledge management

AIMS

1. To show the contributions of intellectual capital and knowledge management in achieving and sustaining competitive advantage;

2. to identify the importance of people contributing their knowledge as a part of developing and sustaining a culture in which information and knowledge are shared.

INTRODUCTION

Knowledge management (KM) is a slippery fish. For some organizations that downsized during the 1980s and 1990s, it was the one that got away, with redundant staff leaving organizations along with large amounts of corporate knowledge and wealth: '. . . the balance sheet offers no hint of a company's memories, traditions and philosophy. It doesn't tell how much they are worth or set off alarms when, through management decisions or employee layoffs, they are lost. The result is often a kind of corporate Alzheimer's, whereby a company busy watching the bottom line loses its institutional memory, and thus itself, without ever noticing the loss' (Edvinsson and Malone, 1997).

Gaps in corporate memory resulting from downsizing or rightsizing, or whatever allegedly politically correct term was used, stimulated considerations as to how corporate information and knowledge could be gathered and managed. Pressures in bringing products to market with greater speed and accelerated innovation have also stimulated the need for the coordination of knowledge and resources across an organization.

Further drivers to the management of information and knowledge have been the development of information technologies that allow the storage, interrogation and distribution of information, the increasing importance of the service sector and the complementary growth in the significance of 'knowledge workers'. However, the information overload experienced by many people means that information and knowledge must be managed if they are to be used effectively as assets in the creation of competitive advantage.

In the past, knowledge was something that was generally netted outside the organization. For example, in the recent past KM for marketers was focused on the external market through a marketing information system that was used to research, monitor and predict future market changes and the activities of competitors. Now, organizations also fish within their own ponds, seeking to catch and release the intellectual capital that lives within its people and networks. However, developing strategies that create tangible benefits from the discovery, translation, protection, transfer and interpretation of knowledge is a huge challenge. Our slippery fish appears to be able to break the surface at every point in an organization, spawn and swim on at will: 'Knowledge management is a fast-moving field that has been created by the collision of several others – human resources, organizational development, change management, information technology, brand and reputation management, performance measurement and valuation. New understanding is generated everyday as organizations experiment, learn, discard, retain, adapt and move on' (Bukowitz and Williams, 2000, p 1).

KM is an emergent discipline and a controversial one in so far as KM, it could be argued, is the most fundamental driver of corporate success. But if an organization is to achieve tangible, measurable benefits from knowledge, people must volunteer relevant knowledge, and in turn, that knowledge must be managed and leveraged. Encouraging people to contribute to the leveraging of knowledge through collaboration is amongst the key challenges of knowledge transfer and management. It may sound like a simple thing to say: 'contribute your knowledge' to people, but actually getting them to do it may require a radical change in an organization's culture, processes and architecture. In the following quotation, Snowden (1999) points to some of the culture-related issues regarding knowledge sharing:

In general, if a community is not physically, temporally and spiritually rooted, then it is alienated from its environment and will focus on survival rather than creativity and collaboration. In such conditions, knowledge hoarding will predominate and the community will close itself to the external world. If the alienation becomes extreme, the community may even turn on itself, atomising into an incoherent babble of competing self interests.

This is of major importance for the emerging disciplines of knowledge management. Organisations are increasingly aware of the need to create appropriate virtual and physical space in which knowledge can be organised and distributed. They are gradually becoming aware that knowledge cannot be treated as an organisational asset without the active and voluntary participation of the communities that are its true owners. A shift to thinking of employees as volunteers requires a radical rethink of reward structures, organisational form and management attitude. It requires us to think of the organisation as a complex ecology in which the number of causal factors renders pseudo-rational prescriptive models redundant at best and poisonous at worst. Managing a complex ecology requires a focus on interventions designed to trigger desired behaviour in the members of the ecology rather than attempts to mandate activity; it requires an understanding of the underlying values around which the various communities that comprise that ecology self-organise their knowledge.

Defining knowledge management

Bukowitz and Williams (2000, p 2) define knowledge management as: '. . . the process by which the organization generates wealth from its knowledge or intellectual capital'. In turn, they define intellectual capital or knowledge as: 'Anything valued by the organization that is embedded in people or derived from processes, systems, and the organizational culture – individual knowledge and skills, norms and values, databases, methodologies, software, know-how, licenses, brands, and trade secrets, to name a few'.

The dilemmas of knowledge management

These definitions provide a dilemma: it is as if almost everything that occurs within an organization can be classified as knowledge. This dilemma is made even greater by considering cases where organizations have redesigned their work environments to encourage casual conversation. A short time ago, such activity would have been considered time-wasting and the antithesis of good corporate practice. Conversations next to water coolers and coffee machines may facilitate the transfer of knowledge within an organization, particularly the kinds of knowledge that are difficult to 'download' from a person and place on an information system. These kinds of practices provide a further challenge regarding the measurement of knowledge creation and learning. How can you measure the benefits of changing an organization's environment to one that encourages conversations around water coolers or access to information held on an intranet?

Knowledge management is obviously at an early stage in its development as a discipline, and in its early evolutionary state we can assume that it is going to extend itself into areas that will yield great insights and others where it will reach a cul-de-sac. This newness presents many difficulties and concerns regarding exactly what might be an avenue of valid investigation and what might be a dead end. Nobody wants to be a dinosaur and nobody wants to be wearing the emperor's new clothes.

Identifying, codifying, analysing and storing relevant information and then distributing or communicating it to others so that further, measurable value can be added, provide the key challenges of knowledge management. Knowledge management is also closely related to considerations of learning organizations and organizational learning. If people will not transfer their knowledge, then an organization will be unable to develop a learning culture. This, in turn, relates to considerations of organizational values. If shared learning is not at the core of an organization's value structure, it will not be adopted as an attitude or behaviour.

Organizational learning and learning organizations

If all of this was not complicated enough, it also important to gain an understanding of the semantics of knowledge and learning. Individual learning will contribute to organizational learning. However, organizational learning should be more than aggregated individual learning. Also, it is helpful to be able to distinguish between organizational learning and a learning organization. Confused? Perhaps Lahti and Beyerlein (2000) can help clarify the situation:

> *Organizational learning entails learning by individuals in a firm that becomes implanted in the structure, culture, and memory of that firm, allowing it to become more flexible and adaptive to its internal and external environments. Organizational learning is more than the sum of individual learning. As with the concept of gestalt, in which the whole is greater than the sum of its parts, there is some synergy among what individuals have learned that enables additional learning.*
>
> *The concept of organizational learning also differs from a 'learning organization'. The latter is a company that continuously tries to become more adaptive and proactive in its environment by intentionally developing and using structures, processes, disciplines, and strategies to maximize what it learns as a whole. Organizational learning, on the other hand, is the action of using these structures, processes, disciplines, and strategies. In other words, a learning organization is what a firm wants to become, and organizational learning is how it achieves this goal.*
>
> *Thus, the nature of the relationship between KM and organizational learning could really depend on how the two terms are defined. Nevertheless, they are not mutually exclusive concepts. They are iterative in nature. Organizational learning enables KM, because it is through learning that the value and application of information is understood, thereby creating knowledge. KM also enables organizational learning, because the knowledge that is managed provides additional opportunities for learning that, in turn, can also create new knowledge. Moreover, formalizing the means and methods of learning helps create a learning organization. Knowledge management is a way of formalizing this learning through strategies, structures and processes.*

Man versus machine

Knowledge management, per se, is not a new concept, but with recent advances in database, network, communications and Web-related technologies, the discipline has taken on new meaning and exploded. This explosion has been partly driven by the companies creating these technological tools. But it has also been driven by the realization that in a global economy where high service and quality standards are the norm, companies must lever their knowledge and discover new and faster innovative approaches if they are to achieve and sustain competitive advantage.

Realizing these two drivers – technology and intellectual capital – provides for what can be two separate approaches to KM. Students of psychology learn of the opposing perspectives of the nature versus nurture argument. Some psychologists believe people are born with a 'ready made' personality, others believe individual personalities are shaped by experience and the environment.

Within the field of KM there are some people who believe that knowledge management is very much about placing information on a database, for example, or a system such as an intranet, so that it can be accessed and distributed. This approach places information technology and systems at the centre of knowledge management. Others take a view that is people-focused, believing that because so much knowledge exists in people's heads, the critical issue is to develop successful strategies for 'downloading' that knowledge from people and making it tangible in some way, so that others can learn from it. This may also lead to considerations of culture, or ecology, as with the earlier quotation from Snowden. However, as with the nature versus nurture argument, an alternative is not to view something purely in terms of black and white, but to adopt an integrative approach that involves both people and technology.

Before exploring 'people' and 'machine' approaches to knowledge management (and why an integrated rather than a mutually exclusive approach, where technology is a supporting or enabling factor, may provide a superior solution), it makes sense to consider how knowledge might be classified. By gaining an understanding of how knowledge can be identified, it becomes easier to consider how it might be managed.

Understanding knowledge

A model that is frequently adopted to illustrate 'how knowledge is made up' is the Hierarchy of Knowledge. If the hierarchy is a pyramid, then we can ascend through levels that should take us from information to insights. At the base of the pyramid is data, and then moving up through levels we reach information, followed by explicit knowledge, then tacit knowledge to the peak of wisdom. To try and place this hierarchy in an everyday picture, the following example is provided.

Starting at the base of the hierarchy is data – for example, individual customer transaction details held on a database by a retailer. On its own, this data is of little value (except for important accounting-related processes) and requires combining with other data and some form of manipulation to provide information. For example, running a report to identify the most popular items sold in the shop and the total revenue generated by each product.

Having gained this information, it is possible to transmit it in a formal, precise way as explicit knowledge that can be used to propose action. For example, identifying the change in sales resulting from different in-store promotions and concluding which type of promotion would be the most likely to succeed in the future. Organizations have large stores of explicit knowledge, such as financial and marketing information, that is used for decision-making as well as patents and documented processes.

Tacit knowledge differs from explicit knowledge in that it is individual, and therefore understood by the person who 'holds' it, but difficult to communicate to others because it relates to individual experiences, beliefs, intuition and values. For example, in reviewing the sales figures following different sales promotions, a person might state a belief that the most obvious conclusion for future promotions is incorrect because of a personal intuition about an aspect of market behaviour that is not apparent from the analysis. Consequently, tacit knowledge is difficult to formalize because it is partly comprised of fragments of personal experiences. A challenge therefore is finding ways to convert tacit knowledge into explicit knowledge so that it can be shared with other people.

To return to the Hierarchy of Knowledge, at the top of the hierarchy is wisdom, representing the use of accumulated knowledge from the lower levels of the hierarchy. However, Snowden (*Knowledge Flow* Not *Information Exchange*, 2000, pp 42–43) challenges the foundations of the Hierarchy of Knowledge, whilst also underlining the importance of differentiating between (and therefore not being confused by) managing information and managing knowledge. Snowden suggests that many KM programmes in companies tend to concentrate on the containers for knowledge, rather than the knowledge itself. An excessive concentration on systems rather than knowledge creation and transfer can lead to problems with seeing the wood for the trees. Snowden also introduces important considerations regarding the roles of language and communications within effective KM projects:

Knowledge is our sense-making capability. It is the means by which we filter incoming signals and structure them in such a way that they have meaning. It is not the third stage in a linear progression from data, through information to knowledge and into wisdom, that some knowledge consultants would have you believe. We make sense of data in two ways: explicitly through the application of defined rules and procedures, such as the use of accounting standards to process transaction data into a set of management accounts; and tacitly through human interpretation and judgment.

The process of sense-making requires the use of an expert language. In the case of explicit knowledge such languages are usually codified and available through appropriate training courses. The process to acquire the expert language of accounting is well known, structured and defined, and the time horizon for its internalisation known. For tacit knowledge the language used is more complicated. It will incorporate some form of professional language – the essential jargon that allows rapid communication of concepts. It will also incorporate less readily codified forms.

For instance, a reference to an article or theory carries a vast complexity of meaning and historical associations that would be difficult to summarise. In organisations common stories also comprise a defining part of the culture and an expert set of references that play a key part in decision-making. All organisations have their successful and unsuccessful programmes and projects. Members of the organisation rapidly learn to reference these common stories to aid understanding; to validate or destroy a proposal.

Understanding this expert language in the tacit domain is the key to effective knowledge management. It is also one of the most frequently ignored activities in building knowledge systems. If we understand the expert language in use – and more importantly we know both the creator and receiver of information share the same expert language – then we can structure the data to create genuine information. Too often information degenerates to data because we fail to understand the range of knowledge needed to interpret it.

The adoption of knowledge management

The adoption of any innovation will occur over time, and different people or organizations will adopt the innovation depending, in part, on the perceived benefits of consuming it. Some people or organizations, of course, may never adopt the innovation. Knowledge management is no different, and companies that are exploiting KM might be classified as innovators or early adopters. Research by Rajan *et al* (1999) provided insights to this adoption process with the publication of a report titled 'Good Practice in Knowledge Creation and Exchange'. The report was based on structured interviews with, and information from, 156 large European and US companies from a broad range of sectors, including many of the world's best-known organizations.

The findings of the research were segmented into several sections that identified the initiatives and approaches being adopted by the companies contributing to the study. The findings from the study included the identification of the common steps followed by organizations as they developed a knowledge culture, the typical constraints in the development of KM initiatives and key influences upon the creation of a knowledge sharing culture. The research identified that for large organizations a typical KM initiative would follow six sequential steps:

1. installing an intranet or groupware to facilitate knowledge sharing;

2. creating a 'yellow pages' of individuals with particular expertise;

3. promoting yellow pages as personal Web sites and facilitating the transfer of knowledge over the electronic system;

4. facilitating personal contacts through electronic media or face-to-face to enable the transfer of knowledge that is hard to formalize and communicate;

5. building a reward system based upon the use of information placed on Web sites to support promotion and reward;

6. the creation of an internal market in knowledge exchange between functions, divisions, businesses and countries.

Of the organizations contributing to the study, the majority were at a pilot stage, but with Skandia at the fifth stage. The study also identified the main inhibitors to the effective conversion and management of knowledge in organizations, from a total of 15 noted constraints the following six were the most commonly found:

■ time pressures on key personnel (50 per cent of organizations);

■ resistance to sharing knowledge as this is viewed as a reduction in individual power – the 'knowledge is power' syndrome (33 per cent);

■ sustained dysfunctional internal rivalries and the perpetuation of functional or product silos – the 'not invented here' syndrome (33 per cent);

■ a lack of a coherent knowledge vision (29 per cent);

■ a lack of ownership of the knowledge vision (24 per cent);

■ a lack of methods for measuring/valuing knowledge (23 per cent).

This research identified that organizations tend to follow the adoption of knowledge management processes in a series of sequential and cumulative steps. The following case studies identify how some organizations have embarked on knowledge management initiatives and the benefits they have delivered.

Mitre Corporation

Mitre Corporation is a non-profit organization based in Bedford, Massachusetts. The organization provides federal agencies such as the Department of Defense and Internal Revenue Service with system engineering and IT expertise. In June 1994 Mitre commenced the development of a corporate intranet to encourage collaboration and to provide a corporate knowledge reservoir. The project was also developed because it was recognized that the company needed to transform its culture based upon internal rivalry and fiefdoms.

Three years after the company's system was rolled out across the organization, Mitre conducted an audit to identify the 'hard' and 'soft' benefits of its Mitre Information Infrastructure. The audit identified that from an investment of $7.2 million in the system, a return of investment of $62.1 million was provided through a reduction in operating costs and improved productivity.

Operating cost efficiencies occurred through employees completing their own HR records or through finding answers to routine questions by searching the system, resulting in fewer HR staff being required to carry out administrative activities. Cost savings were also achieved in other areas of the company including information systems management and technical and financial operations.

A further area of improvement was in cost avoidance. The system supported Mitre in meeting its extensive contractual obligations and to avoid non-compliance penalties. In addition, potential costs through employee turnover were reduced as the system supported remote working, which in turn assisted employee retention and therefore reduced the costs of hiring and training new staff.

Mitre also audited the 'soft' benefits of its system, including the volume of content being posted to the system, the number of times content was being accessed, and the use of the system as a collaborative environment. For example, a survey of all Mitre employees indicated that 91 per cent of respondents felt the system positively impacted their productivity and the ability to find quality information or expertise when needed.

Mitre has experienced extensive 'hard' and 'soft' benefits from the implementation of the Mitre Information Infrastructure, both through cost savings and productivity efficiencies, as well as improved knowledge sharing and collaboration within the organization (Young, 2000).

Frito-Lay

Organizations will frequently develop knowledge systems due to the frustrations of finding relevant information and the realization that people are repeating the same tasks ('reinventing the wheel' syndrome) because information is not readily accessible across the organization. To address these kinds of issues the customer development team of Frito-Lay, the snacks manufacturer, built a knowledge management portal on the corporate intranet. The portal provided access to information related to customer activity and news as well as details about employees (commonly known as 'yellow pages'), to make searching for relevant experts an easy task. With a sales team that was spread out across the United States, it was anticipated that the portal would provide substantial knowledge sharing and collaborative benefits given the geographic dispersal of employees.

The portal was launched in January 2000 to a pilot team. Results for the pilot team showed a doubling in the growth rate of customers' business in the salty snack category. Further benefits were generated through a reduction in travelling time and travel costs, increased collaboration between team members and the posting of sales presentations that could be edited for use by other colleagues. The portal is also credited with improving employee retention rates because of team building and a reduction in the frustrations experienced by sales people in finding information and communicating with colleagues.

Due to the success of the portal, it was decided to roll it out to other divisions within the PepsiCo organization so that information on clients could be integrated across different brands and product lines, leading to co-promotions of drinks and snacks, whilst also promoting greater collaboration between units within PepsiCo (Shein, 2001).

IBM – rewarding cooperation

Knowledge management and knowledge sharing are closely related to organizational or community culture, and changing that culture may be required if new opportunities are to be exploited. The following short case regarding IBM shows how changes in reward systems changed the culture of one of its sales teams, leading to improved performance. Typically, sales people are rewarded by results, and competitions will often be used as carrots for higher levels of sales performance by creating strong competitiveness amongst sales teams. This approach can encourage competition between sales people in a team rather than cooperation that might be to the greater good of the organization and its customers.

IBM provides an example of how rewards can be used to encourage knowledge sharing and cooperation. One of IBM's sales forces was motivated by a quarterly competition where the prize was a holiday in Acapulco for the winner and his or her family. The downside of this promotional approach was that it discouraged knowledge sharing and encouraged high levels of competitiveness amongst members of the team. As a result, they were unwilling to share information about sales techniques, as this was considered to make the possibility of winning the next competition less likely. In addition, customers were complaining about being overloaded with products at the end of each quarter.

To change this situation whilst retaining the competitive spirit of the team, a different approach to rewards was adopted. Rather than competing on sales levels, the team participated in a quarterly event where they all provided details of what they had learned from customers in the previous quarter. Members of the team then voted who should be winner of the competition based upon the value of the information provided to them as individuals.

The results of this change of emphasis in the nature of the competition meant that members of the team spent more time listening to their customers and passing this information to their colleagues. Team sales increased by 38 per cent and the gap between the best and worst sales achieved by individuals was reduced by 50 per cent. In addition, the person who had sold the most in the previous quarter was frequently the competition winner.

This example of rewarding knowledge sharing is but one case within IBM. There are many other situations where people at IBM can be rewarded for creating, contributing and sharing knowledge, including: developing a patent; authoring a certain number of articles and creating material on knowledge databases, with rewards for contributions that are frequently used by colleagues. All of these approaches are used by IBM to encourage knowledge sharing – which is fundamental to a business that is driving increasing amounts of revenue from the delivery of value-adding services to clients (Hampden-Turner, 2000).

Using knowledge

The 'collection' of information in itself is insufficient for the leveraging of that information into new assets. In a paper published in 1999, Pfeffer and Sutton go to great lengths to demonstrate that, for many organizations, there is a gap between knowing that something is important and actually doing something about it. In simple terms, they believe that many organizations have access to information that would allow them to improve their activities, but they fail to implement actions based upon this information. The authors state:

> *If there is widespread diffusion of information on 'best' (or at least 'better') practices, and if the evidence suggests that many successful interventions rely more on implementation of simple knowledge than on creating new insights or discovering obscure or secret practices used by other firms, then our position that the gap between knowing and doing is important for firm performance follows logically. This conclusion means that although knowledge creation, benchmarking and knowledge management may be important, transforming knowledge into organizational action is at least as important to organizational success.*

The authors also emphasize the importance of learning through interaction and observation, stating the greater value of these forms of learning versus knowledge that is commonly stored on systems:

> *Formal systems can't store knowledge that isn't easily described or codified but is nonetheless essential for doing the work, called tacit knowledge. So, while firms keep investing millions of dollars to set up knowledge management groups, most of the knowledge that is actually used and useful is transferred by the stories people tell to each other, by the trials and errors that occur as people develop knowledge and skill, by inexperienced people watching those more experienced, and by experienced people providing close and constant coaching to newcomers.*

The authors go on to identify common themes of why organizations typically fail to turn knowledge into action. These themes can be described briefly as involving:

▌ The philosophy or values of an organization.

▌ Leadership behaviour and the influence upon encouraging behaviour related to learning, including experimentation.

▌ Learning by doing and reflection, coupled with an action orientation. Learning through action must involve an acceptance that some efforts will fail, that failure is not a 'punishable offence', as well as the ability to learn and grow from mistakes. This means organizations that turn knowledge into action must eliminate the fear of failure. Turning knowledge into action also requires that an organization works in a collaborative, cooperative way, with competitive activity being directed at competitors rather than colleagues

A further key point raised by the authors is in relation to measurement. They put forward the view that many organizations fail to measure knowledge implementation, focusing instead upon the stock of knowledge: the number of patents, skills inventories, and so forth. The authors question whether these systems can capture tacit knowledge; they also emphasize again the importance of experiential knowledge, and question whether these systems capture whether this knowledge is being turned into action.

Action is therefore a keyword for Pfeffer and Sutton, and they question whether organizations are doing enough about turning knowledge into meaningful outcomes. They suggest the majority of organizations are placing an overemphasis upon systems and explicit knowledge rather than knowledge that is gained through doing and action. In a nutshell, there is more to knowledge management than information systems, and not all tacit knowledge can be reduced to information on a database.

Cultural change

A further consideration identified by Pfeffer and Sutton concerns the influence of culture and values on knowledge management and action based upon knowledge existing within organizations. For organizations where there is a reluctance to share knowledge, a range of issues will provide resistance to the development of knowledge management initiatives. In his book *The Springboard* (2001), Stephen Denning provides what is in effect a case study of how he led the World Bank's knowledge management programme where the aim was to develop a culture based upon learning and knowledge transfer.

The World Bank

Denning illustrates the value of storytelling as a 'springboard' to creating organizational change. Denning faced a culture that was used to working in silos, where people saw knowledge as power (and therefore something not to be shared) and where there was resistance to adopting new working methods.

The Springboard tells the story of Denning's successes and setbacks as his programme gathered momentum and created positive change within the organization. A key enabler in this process was the use of storytelling. Denning used stories to encourage people to chunk up to 'big ideas' or visions that received universal acceptance. The advantage of this approach was that it achieved buy-in at a mental level that would not have been achieved if knowledge management or other aspects of change were introduced at a process or structural level. (This 'chunking up' and 'chunking down' approach to communication will also be identified in the case study of Focus Central London in the next chapter, but where storytelling was not used as a change tool.)

To overcome resistance to change and the adoption of knowledge sharing and management, Denning recognized that he needed an approach that would, somehow, break down individual and silo-based thinking. To begin the process, he used a very short story that illustrated how technology and the sharing of knowledge provided by a variety of people managed to save the life of a person in a remote village in Africa. This story was powerful in that it allowed people to 'chunk up' to a big idea, and accept that knowledge sharing as a broad concept was a positive activity. Denning describes it in this way:

> . . . when I tell listeners about a health worker in Zambia who logged on to a Web site in Atlanta on the other side of the globe and got the answer to a question on how to treat malaria, I am implicitly inviting the listener to live the story with me, to follow the experience of the health worker. To relive the momentary professional dread of being asked a centrally important question and not having an adequate answer, as well as the imminent triumph that derives from finding it in minutes on the World Wide Web. It is a brief experience, but nevertheless – if the listener understands the context – a living experience. For anyone who has been in an out-of-the-way place and baffled for lack of the answer to an urgent and important problem, the experience of listening to such a story can be vivid enough to spark the mind into having further important thoughts that could lead to meaning, generate understanding, give impetus to the will, and eventually catalyze action.

Denning then had the difficult task of using this story, and others, to bring about change within the World Bank. Storytelling was used as a wedge to drive change through the organization. The wedge was then driven further into the organization through knowledge champions, the adoption of information systems, yellow pages, 'knowledge shows' and other activities that encouraged the creation of communities of specialists who provided access to their knowledge to others in the organization. This sharing and management of knowledge created cultural change in the World Bank and improvements in service delivery.

This quick reference to the use of storytelling in the World Bank does not describe the difficulties that Denning had to overcome in creating cultural change, and there were many. But it does illustrate the relationship between organizational learning, organizational change, systems, processes and individual behaviour and knowledge management. Also, reference to *The Springboard* illustrates that innovative and risky approaches may be required as a part of knowledge management initiatives, but that storytelling has a potentially meaningful role within these initiatives.

Professional services firms

Chapter 6 of this book concerns HR strategy and includes a case study of a professional services firm (a legal firm: DLA), which has gone through great cultural change. Professional service firms are of great interest from a perspective of knowledge management and change because they rely so heavily on knowledge management and knowledge transfer for wealth creation, yet they have traditionally been perceived as having cultures that acted against the encouragement of learning and sharing.

A study by Liedtka *et al* (1997) identified what the authors considered to be key attributes of professional service firms that had broken the cultural mould of 'contentiousness and self-interest, fiefdoms, insensitivity to clients, exploitation of staff professionals, and slow, inefficient decision-making'.

The authors state the following regarding what it is that they consider differentiates the successful from the not-so-successful professional services firms (PSFs):

> Our thesis is that outstanding PSFs across a variety of industries mutually reinforce the processes of employee and market development. Processes for recruiting, developing and retaining professional staff develop a capability for collaborative learning, which, in turn, produces valued outcomes for clients, which further support professional development. Taken alone, none of the elements of the cycle are remarkable; in conjunction, however, they produce extraordinary results.
>
> The advice to hire the best people, train them well, retain them, and get them to look for new opportunities and treat clients well is hardly revolutionary. But, explored together within a strategic context, the process of individual professional development and business development reinforce each other to produce significant strategic value. The key elements of the model are (1) the process through which, and the context within which, a firm enhances and extends individual expertise through collaboration, and (2) the process through which a firm leverages

individual learning to create a capacity for collaborative learning.
Together these translate into new organizational opportunities.

For these PSFs it is possible to identify how HR strategy and cultural change combine with learning to create competitive advantage. Integrating HR and learning strategies will, for many firms, require cultural change, as with the example of the World Bank. According to Liedtka *et al*, for PSFs, this requires hiring people whose skills go beyond a technical specialization, to include entrepreneurial ability and interpersonal skills. For the firms studied by Liedtka *et al*, it is possible to identify the close links between several of the chapters in this book, including business values, knowledge management, HR strategy and internal communication, as adopted routes to competitive advantage. In this quotation from the study, the interrelationships of these approaches are clearly shown. The quotation also raises some of the issues connected with cultural change, which will form a large part of considerations in the next chapter of this book.

> *In the successful firms, the magic is not in what they **do**; it is in what they **are** and what they stand for. What they do flows naturally from what they are – communities of practice committed to both the development of people and value creation for clients. What they do turns out to be fairly self-evident activities, given their value. They act as if they really care about their members' development by selecting them carefully, investing in their ongoing learning, rewarding them appropriately, offering them a voice in firm governance, and, in general, giving them good reason not to leave. They create value for their clients by caring more about issues than internal politics, sharing their knowledge with each other as efficiently as possible, and constantly looking for better ways to solve their client's tough problems.*
>
> *This should be simple, except that firms have gotten it so wrong for so long by hiring people without concern for their long-term fit with the business's principles, by treating them as commodities, by denying them a voice in decisions that affect them, and by giving them reason to leave for more lucrative offers. Firms have failed customers in similar ways – by caring more for their own comfort than client issues, by guarding turf and creating inefficient hand-offs, and by targeting the easy problems and convenient answers. What makes this all so difficult for many organizations is that they are not starting at ground zero. It is often easier to build a new community from scratch than to attempt to reform an existing one. Yet reforming existing organizations into new communities of practice is a challenge that senior executives must embrace.*

*Such a process begins, we believe, with value-driven leaders willing to fundamentally re-examine organizational capabilities, values, and practices and ask, 'What kind of firm are we committed to **being**?'*

THEORIES, MODELS AND PERSPECTIVES

So far in this chapter some of the issues relating to knowledge management have been highlighted. These issues include developing a culture in which knowledge sharing is a daily occurrence, creating systems that enable some aspects of knowledge transfer and management, and ultimately, how it is that knowledge and learning can be leveraged to create constant innovation.

In this section, some approaches to resolving these issues will be presented. However, before looking at some of the issues surrounding the evaluation and management of knowledge, it makes sense to develop further some of the considerations surrounding organizational learning (which relates to considerations of intellectual capital that were introduced in the previous chapter), to provide a context to why organizations are placing so much importance upon learning, information and knowledge as drivers of sustainable competitive advantage.

Senge – the learning organization

With the need for organizations to be more flexible, adaptive and innovative if they are to survive and thrive in an increasingly competitive, extreme and global economy, Senge (1990) presented his approach to organizational learning in the book *The Fifth Discipline*, and used the term 'The Learning Organization'. At the core of Senge's approach is the view that organizational learning provides a route to survival and creativity through the encouragement of learning and innovation.

Creating a culture where individual and organizational learning and sharing occur as natural activities will be a challenge for many organizations, particularly those that operate a command and control structure and are driven solely by financial considerations. A command and control structure is the antithesis of a learning organization, which would be characterized as a workplace with a focus upon people where:

▌ Experimentation and learning by mistakes would be encouraged.

▌ People work in teams rather than in competition with each other.

▌ Learning is facilitated and rewarded.

▌ Knowledge is developed and maintained.

▌ Creative solutions to problems are sought through new approaches.

Senge's approach identifies that the journey to becoming a learning organization includes individuals mastering five interrelated disciplines:

1. Systems thinking – Systems thinking is of great value when analysing cause and effect through the decisions, attitudes and behaviours that have impact upon a situation and their results. It is quite possible that recurring behaviours have an increasingly negative impact on situations and that by understanding why these behaviours occur, the system can be brought 'back to normal'.

2. Personal mastery – A driver to personal mastery is where a gap exists between individuals' vision and the perception of their current situation. This creates tension that may drive such people to develop ways of thinking that will take them towards their vision. In relation to organizational behaviour, personal mastery involves providing people with a culture that will motivate them to want to contribute and make a commitment to the organization because they wish to learn, find fulfilment in their work for its own sake and receive recognition as people, rather than purely financial rewards. This also means aligning or 'sharing' corporate and personal visions, which takes us to the next discipline.

3. Shared vision – Shared vision involves building a common sense of purpose and commitment by developing shared images of the future that people wish to create. This has implications for the contribution that employees make to the creation of that vision as a route to realizing a purpose that binds an organization and its people. This will also lead to considerations of values, goals, the nature of the work people do and why it is important. This in turn has implications for an organization's culture, as it supposes that

people can share their visions and mental models with others in that organization and be listened to.

4. Mental models – Within organizations, learning of the mental models of colleagues can provide insights to the behaviour that results from assumptions made about the actions of others. Incorrect assumptions about colleague motivations and behaviour can lead to conflict and a misunderstanding as to why certain things happen. Understanding other people's mental models can lead, through discussion, to the resolution of issues by addressing underlying assumptions that may not have a basis in real activity.

5. Team learning – Team learning involves the creation of a 'team gestalt' by generating collective thinking skills so a team can develop intelligence and ability that is greater than the sum of individual member abilities. Team learning involves considerations of the other disciplines so the team thinks and acts in new, innovative ways that recognize the whole is greater than the sum of its parts.

Senge's approach may appear too extreme or removed from practical reality for some businesses, but 3M, IBM and many others have adopted aspects of Senge's theories. In the *Fifth Discipline Fieldbook* (1994), Senge and other practitioners provide a large number of case studies and exercises to illustrate the application of the underpinnings to each of the five disciplines and the resulting benefits. But for people that prefer viewing organizational learning from a more direct perspective, there are alternative, or perhaps complementary, approaches.

Burgoyne, Pedler and Boydell – the learning company

Similarly to Senge, Burgoyne, Pedler and Boydell (BPB) recognize the importance of organizational learning as the key to organizational survival and sustainable development. In 1994 they published a book titled *Towards The Learning Company* in which they identified 11 characteristics of a learning company, with each characteristic supported by five clusters or supporting statements. The characteristics are linked through policy, operations, ideas and action. The book also provides guidance on how organizations might be transformed into learning organizations.

For managers seeking an understanding of what it is to be a learning organization/company, the BPB approach may be far easier to grasp than through a reading of Senge's work. Also, the characteristics and clusters identified by BPB can be illustrated on a sheet of A3 size paper. The 11 characteristics of a learning company as identified by BPB are:

1. learning approach to strategy – where policy and strategy formulation, as well as implementation, evaluation and improvement are structured as a learning process including deliberate small-scale experiments and feedback loops;

2. participative policy-making – involving stakeholders in the development of strategy and policy;

3. informating – where IT is used to inform and empower people;

4. formative accounting and control – where systems of accounting, budgeting and reporting are structured to assist learning and support internal service quality;

5. internal exchange – where internal units and departments see themselves as customers and suppliers, with the aim of delighting internal customers through high levels of internal service quality;

6. reward flexibility – seeing rewards as not simply money, but considering other forms of reward that provide satisfaction and are in line with the aims and values of a learning company;

7. enabling structures – having a structure that has flexibility to allow for meeting current needs and responding to future changes;

8. boundary workers as environmental scanners – where employees have contact with external customers, suppliers and other stakeholders, and collect information that is then used within the organization to support its purpose;

9. inter-company learning – where learning occurs as a result of contact between companies, including benchmarking, joint training and shared research and development;

10. learning climate – encouraging an atmosphere of continuous improvement through learning, feedback and questioning;

11. self-development for all – where resources and facilities for self-development are made to everybody in the company.

The Learning Company profile places great emphasis on the importance of internal service quality and a range of other factors that are significant in relation to internal marketing strategy. These factors include considerations of values in the development of policy, the use of IT to assist understanding, the need to have a flexible structure, the use of benchmarking and bringing information from the external environment to help improve performance. Links can also be made between the characteristics and clusters and the elements of the EFQM Excellence Model.

Through the Learning Company profile, BPB provide an overview of how a Learning Company might appear to someone working within such an organization and emphasize that it is a people-based strategy. They also emphasize that organizational learning will only occur if behaviour, communications, processes, policies and the working environment create a culture in which learning is encouraged as a daily activity and where that learning is directed at delivering the organization's purpose.

Bukowitz and Williams – implementing knowledge management

The case studies in this chapter provide examples of a number of KM initiatives that have been implemented by a small number of organizations. Through the theoretical underpinning provided in this section, an attempt has been made to try and explain why organizational learning, KM and knowledge transfer are critical to the development of sustainable competitive advantage at a corporate and individual level. In addition, links have been provided between corporate strategy and an organization's culture and people.

However, this still begs the question as to how knowledge management initiatives might be created and implemented within an organization.

Knowledge management is a broad field, and biting off more than you can chew could be the first step towards failure. In their book *The Knowledge Management Fieldbook* (2000), Bukowitz and Williams present a 'how to' guide to developing and implementing knowledge management initiatives. The book draws in part from knowledge gained by the authors as members of the Intellectual Asset Management group at PricewaterhouseCoopers, and their approach is based upon knowledge from project implementation and research.

Central to the Bukowitz and Williams approach is the Knowledge Management Process Framework, which incorporates the strategic and tactical aspects of KM. The framework allows for considerations of the immediate needs for knowledge to meet market demands and opportunities, as well as the longer-term needs of matching intellectual capital to strategic requirements. The tactical aspects of the model cover four steps:

1. Get – where people get the information they require to do their job. Given the level of information overload people face, it is important that resources are available for people to find the relevant information with speed.

2. Use – having obtained information, people need to add value to it in some way so that new and innovative solutions are found to resolve problems and issues. This kind of innovative thinking is more likely to occur in organizations where creativity, experimentation and communication are encouraged.

3. Learn – people need to be able to learn from their successes and failures and therefore a structured approach is needed for people to reflect upon projects and other work activities, and for the resulting learning to be used to the benefit of others.

4. Contribute – where people see knowledge as power, they will wish to retain their knowledge as a lever against a perceived potential loss of status or occupation. Therefore encouraging people to contribute their knowledge and illustrating that doing so will provide personal and organizational benefits is an important aspect of KM.

The strategic aspects of the model cover three steps:

1.   Assess – where evaluating intellectual capital becomes a part of the strategic planning process, and the organization defines its mission-critical knowledge and identifies the gaps between current and anticipated needs. Reference to the Skandia intellectual capital model in the previous chapter provides an example of how one organization goes about this process.

2.   Build/sustain – this step involves reviewing the management approach adopted within an organization. As identified in the Skandia intellectual capital model and in the final chapter of this book where reference is made to Lynch's Four Links Model, intellectual capital will be increasingly derived from an organization's relationships. Building and sustaining relationships with employees, suppliers, customers and other stakeholders will force managers to take a less controlling style and move towards a facilitating, enabling approach.

3.   Divest – organizations may wish to divest some of their intellectual capital because the opportunity costs of retaining it are greater than the benefits of retention.

Bukowitz and Williams have developed short, diagnostic questionnaires related to each step of their model. By evaluating a part of or an entire organization's activities in relation to knowledge management, scores from each section provide a relative position (or gap) for knowledge management activity relating to each step, and consequently help the prioritizing of action planning and activities.

Snowden – the social ecology of knowledge management

David Snowden is the IBM Director of the Institute for Knowledge Management, Europe, Middle East and Africa. He is a frequent speaker at knowledge management-related events, and has written extensively on the subject. Snowden (1999) defines knowledge management as: '... the developing body of methods, tools, techniques and values through which organisations can acquire, develop, measure, distribute and provide a return on their intellectual assets. It is fundamentally about creating self-sustaining ecologies in which communities and their artefacts can organically respond to, and confidently proact with, an increasingly uncertain environment'.

Expanding on the use of the words 'communities' and 'artefacts', Snowden, in another work (*Thresholds of Acceptable Uncertainty*, p 10) writes: 'The management of artefacts and communities is the essence of what we know as Knowledge Management. In order to arrive at this point we need to start with an understanding of what we have, its nature, what we need and, maybe, what we can discard. Once we know this we will have a powerful means of achieving competitive advantage through the effective deployment of those assets'.

Snowden places great emphasis upon the applications of knowledge management as a way of helping people operate in complex and changing environments or markets. An approach to encouraging consistent behaviour proposed by Snowden is the adoption of a heuristic-based strategy. Heuristics provide a value/rule system for teams to operate within, with the aim of teams adopting consistent behaviour in the face of uncertainty and complexity.

Snowden and his colleagues have identified and adopted an approach for eliciting values and rules. This process involves, in part, eliciting anecdotes. To provide a more easily visualized picture of an aspect of the approach adopted by IBM, and its potential benefits, Stewart (1998) provides this commentary:

> *To improve its ability to sell large contracts, IBM is using a novel way of constructing narratives. That experiment highlights another virtue of storytelling: It helps organizations bring tacit knowledge to the surface. Explicit knowledge is stored in manuals, file cabinets, documents, databases, and so on. It's often a mess, hard to search, and incomplete but it can be found. Tacit knowledge, by contrast, resides in narratives – and the more complex it is, the less likely it is to be documented. Says David Snowden, an expert on tacit knowledge at IBM Global Services: 'Stories are the way we communicate complex ideas'.*
>
> *One of IBM's most complicated tasks is selling global accounts. These are big deals, multiyear contracts across multiple lines of business, involving millions upon millions of dollars. Prospecting, courting, negotiating, and closing such deals can take years. Each deal is different, yet there are things to learn from past successes and failures, and the deals are so big that even a small improvement in the success rate or time involved could be worth millions of dollars. To get at the knowledge,*

IBM has been reassembling the people who worked on a deal and asking them to relive the story – interrupting, correcting, supplementing, reminding each other of who did what when, and why – while video cameras record the event. The result, says Snowden, is a pirate's caveful of ideas that can be lifted from the tape and shared as best practices; more than that, dealmakers get a feel for how the process works when it's going well, and for the kinds of things – remember, they'll be different every time - that derail it.

Using IBM's approach, from the stories that are provided, particular factors will be searched for, as well as values and rules. These factors are identified through the application of the ASHEN model to knowledge disclosure points (KDP). Through this overall process, the aim will be to deconstruct the stories and anecdotes and to identify story elements and archetypes that may later be used as parts of teaching stories that are communicated within communities, as well as an asset register relating to the ASHEN elements and the identification of processes involved in particular decisions. The aim of disseminating new, constructed stories will in part be to replace previous values/ rules with new, shared values/rules and the creation of new knowledge. The ASHEN model is comprised of the following elements:

▌ artefacts;

▌ skills;

▌ heuristics;

▌ experience;

▌ natural talent.

Snowden writes: 'By asking the ASHEN question in the context of a KDP we can achieve a meaningful answer which itself leads to action. When you made that decision, what *artefacts* did you use, or would you like to have? What *skills* did you have or need and how are they acquired? What *heuristics* do you use to make decisions quickly, what is the range of their applicability? What *experience* do you have and what experience do the people you respect in this field have? What natural talent is necessary? How exclusive is it? Who else has it?' Through an understanding of the combination of ASHEN elements that have contributed to a particular decision, it is anticipated that a shift in understanding and consequent action can take place:

> *This understanding allows a key psychological shift from saying, 'Only Linda really knows how to launch a new product' to, 'In order to launch a new product we need: this market research and information from Manufacturing (A); a team who've all been through basic marketing training (S); a leader who we trust to make those gut decisions under pressure (H); who has had success and failure in similar markets (E); who's got the sparkle to make it happen (N). The trouble is that only Linda's got it all.' Articulating issues in this way helps point towards the eventual solution.*

(Knowledge Flow *Not* Information Exchange, 2000, *p* 44)

Snowden also advocates the use of storytelling as a change tool. As noted above, new stories may be disseminated within an organization to replace previous values/rules with new, shared values/rules. The aim here would be to disseminate carefully constructed stories within an organization that (to return to Denning) act as a springboard for change. The following quotation provides insights to the approach adopted by Snowden and the results achieved:

> *Over the last two years we have developed techniques that use the age-old capacity of humans to tell stories about their lives that reveal those underlying values or rules. Elicitation of these stories (which is very different from focus group techniques) is a mixture of science and art, but is largely trainable. Experimental evidence demonstrates that gathering thirty-plus anecdotes is sufficient for a subgroup of the storytellers to identify and articulate the underlying values.*
>
> *What can we do with this? A few highlights from a recent story-based project will illustrate the point.*
>
> *In a programme to convey brand values to client-facing staff, a pervasive story was constructed using real characters and built from components of several anecdotes. That story, told around a water cooler in head office on a Wednesday afternoon had been retold in hundreds of stores nationwide within 48 hours. Within two weeks it self-generated similar stories from individuals' own experiences and this reinforced and authenticated the desired switch in behaviour.*
>
> *By using one of the universal story constructs (in this case Beauty and the Beast) a complex set of values was naturally communicated to a broad population at low cost. The initiative was designed to share lessons*

learned (a better term than 'best practice' because we learn from failure, not success) across groups working on all continents of the world, using storytelling as a means of disclosing how knowledge is used well and badly.

Two classes of story were then constructed to spread that knowledge worldwide. The first group were pervasive stories designed to self-propagate; and the second were constructed to be told consistently by storytellers. Writing down best practice would have resulted in the documents being ignored or slavishly imitated, but stories allowed learning to take place.

Anecdotes were captured from selected groups of customers and in parallel from a group of buyers in the selling organisation. Having captured the anecdotes, the rules and values were extracted and compared and the five underlying components were identified. Based on this, interventions were devised to alter the rules and values of both groups so that they would interpret data in the same way. The organisation was not just pumping out information but had started to create knowledge flows.

(Knowledge Flow *Not* Information Exchange, 2000, p 45)

This quotation is provided here for two reasons. Firstly, it provides an illustration of the use of storytelling. Secondly, the following two chapters are concerned with internal communication, change and HR strategy. A key underpinning to successful organizational change is effective internal communication. If storytelling is a potential communications device for creating change and the adoption of brand values, then its importance stretches from change in relation to knowledge flows to cultural change. Points that will be raised in the chapter on HR strategy include criticisms of branding and certain marketing techniques, and an increased resistance to change programmes where people are encouraged to 'live the brand'. It might be that storytelling provides a route to change that eliminates resistance to the adoption of brand values where more traditional approaches of workshops or direct communication may be resisted.

Whilst the telling of stories has been going on for centuries, the application of storytelling to knowledge, change and communications within organizations is far more recent. The use of storytelling as described in the above example by Snowden within a network of stories, introduces storytelling as an almost subliminal form of communication. What remains to be seen is whether storytelling, as knowledge of its applications and processes becomes more widely known, will face resistance from people within organizations if coupled to branding messages. Subliminal advertising was banned because it was seen as placing an unfair advantage in the hands of the advertiser and an unethical marketing tool. In relation to change and branding this raises the question as to whether storytelling will be viewed by some employees as an unethical approach to cultural change and communication. A further concern must be that 'a little knowledge is a dangerous thing'. Just as storytelling has been used for centuries, so has rumour mongering, suggesting that organizations may need to pay more attention in the future to 'unofficial' storytelling in organizations and the channels through which these stories are communicated.

KEY LEARNING POINTS

1. With the increasing importance of service-based organizations and the evolution of the 'knowledge economy', organizations are increasingly driven to considering ways of leveraging their intellectual capital as a route to sustainable competitive advantage.

2. KM can be defined as the process by which an organization generates wealth from its knowledge or intellectual capital, and this will involve considerations of an organization's culture, architecture, communities and communications.

3. Considerations of intellectual capital involve aspects of individual learning and organizational learning, and how organizations can best structure themselves to maximize the benefits of learning and knowledge.

4. Encouraging people to volunteer their knowledge and participate in communities where knowledge is organized and shared is a key challenge for organizations embarking on a programme of change where an aim is to encourage knowledge creation and sharing.

5. At a basic level, knowledge is segmented by explicit knowledge (for example, financial information, patents, processes) and tacit knowledge (knowledge that is specific to individuals and 'held in their heads').

6. With the development of technologies that support the storage of information, KM as a discipline has grown with great speed. However, creating information systems for storing information does not necessarily lead to improvements in knowledge creation or sharing. Information management is not the same thing as KM. A great deal of 'hard to discover' tacit knowledge may be best 'discovered' and communicated through speech and face-to-face contact.

7. Effective knowledge creation and management involves considerations of language as a factor in the transformation of information to knowledge and the benefits of generating knowledge through experiential learning and experimentation.

SOURCES

Kransdorf, A (2000) The Other 'Virus' that is Bugging Industry, *Market Leader* (Winter), pp 27–29, The Marketing Society

Leidner, D (2000) Editorial, *Journal of Strategic Information Systems*, **9**, pp 101–05

Nonaka, I and Takeuchi, H (1995) *The Knowledge-Creating Company*, Oxford University Press, Oxford

Pedler, M, Burgoyne, J and Bodell, T (1991) *The Learning Company*, McGraw-Hill Europe, Maidenhead

Senge, P, *et al* (1994) *The Fifth Discipline Fieldbook*, Nicholas Brealey Publishing, London

Snowden, D (1999) The Paradox of Story: Simplicity and complexity in strategy, *Journal of Strategy & Scenario Planning* (November)

The Economist, anonymous (2001) A Survey of E-Management, 18 November

Wu, J (2000) [accessed 3 May 2001] Business Intelligence: The Transition of Data into Wisdom, *DM Direct*, November [Online] http://www.dmreview.com

REFERENCES

Bukowitz, W and Williams, R (2000) *The Knowledge Management Fieldbook*, Pearson Education, pp 1, 2

Denning, S (2001) *The Springboard*, Butterworth-Heinemann, Woburn, MA

Edvinsson, L and Malone, M (1997) *Intellectual Capital*, p 9, Piatkus, London

Hampden-Turner, C (2000) The Dilemmas of Managing Knowledge, *Market Leader*, **7** (Winter), pp 30–35, The Marketing Society

Lahti, R and Beyerlein, M (2000) Knowledge Transfer and Management Consulting: A look at 'the firm', *Business Horizons*, (January–February), pp 67–68

Liedtka, J *et al* (1997) The Generative Cycle: Linking knowledge and relationships, *Sloan Management Review* (Fall), pp 47–58

Pfeffer, J and Sutton, R (1999) Knowing 'What' to do is Not Enough, *California Management Review*, **42** (Fall) pp 83–108

Rajan, A, Lank, E and Chaple, K (1999) *Good Practice in Knowledge Creation and Exchange*, CREATE, Tunbridge Wells

Senge, P (1990) *The Fifth Discipline – The art and practice of the learning organisation*, Century Business, London

Shein, E (2001) [accessed 3 May 2001] The Knowledge Crunch, *CIO Magazine*, 1 May [Online] http://www.cio.com

Snowden, D (1999) Liberating Knowledge, from *Liberating Knowledge*, ed J Reeves, CBI Business Guide, p 18, Caspian Publishing, London

Snowden, D (2000) Knowledge Flow *Not* Information Exchange, *Market Leader*, The Marketing Society, **7** (Winter 1999/2000), pp 42–45

5

Internal communication

AIMS

1. To show why effective internal communication is critical in creating organizational change;

2. to identify the key components of effective internal communication strategy.

INTRODUCTION

A further key component of IMS is internal communication. If an organization's vision, mission and values are to have a chance of being adopted by the people in an organization, then these components must be communicated effectively within the organization. Internal communication supports the 'living' of the organization's strategy, values and personality and therefore has a part to play in creating competitive advantage. At the most simple level, internal communication should be about creating desired behaviour that contributes to competitive advantage. Creating that behaviour may require significant culture change which, in turn, must be enabled by effective communication.

Living the brand is about living a culture and internal communication is, in part, about helping to build and sustain a competitive culture. This implies openness in communication for successful companies that recognize the importance of internal drivers and resources in creating competitive advantage. This openness should be reflected in communication that recognizes the importance of all people to an organization's performance, not just a favoured few.

Internal communication also plays a critical role in organizational change. Nelson and Coxhead (1997) state this very clearly in a paper that explores organizational change and internal communications: 'Internal communication is never the first thing on anyone's mind, but nothing meaningful will be changed without first communicating the intent to change to those involved or affected. Internal communication is fundamental to creating change, and most people after thinking about it should be willing to acknowledge this'.

Effective change cannot occur within an organization without appropriate internal communication, which in turn must be integrated with the company's interactive and external communication to ensure continuity of messages. However, Nelson and Coxhead also provide this warning: 'Internal communication is the shadow lurking behind everything attempted during a re-engineering/culture change project and poor internal communication has been identified as one of the single most destructive elements in an environment undergoing change. . .'

All organizations face change on a daily basis in some form, and on a much larger scale when step change is made to strategy and objectives. If people working in organizations are to understand where, why and how they need to change, then they must be communicated with and be able to communicate effectively up, down and across an organization in a consistent way.

Internal communication is not just about sending out e-mails or holding briefings, it is also about culture, leadership and behaviour. Communication is more than the spoken or written word. People do not just interpret messages based on what they hear. The spoken word may account for only 7 per cent of communication, with tone, inflection and delivery contributing 38 per cent and body language 55 per cent. Consequently, to use a frequently heard expression, you have to walk the talk. Talking the talk is not enough. Or to use a further expression, actions speak louder than words. Inconsistencies between messages and behaviour will soon be spotted by people and may lead to cynicism and obstruction.

Some words of warning

In this chapter reference will be made to some of the writings of Kevin Thomson. Thomson is the Chairman of MCA, a leading internal communications consultancy. In 1990 Thomson wrote a book titled *Corporate Internal Marketing*, where amongst other points, he suggested a growing fusion of marketing and HR. This chapter and Chapter 6 on HR strategy are closely related because internal communication frequently falls within the responsibilities of HR departments, and because communication and change are ultimately about changing people's behaviour. The view presented in this and the following chapter is that marketing and HR, particularly within service-based organizations, are increasingly concerned with similar issues: culture, communication, relationship management and measures of effectiveness. Chunking up from these issues leads us to living the brand.

Not everybody shares the views presented in Thomson's book, and some points made by Tony Greener (2000) are of particular value for consideration because they challenge some fundamental underpinnings to this book. Greener has a track record of senior and high-profile communications roles in service and product sectors, has written extensively on internal communication and at the time of writing was running his own training, PR and marketing business.

Greener is critical of internal marketing, describing it as an 'outworn term'. His criticisms are in part based upon the view that internal marketing relies heavily on the principles of total quality management and process engineering, and a focus upon internal customers. Greener does not believe these approaches provided meaningful business benefits in the 1970s and 1980s.

To return to Thomson's book (1990), Greener believes Thomson failed to address key issues, skills and problems relating to internal communications and the relationship between internal communications and internal marketing (though Thomson wrote extensively on internal communication in a later book). Greener writes:

> *For these reasons, and because it is still being hawked around as an idea a decade and more after this book was published, internal marketing may turn out to be a flash in the pan, a Thatcherite backwater with little lasting credibility. It may just, however, turn out to be a way of making responsible internal communications more appealing and more relevant to more managers. . .*

The other main problem with internal marketing is that its concepts are not in the realms of the thinking for most non-profit making organisations where marketing as a concept is not fully developed, if it exists at all. Thomson assumes a marketing function and role for his organisations – with reason. However, when canvassed for her opinion on internal marketing, an internal communications manager in a major local authority asked whether it included team briefings, if it didn't, she didn't want to know. That type of approach may be a hurdle which is simply too steep to overthrow within the reasonable future.

Greener continues by considering whether Thomson's ideas about internal marketing are too complex and ambitious for many people undertaking internal communication, and whether they are more appropriate for large-scale, highly commercial organizations. Greener doubts their relevance to small and medium-sized companies and the public and non-profit sectors. He also wonders how internal marketing can be blended harmoniously with modern developments such as intranets.

In this chapter, hopefully some of these questions are addressed. One of the chapter's case studies shows how internal communications supported significant change in a mid-sized (200-employee) quasi-public sector organization. It is also worth considering that the British government promotes programmes that encourage the use of the EFQM Excellence Model, benchmarking and work-life balance. The EFQM model provides a route to integrating approaches to issues including leadership, quality and communication. Government bodies also hire internal communication and change management specialists to support a greater awareness and response to public needs in a drive to delivering 'best value'.

Arguably, internal marketing is relevant to all organizations, but competitive external environments may push private sector organizations that truly value their people further and faster up a learning and relevance curve in relation to internal market. As initiatives that promote closer relationships between the private and public sector take on greater significance, the importance of internal marketing will become of greater relevance to non-private sector organizations. Competition, environmental change and considerations of differentiation through branding are key drivers to internal marketing, and public and non-public sector bodies are increasingly exposed to these factors. Internal communication has a key role to play as organizations adapt to these changing circumstances.

For example, the education sector in the United Kingdom is going through extensive change. This change is being driven by government policy and funding. Government policy for schools involves several thrusts, including the need to improve student attainment and the integration of information communications technology within the curriculum. The drive for higher standards is supported through a range of programmes that encourage schools to be innovative in finding new approaches to issues surrounding student achievement. Some head teachers have created massive positive change within schools, acting as entrepreneurial leaders and change agents that should be role models for some private sector business managers. At Cranford Community College near Heathrow Airport, London, for example, the college has a wireless IT system that many businesses would be envious of. The college has gone beyond being wired for change, to being wireless. From a position of poor attainment, the college is now one of the leaders in the country. This position was achieved through radical cultural change that included making IT ubiquitous so that it became just a part of the way things happen at the college. There are many people working in the education sector in the United Kingdom who have used innovation, cultural change and communication to effect massive change. Whether consciously or not, they have adopted the underlying principles of IMS to create and mange that change. Therefore IMS is of great relevance to the public sector.

Greener also refers to comments made by an employee of a local authority, and the view expressed that if internal marketing did not include team briefing, it could not be considered as relevant. To consider internal marketing as a different title for internal communication suggests a lack of understanding as to the breadth of internal marketing. Internal marketing is more than internal communication, and tactical approaches to internal communication adopted by organizations may or may not include team briefings. Government departments and agencies (including local authorities) in the United Kingdom have been encouraged by central government to achieve the IiP standard, and one of the frequently implemented communication processes as a part of achieving the standard includes team or cascaded briefings. This form of briefing may or may not be the most appropriate way for disseminating information in an organization. For an organization where its workforce is widely dispersed and linked electronically, an e-briefing rather than a face-to-face approach may be the only route to getting information to people within an appropriate timescale. Also, with the need to communicate messages to people with great speed, during a merger or acquisition, for example, team briefing may be too cumbersome a route. Intranets and television may be the only media where people can learn first-hand about changing events, rather than learning second-hand through mass media.

As events, competition and technologies change, so must communication and the people delivering those communications. Communications, channels and the people involved in communication must be fit for purpose.

The importance of internal communication

In *The Twelve Dimensions of Strategic Internal Communication* (1999) Thomas Lee stated: 'The fundamental purpose of communication in an organisation is to enable and energise employees to carry out its strategic intent'. Lee also emphasized the importance of internal communications being timely, credible, sensible and relevant, with messages communicated up, down and across the organization 'so as to bring all their resources to bear on the execution of their strategic intent'.

Bill Quirke, Managing Director of internal communication consultancy Synopsis, views internal communication as a core business process: 'In an information age, internal communication is the core business process which enables businesses to engage their people's intellectual and creative assets to produce value. Despite the increasing complexity of the world, people still want to know some simple truths about what is going on, and they want to be treated as if they matter' (Quirke, 2000).

If internal communication has a role to play in improving business performance, then there is ground to catch up in many organizations. In a presentation given by Kevin Thomson of MCA in 2001, he quoted these research findings from a 1998 study involving 350 people from British organizations with over 1,000 employees:

I Only 27 per cent strongly agree they have a clear sense of their organization's vision.

I Only 40 per cent of respondents strongly agree that they play an important part in meeting customers' needs.

I Less than 25 per cent of respondents are fully committed to giving their best.

These results suggest many organizations are failing to enable and energize employees to carry out strategic intent.

Push and pull

Organizations that wish to stimulate commitment from their employees and manage change have to manage their internal communications effectively. People need to know where the organization is going, their part in that journey and the results of their work. They also need to want to go there. Simply telling people to change is unlikely to produce the desired change in behaviour or respect and commitment for the message deliverer. We do not buy every product where we are exposed to advertising, and neither do people 'buy' every message that is communicated within organizations. People buy products because they meet some kind of desire, want or need, which leads to considerations of psychology and motivation: 'Many of the behavioural concomitants of sought after values are sufficiently subtle to be virtually unenforceable: people must *want* to behave that way. They will only do so if their own goals of fulfilment, development and self-actualisation stand a greater chance of being achieved along the way. This will in turn only be the case if their needs for resources and quality of working life have been taken into account in the planning of the change process' (Wood, 1995).

If an aim of internal communication is to create changes in behaviour, then internal communication should be viewed as broader than tactical activities such as newsletters and team briefings. Internal communication also involves considerations of culture, leadership, management behaviour, the working environment, the systems and networks through which communications occur and, related to these factors, KM.

Internal communications are not about 'spin'. If an organization wishes to energize its employees and uses internal communication as one tool, along with HR policies such as reward structures to motivate its people, then those communications must be perceived as integrated, trustworthy, transparent and two-way. People must be able to question the messages they receive and, in turn, have their questions answered. Top-down communication alone will not lead to the creation of an atmosphere of trust, participation, commitment and respect.

The medium and the message

A further important consideration for internal communication is the selection of channels or media for those communications, and the messages they will carry. The medium must be appropriate for the message. The introduction of e-mail, intranets and other electronic media should not wholly replace face-to-face communication. There is a need for both electronic and human relationships: 'high tech' and 'high touch' communications, as Gummesson would say.

Gummesson also emphasizes the need for total relationship marketing where customer relationship marketing becomes an integrated aspect of internal and external communication and behaviour. A role for internal communication is therefore ensuring that employees understand their part in delivering customer satisfaction, and how they can contribute to the improvement of satisfaction levels. Reardon and Enis (1990) provide four steps for persuasive internal marketing regarding customer relationships:

1. *define the customer satisfaction link for each employee,*

2. *encourage feelings of self-efficacy among employees with regard to their ability to serve the customer more effectively,*

3. *provide rewards for actions that enhance customer satisfaction,*

4. *elicit commitment to long-term efforts directed at customer satisfaction.*

Whilst considering the benefits of communication opportunities provided through technology, it is important to recognize the value of face-to-face communication:

Face-to-face communication is potentially far and away the most effective form of internal communications. By its very nature, it is two-way, inviting response, reaction and motivation to action, on both sides. Within it, and with goodwill on all sides, participants are able to make sure they understand and have been understood.

Face-to-face communication is also the form of communication which most people prefer both in order to hear from their manager or supervisor what is happening in the organization, and in order to make known to management their feelings and ideas.

(Farrant, 2000)

From simplicity to complexity

In thinking about messages and how they are delivered, it might appear that internal communication is a simple process, whereby people in an organization agree messages, and then media or channels are agreed upon for the communication of these messages to specific people. An assumption is then made that these messages will be received and correctly interpreted by people who will then change their behaviour in line with the messages provided.

This is clearly an over-simplification of communication in organizations. Just as in the external environment, people are bombarded by messages on a daily basis in the workplace. Behaviour is not just influenced by 'official' communication but also by word-of-mouth communication (and particularly by who it is that is delivering the message), the environment in which the message is received, competing messages and the content of messages.

Within organizations, messages may be cascaded through briefings and the content of the briefings may be altered by the people delivering the briefing to meet a particular political agenda, or because they do not wish to pass on bad news. Briefing and communication also require individuals to have the appropriate skills so that information can be communicated effectively, and for questions to be responded to in a similar fashion.

Communication becomes even more complex during times of great change, such as during mergers and acquisitions or where an organization is going through strategic change or restructuring. If rumours or press reports reach employees before 'official' internal communications, the internal communication processes can be seen to have failed. Similarly, conflicting 'official' messages over time will lead to a lack of credibility for the messages and the messengers. Consequently, internal communication is a proactive activity that may be steered or directed by a group of people, but where the delivery processes become the responsibility of all people working in an organization. For global and matrix organizations this becomes even more complicated, as considerations of the relative importance of corporate and local messages come into play. Organizations therefore need an ongoing internal communications strategy that ensures they are delivering, measuring, evaluating and responding to the right messages that are being delivered to the right people.

Approaches to internal communication strategy development

The development and implementation of an internal communication strategy must be an integral part of strategic planning. If organizational performance is to be continuously improved, then people need to know where the business is going, what the business strategy is, how they can contribute to the strategy, how business performance is to be measured and how their performance will be measured and rewarded.

An internal communication strategy is not just a single burst of activity, but an ongoing process. Similarly to any other kind of strategy, internal communication must be linked to specific objectives and measures. It is necessary to concentrate internal communications on a tight range of messages, with the emphasis upon selecting the messages, audience, language and channels that will have the greatest impact on delivery, interpretation, understanding and performance. Over-communication can lead to 'turn off' and time lost on other activities. A balance therefore needs to be struck to ensure the volume and value of communications are maximized. Quirke (2000, p 162) proposes the following key considerations for the development of an internal communications plan:

1. analyse your audiences;

2. set communications objectives;

3. select the communication approach;

4. develop key messages and themes;

5. match communication vehicles to your approach;

6. measure the outcome.

Managing internal communications

For the majority of organizations, internal communication will be managed through the HR function, though this is becoming less the case. For organizations not following this approach, prime responsibility for internal communication may form a part of corporate communication, PR or marketing department activities. Regardless of where internal communications 'sit' in an organization, a cross-functional approach is required for the development and implementation of an internal communication strategy that integrates HR, information and KM, corporate communications, customer and partner communications, operations and marketing activities.

Whilst 'placing' responsibility for internal communication within a particular team may be attractive from a perspective of accountability, internal communication processes should move across an organization, not within functional silos. Major cross-team initiatives may require their own communications plans for integration with corporate internal communication plans to ensure control and consistency. Strong 'gate keeping' is therefore required to manage the volume, content and tone of communications and to stop the personal agendas of individuals creating interference and noise in communication channels and people's minds.

Communications media

As with external communication, there are many media or channels that can be used to communicate internal messages. Some of the frequently used media are:

▌ face-to-face cascaded briefings;

▌ team meetings;

▌ direct personal presentations or briefings using video or other electronic channels such as the Internet or TV;

▌ conference calls;

▌ road shows;

▌ pre-prepared presentations;

▌ intranet and news bulletins;

▌ internal radio;

▌ newspapers/magazines;

▌ newsletters;

▌ bulletins;

▌ memos;

▌ letters;

▌ noticeboards;

▌ ambient advertising;

▌ promotional gifts and other items such as mouse mats;

▌ entertainment, such as parties.

This is a lengthy list of potential media or channels for delivering messages but, as in the development of advertising plans, there is a need to obtain the greatest impact from the delivery of messages to target audiences as cost-effectively as possible. This may require a single or a multimedia approach. Internal communication, like any other business activity, has to be able to demonstrate that it delivers real business value.

It is also necessary to consider the richness of particular media in relation to the target audience for communications. A global presentation by the CEO via television may deliver core messages to large numbers of people instantaneously (putting aside cultural, language and time zone issues). But as with all mass media, it will not be of value in communicating specific issues that exist at local, team or individual levels. Face-to-face discussion may be the most appropriate form of communication for answering the 'what's in it for me' questions.

The above list of media relates to formal networks of communication. But informal networks should not be forgotten. Every organization has informal networks of people and particularly influential people at nodes in those networks. Where possible, informal networks should be considered for the dissemination of messages and receiving feedback. Informal groups can include people who get together outside a building for a cigarette, groups with social ties resulting from companies that have previously been merged or acquired and people that have previously worked together in project teams. The following brief cases illustrate how some companies use different media for different messages at different times.

British Telecommunications (BT) – wired and wireless

BT has developed a range of media to deliver communications to its employees, some of whom work remotely, such as engineers. The internal communication media used by BT include an intranet, a Web-based newsdesk, e-mail, an audioline that provides information to people who are on the road, and a newspaper. The company is experimenting with text messaging, video casting and communications that can be experienced through PDAs.

The company's intranet includes access to a range of services including HR support, facilities management, job pages, policies, group work and the Web sites of some senior executives, which are used to communicate specific information regarding the activities of that executive and to seek feedback.

Internal communication at BT is not dissimilar to running a 24-hour news station with the aim of providing employees with up-to-date information on events that impact the organization and its people. Information is segmented by business sector and unit for ease of finding information that is directly relevant to the people working in those areas.

A benefit of the approach adopted by BT to internal communication is that important news can be distributed instantly to all employees, providing the various channels with credibility, as people can learn of events through the company's own media rather than hearing of them first through television, press or radio.

Shell Chemicals – from global to local

Shell Chemicals has business units operating in countries around the world, where the benefits of good communication include the sharing of best practice and greater efficiencies. The company's internal communication strategy has changed in parallel with a move from local companies operating as largely separate businesses, to a regional and then to a more networked approach. This approach includes extensive travel for senior managers who visit local business units to gain an understanding of local issues and a network of communications professionals around the world to support the communication of business objectives and strategy at a local level.

Whilst English is the official language of Shell Chemicals, the company recognizes that if communications are to be effective at a local level, they must be sufficiently flexible to ensure that ideas and information can be communicated in the language and culture of a particular country.

Formal communication takes place through a weekly electronic newsletter for communicating global news to Shell Chemicals' employees. The newsletter provides brief summaries of important business news (with hyperlinks for people wishing to obtain more in-depth information), and therefore acts as a medium for sending a limited number of global messages to all employees.

At a local level, individual business units may also produce newsletters in the relevant language for communicating local news. To ensure consistency of corporate branding for these newsletters, Shell Chemicals provided templates for these local newsletters, where locally relevant copy can be dropped into the template.

The case study of Pret a Manger in the next chapter provides further details of specific internal communication activities.

Communication and behaviour

The discussion so far has provided a fairly clinical view of internal communication. However it cannot be assumed that, because strategy, audiences, messages and channels have been defined, a simple rollout of a 'one-off' communications plan will deliver immediate changes in behaviour and organizational performance. Internal communication is an ongoing process where messages must be integrated and controlled in terms of frequency, target audience and content. To use a term provided by Tim Greenhill (2000), Managing Director of corporate communications consultancy Basten Greenhill Andrew, 'Irrigate not flood'.

Greenhill's advice suggests a need to manage internal communications in such a way as to provide a flow of communication without drowning people in an excess of messages or too much repetition. However, as with external communication, the repetition of messages may well be required to ensure awareness and understanding. With many organizations using intranets as a communications channel, new opportunities are provided for electronic forms of communication to reinforce key messages. For example, Wide Learning, an e-learning provider, has developed 'quicksights'. Quicksights are short e-learning episodes that can provide sound, vision, animation, interaction and testing for the viewer. These short bursts of content can be used for disseminating key messages in a concise way, whilst appealing to more learning styles than is possible through simply reading or listening to a piece of communication. This approach can also be used for disseminating stories, and therefore has value as a route for disseminating information and knowledge within communities of practice where people are located in a variety of geographic locations.

As noted earlier, communication has the aim of influencing behaviour. An assumption that can be made about the workplace is that people are more likely to perform well if they believe they are valued, they are able to speak openly and contribute their ideas, they receive frequent feedback on their performance, knowledge is volunteered and shared, they can progress and develop and they are appropriately rewarded for their contribution. In short, people have to be emotionally committed to doing things if they are going to do them to the best of their ability. Creating or enhancing an environment in which these activities and approaches are a way of life requires the development of a supportive culture where people are encouraged to do their best as individuals and as members of teams. Communication is fundamental to the creation of this kind of culture.

If an organization has identified gaps in its values and behaviours that require closing, then cultural change must be driven from the top of the organization, with leaders and other highly visible people acting as role models for new behaviours, as described by Williams *et al* (1996): 'The use of a cultural change strategy that uses role models and methods of participation and persuasive communications, targeted at specific levels, attitudes and behaviours, is likely to promote cultural change. This is particularly the case when methods are cascaded down the organization and there is top commitment'.

Training and mentoring may be required to create broader change as, for example, with the Barclays case in Chapter 2 on corporate strategy. John Tiebout, managing director of Banner McBride North America, an internal communications and change management consulting firm, reinforced the importance of leading by example in an article published in *Internal Communication* (2000, p 8): '. . . we don't help leaders get there by drafting a "we're-going-to-change-the-culture" memo. We help them get there by helping them change behaviour and by making damn sure that as many people as possible get to see these new behaviours in action. While this form of communication has nothing to do with the tools of our trade (eg, newsletters and PowerPoint), it is communication at its most basic (and, perhaps, its most powerful)'.

There are many approaches to creating behaviour change. The approaches adopted will vary by the situation to be addressed, the culture of the organization and its leaders, the speed at which behaviour change is required and available resources. There is no off-the-shelf solution:

> *Every effective internal communication programme should be unique because it will be designed and governed by the parameters of the specific project. Just because an internal communication programme has operated successfully for one organization it should not be expected to be effective in another organization. Just because an existing internal communication programme has appeared to work in the past it should not be expected to be effective during the forthcoming period of radical change.*

> (Nelson and Coxhead, 1997)

This quotation from Nelson and Coxhead acts as health warning regarding the potential success of internal communication programmes and just how much might be learned from the experiences of other organizations. However, the following brief cases provide illustrations of how aspects of behaviour change have been achieved through very different approaches.

Pfizer

Following research to identify employee perceptions of the company and its philosophy, Pfizer, the pharmaceutical company, identified seven corporate values. To embed the values, the company took a behavioural approach using a drama-based development programme. The programme used actors in role-playing exercises. The exercises covered a range of typical workplace activities. At various points during the role-playing, employees were asked to provide suggestions as to how they should proceed with the situation. Through these 'dramas' employees were able to identify how the values influenced behaviour in these situations and what kinds of behaviour were consequently inappropriate (Dawson, 2000).

GE

When GE prioritized e-business as a part of its strategy, fundamental change in the way the company did business was required, with each division encouraged to reinvent itself. To achieve this change, the approach adopted included both carrot and stick. An article published in *The Economist* (May 2001) identified some of the challenges faced and the disciplines that were put in place:

> The greatest hurdle has not been technology but culture. Sales staff, worried that they might be destroying their jobs, had to be offered bonuses for helping customers to use GE web sites to order. Managers had to watch carefully for reprobate employees using 'parallel paths' (the telephone, for instance, or a walk to a store) to order supplies, say, or arrange travel. Some offices even closed their mail rooms for all but one day a week (and that only for the incorrigible legal department) to stop employees from using regular post. Others locked their printer rooms except for occasional days when bosses would station themselves at the door and demand from those who came through an explanation for their sad inability to shake old paper habits.

Jaguar Cars

Jaguar is producing its X-400 model at Halewood, near Liverpool, England. Ford previously used Halewood as a manufacturing plant. The location developed a reputation for poor quality, poor industrial relations, poor performance and poor conditions. Halewood was a case study of the 'English industrial disease'.

Ford transferred Halewood to its Jaguar subsidiary, with Jaguar carrying out radical change to the environment and working practices. Changes to communications included providing details of production and quality performance in refreshment and meeting rooms. More radical changes included the creation of a 'Halewood Charter' that detailed working relationships, behaviours and quality principles. The contract for each employee included key aspects of the charter, and those refusing to sign (600 out of 3,000 employees), left the company (The Economist, March 2001).

Philips Electronics

Similarly to Jaguar, Philips Electronics introduced new contracts as a part of changing the nature of the relationship between employer and employee, and as a component of a broader programme of radical change. This example also illustrates the tough approach taken to changing a culture that was characterized by politics, fiefdoms and networking as routes to lifetime employment and loyalty.

The need for change at Philips was evidenced by falling market share and revenue. Jan Trimmer became CEO of the company in mid-1990 and embarked upon a shake-up of the company's management structure and contractual relationships.

Trimmer began his attack by meeting with the company's top 100 executives, explaining to them all as a group the desperate situation the company was in and the need to take urgent action. Trimmer then presented a number of targets that these managers were required to meet, including reductions in costs and headcount. Managers agreed to targets and plans of how to achieve them signed contracts to that effect. Performance in relation to the targets was then used for evaluating bonuses and career development. Those managers who did not believe they could work to this new approach were encouraged to leave the company.

Performance reviews and meetings were used by Trimmer to drive home his messages and develop longer-term plans. The programme of performance-related contracts was extended deeper into the organization in parallel with communications activities, including question and answer sessions held by Trimmer with employees. At these meetings Trimmer communicated the company's objectives, values and procedures, and demanded that if people wished to remain in the organization they would have to commit to the new way of doing things.

By mid-1994, of the original group of 100 managers that met with Trimmer, only four remained with the company. Over the same period, both operating income and share price improved. As the company's performance improved, Trimmer began a different approach with communications, placing greater emphasis upon the company's values and achieving consensus. Having taken drastic steps to change the organization's culture and performance, Trimmer's approach moved to one of trying to build loyalty to the organization and improve social networks amongst employees.

Change management

These four brief cases illustrate aspects of change management and where internal communication goes beyond simply delivering specific messages to target audiences. In 'everyday situations' internal communications might be about delivering news, performance feedback and so forth. But in almost all organizations, substantial change will be occurring where internal communication will be required to play a strategic role in supporting change. This change might be a result of a radical reorientation in strategy brought about by external forces, new internal initiatives or mergers and acquisitions. Whatever the driver of the change, behavioural and attitudinal change within an organization will almost certainly be required, and internal communication has a meaningful role to play in moving it forward.

Change programmes are notoriously difficult to implement successfully. An article published in *The Economist* (July 2000) gave details of two surveys conducted by business consultancies. Highlights from the results of these surveys include:

▌ Only 20 per cent of change-management programmes succeed.

▌ Sixty-three per cent of change programmes yielded some temporary improvements, but these improvements were not sustained.

▌ Seventeen per cent of change programmes did not provide any improvements at all.

▌ A positive correlation exists between companies that are more successful with change programmes and those that involve top managers in the project and have proactive policies for communicating change.

▌ More successful companies tended to have 'embedded' change expertise as a functional capability within the organization, rather than relying on consultants.

These highlights provide insights to the management of change and an organization's capability to carry it out effectively, suggesting that change is a competence that organizations need to develop so that change is an instinctive rather than a reactive activity. However, there is little point in trying to provide a prescriptive response to a question such as: How can I be sure my change programme will be 100 per cent successful? The type of change required within an organization will obviously vary from organization to organization, and that may well include changing its leadership. Similarly, the response to a need for change will vary from organization to organization. Considerations in developing an approach will include the degree of change required, the cause of the change, organizational culture, leadership and processes and the speed with which change is required. Overall, this means considering what changes in behaviour are needed, and what is the most effective way of achieving the desired outcomes at corporate, team and individual levels. This may not mean launching a massive, intimidating, branded programme that has people rushing under their duvets. Communications need to be targeted, and that includes people knowing exactly what change means to them as individuals.

Time and tide wait for no man

Some organizations take the approach that a cultural change programme lasting four years is acceptable and realistic (as with the Barclays example provided in Chapter 2 on corporate strategy). Others may decide that a far speedier approach is required. This might mean launching a series of small projects related to a particular vision rather than announcing a massive programme. Feldman and Spratt emphasize the need to move quickly when managing change resulting from mergers and acquisitions to maximize the likelihood of delivering the promised benefits:

> _Speed means rapidly putting the piers in place and laying down the platform for the timely capture of economic value. It is about how to launch all the critical actions in a merger, acquisition, or large-scale change in the first one hundred days, the outer limit of employee enthusiasm, customer tolerance, and Wall Street patience. It's about accelerating any transition – by maximising the value sought as early as possible while minimising the decline in performance that inevitably accompanies unsettling change. It's about treating change like removing a Band-Aid. No hesitation. No delay. One quick movement. Rip. Sting. Done._
>
> _(Feldman and Spratt, 1999, p 36)_

This quotation also raises considerations regarding the objectives of a change programme, and the relative importance of differing audiences such as employees, shareholders and customers to those making decisions about change. The relative importance of those audiences may change during the life of a specific programme, requiring differing leadership approaches over time. For a company facing a financial crisis and requiring fast, drastic surgery, this might mean a strong top-down approach in the early stages, with a move to a more collaborative approach if performance improves.

A further point regarding time and change is the duration of a change programme. Typically a change programme or series of programmes will be announced to employees, and each programme will have a name. The name might be an acronym that few people will understand (and as a result they may make up their own cynical versions), or something that appears to have been dreamed up by the military in the wake of Operation Desert Storm. As the project drags on, the project name gets included in all kinds of communications and as new projects and initiatives are launched, the original initiative competes for increasingly cynical and congested brain share. Not surprisingly, without adequate management of communication volume and value, people tune out and turn off. When people's interest falters, so does their potential commitment to change.

If a change programme is to last for several years, then it begs the question as to whether it will be perceived as a change programme at all, or just a general drift that has little immediate need for attention and action. If four years is greater than the anticipated period of employment for an individual with an organization, then why not just duck and stick to business as usual? If creating a sense of urgency is a critical success factor for a change programme, then its structure and communications must reflect that priority. Those communications might include exposure to the activities of competitors and the needs of customers.

Changing change

One of the problems with change management, therefore, is the use of the term 'change management'. Like other terms used in this book, including 'internal marketing strategy' and 'employer branding', these terms are inappropriate because they do not describe adequately what they are. For change management, this assumes that change can be managed (which is only a part truth because neither people or change are entirely predictable or manageable), and that when used in relation to a defined change programme, that change has a finite lifecycle.

The implication is that an organization embarking on a lengthy change programme can breathe a sigh of relief at the end of the time span of the programme (assuming its objectives have been met) and say: 'Phew, I'm glad that's over. That change thing is really tough. Now let's do something else that's a bit easier'. But the reality is that change is occurring all the time and does not have a finite time span. Singling out and communicating change as a series of events or projects that have defined outcomes and time spans may provide a false sense of what is required to achieve and sustain competitive advantage for an organization. Celebrate success, but do not communicate that change is just a new management initiative that will be over in a while.

For the majority of organizations that fail to achieve the desired outcomes of change programmes this requires the question as to whether one of the reasons they failed was because they communicated change as something that had finite sides, rather than something that you just need to be accomplished at. People are frequently reluctant to change and so the word is loaded for many people, translating into insecurity, redundancy, loss of status, loss of income, hell. Just using the word 'change' means you are probably creating resistance. There is a need to find a new word (and new behaviours) to replace change in terms of communications and routes to competitive advantage.

Change is like air. We know it's there, and we breathe it, but we tend to speak about living. Breathing is something we are generally not conscious of. We just do it. That's how we're wired. Living breaks down into experiences, thoughts and actions – hopefully, enjoyable ones. If we concentrate on the process of breathing it becomes difficult to focus on living because our senses concentrate on your lungs and the way they function, rather than getting on with the things we want to do. So an excessive concentration on process stops meaningful behaviour because, to change metaphors, you can't see the wood for the trees.

For a change programme to be considered effective, change should become eradicated from the organizational vocabulary and replaced by anticipation and proaction. Organizations need to wire anticipation and proaction into the collective subconscious. If an organization staggers from unsuccessful change programme to unsuccessful change programme it clearly has not developed a competence in change. This might be due to an inability to adequately separate process from vision.

To try and illustrate what might otherwise appear an abstract line of thought, the experiences of people working at the British Broadcasting

Corporation (BBC) provide a consideration of change and process (Felix, 2000). During the 1990s the BBC went through a lengthy and bitter period of change, with the aim of providing greater accountability. The organization is now going through further change, in part as a response to change in the external environment, and in part in response to some of the negative cultural consequences of the earlier programme.

The earlier programme did change many of the processes within the organization, creating greater accountability in relation to the development of programmes and business units. However, the change programme was criticized for being prescriptive, relying too heavily on large numbers of expensive consultants, an overemphasis upon process, the creation of a culture that was driven by accounting rather than creative considerations and where 'management speak' created a cultural divide. Amongst the unintended consequences of the programme were key members of staff leaving, poor morale and commitment, high levels of stress, a fragmentation of the organization, inter-departmental warfare and criticism of the BBC for lowering its programme standards. It is possible to conclude that an overemphasis upon process contributed to this disappointing and highly controversial programme of change.

Pfeffer and Sutton provide a further example of the difficulties that can be experienced through an over-emphasis upon process in change:

A while ago we worked with the World Bank as it was trying to transform its culture. One of the problems the bank faced was a set of human resource policies and practices that clashed with the culture the bank thought it wanted and that it needed to implement to fulfil its evolving role in the world economy. So the bank embarked on an effort to change those practices. But what this particular change effort entailed, and this was true in many other instances of change in the bank, was preparing a white paper laying out options, providing rationales, talking about implementation plans, and providing supporting data. The white paper on human resources practices was then critiqued by senior officials and revised on the basis of those critiques. And the process continued – analysis, writing, critique and revision. There was great concern to produce an outstanding paper about human resource policies and practices, but much less concern with actually making changes. This sort of process came naturally in an environment of people with advanced degrees who had learned to write journal articles in precisely this way – write, get comments, revise, and produce yet another draft. But behaviour that may be useful for writing articles in scientific journals can be quite unproductive for organizations trying to change. In the time it took the people at the bank to analyze, document, propose, and revise descriptions of possible changes to management practices, they could have imple-mented many actual changes, learned what worked and what did not and why, and could have made revisions based on that experience numerous times.

(Pfeffer and Sutton, 1999)

Managing change and managing expectations

It is unrealistic to believe that change can always be modelled and executed with precision and 100 per cent involvement and enthusiasm from people because internal communication did a truly remarkable job. Change always hurts some people and the expectation that all carefully constructed communications are interpreted exactly as required by everybody is also wholly unrealistic. So what level of success might be considered realistic?

From the survey noted above in the quotation from *The Economist* (July 2000), we already know that the majority of change programmes fail to deliver the anticipated benefits. We can also assume that with the changing contract between employers and employees, some people move jobs more regularly. Simple mathematics and logic therefore suggest that more and more people are being exposed to unsuccessful change projects. Following from this we can conclude that the future potential success rates of change programmes will be diminished unless new approaches to change are developed and implemented, because people will become increasingly cynical about them and more resistant to them.

Also, it is unrealistic to believe that all the people in an organization think the same thing about the same things at the same time. There will always be people who will not wish to go in a direction that a corporate body desires to go in. In the Jaguar example above, those people left the company, and Jaguar is not alone in taking that perspective.

If people within an organization are placed upon a continuum that stretches from 'want to change proactively' to 'no way am I doing this', then a segmented approach to the workforce might be valuable as a consideration in managing change and communications.

The market research company MORI (Brown, 2001), for example, has a specialist unit carrying out research into HR issues, including related aspects of internal communications. The work carried out by the company includes research to identify the effectiveness and impact of internal communications, employee satisfaction surveys, the alignment of brand values and behaviour/attitudes and internal segmentation.

Internal segmentation can include identifying clusters of people in relation to their understanding of organizational priorities and their commitment to making a company's mission a success. These clusters can be identified by such terms as 'loose cannons', 'apathetic', 'disenchanted', 'fence sitters' and 'advocates'. Some of MORI's analysis has indicated that communication is a significant factor in explaining why people 'sit' in a particular cluster. Therefore an aim might be to move people from one group, up through a hierarchy towards being 'advocates', by developing specific communications for these different clusters. The following example, drawn from research by MORI regarding attitudes and behaviours and the workplace, provided the following segmentation based upon employee commitment and satisfaction:

▌ Apostles (35 per cent) – high levels of satisfaction and commitment, actively positive, employee role models with 80 per cent satisfied with communications.

▌ Hostages (38 per cent) – low satisfaction but high commitment, likely to have low productivity, only 40 per cent satisfied with communications. People in this group tended to be long-time servers with the organization working a 9–5 routine and having strong social networks, but resistant to change and 'hand-cuffed' to the organization for financial reasons.

▌ Mercenaries (17 per cent) – highly satisfied, but with low levels of commitment, difficult to retain in the organization, only 20 per cent satisfied with communications. People in this group are likely to leave the organization if offered a better remuneration package elsewhere and tend to be people who have worked for the company for a short time and in their first or second job.

▌ Saboteurs (10 per cent) – low satisfaction and loyalty, actively negative about values, employee terrorists, only 5 per cent satisfied with communications.

Even this brief overview of employee segments provides an indication of the difficulties that will be encountered if trying to influence behaviour through internal communication. If an organization applied similar considerations to the integration of communications and HR strategy to its workforce as are used in customer relationship management, it might develop targeted communications and policies aimed at people within these groups.

For saboteurs, the obvious route is to move them out of the organization. Mercenaries are difficult to retain and will probably leave of their own accord in a short time. Attempts at moving members of this group to the apostles group might be considered, given their high level of satisfaction with the company, by encouraging higher levels of commitment. Hostages might be approached from two perspectives, one to reduce 'deadwood' and another to redeploy them to new areas with strong performance targets to encourage higher levels of satisfaction and encourage some members of the group to become apostles. The apostles are the kinds of people the organization will almost certainly wish to retain, in part because they are key role models and communication channels.

This kind of internal segmentation analysis therefore has potential value in contributing to the development of internal communication activities. Managing communications and HR policies in response to an understanding of internal segments can assist in improving the likelihood of the successful implementation of a change programme.

Adopting this kind of approach to internal segmentation and research may not suit all organizations, in part because of the resources required to conduct the research. Jack Welch adopted a different and more easily defined approach to evaluating and segmenting employees during his time as CEO of GE. At GE, on an annual basis, all of GE's businesses ranked their executives in terms of the top 20 per cent, the 'vital' 70 per cent and the 'bottom' 10 per cent. Varying approaches to rewards, development and retention were applied to the top 90 per cent of executives, and the remaining 10 per cent were moved out of the company. Ford has taken a similar approach to that of GE, but with the following result:

> *The Ford Motor Company, for example, had a system which identified its lowest performers by grading them as Cs – 10 per cent of its 18,000 top managers were annually placed in this category. Two consecutive grade Cs were grounds for demotion or dismissal. In July 2001 the company changed this system after being sued by 150 managers who claimed the process was used to increase diversity by getting rid of older white male managers. The voluntary approach to redundancy avoids such risks and appears to have the least negative impact on morale.*

> (Abbey, 2002)

Understanding the key drivers of successful communication can also improve the likelihood of success, as with the Sears, Roebuck and Company case study in Chapter 3 on processes, standards and measures.

However, this kind of information may not be available when making decisions about internal communications and there may not be time to conduct extensive studies, such as when communication plans for mergers and acquisitions are being developed.

Mergers and acquisitions

The importance of communication during change resulting from mergers and acquisitions has been emphasized in a book written by Feldman and Spratt of PricewaterhouseCoopers (1999), *Five Frogs on a Log*. The book draws on the authors' experiences in helping organizations manage change and disruption resulting from mergers and acquisitions. (But note the final bullet point above from the article published in *The Economist*, July 2000, regarding the success or otherwise of change programmes and the use of consultants!) On the importance of internal communication, the authors state:

> *Securing stakeholder acceptance and support for the change is one of the most powerful ways to stabilize the company during the transition period. It helps to accelerate the transition and drive higher levels of performance.*
>
> *The recent PricewaterhouseCoopers survey of 124 mergers and acquisitions provides dramatic support for this conclusion. Companies that implemented an effective post-deal communications strategy shortly after announcing the change reported significantly better results in such areas as customer focus, employee commitment, clarity of company direction, speed of decision making, and productivity than did those that delayed implementation of a communications strategy for three months or more.*
>
> *The communication of change is not about announcements. It's about gaining support and capturing buy-in. Candid communication is a defensive perimeter and tactical edge – not just to transmit information or even to create awareness, but to build stakeholder acceptance, early support and full participation. It must be wielded like a weapon, a powerful tool for establishing leadership and direction and rallying the troops to the cause.*
>
> *(Feldman and Spratt, 1999, pp 69–71)*

The high road and the low road

Birkinshaw (1999) provides alternative considerations to those presented by Feldman and Spratt regarding the integration of companies following an acquisition or merger. Birkinshaw proposes two potential routes: the High Road and the Low Road. In very simple terms, the High Road represents an approach that places great emphasis upon human integration (generating satisfaction and a shared identity) with less emphasis on task integration (the transfer of capabilities and the sharing of resources). The Low Road represents an emphasis upon operational synergies through task integration with less consideration given to human integration. Regarding time frames, the Low Road would be typified as a speedy route to integration, whereas the High Road would take much longer.

Birkinshaw concludes that the High Road is the best route to be adopted when the acquired company is knowledge-intensive and where, as a result, it is important that knowledge workers continue to work to the best of their ability and not leave the company. Where an acquisition involves the acquisition of assets such as brands, products or market share, the Low Road may prove to be a better approach.

Individual communication

Achieving buy-in to a new vision or strategy will almost certainly involve not only the communication of a big picture to people so they can understand the direction a company is to take, but the chunking down from the vision (if developed) to strategy and on further to individual action. John Tiebout (2000, p9) writes: 'Once a general understanding of the new direction has been achieved, any effort to personalize that call to action is usually well spent. Our client partners who have been able to dialogue with employees to create a well-defined individual picture of the future, that is an understanding of "how I fit and what I can do to contribute to our success", seem to be able to attain the biggest results quickest'.

Feldman and Spratt take a similar view, but extend their considerations to a broader range of stakeholder communications, reinforcing the importance of integrating internal, interactive and external communications:

> *Successful communication of change begins by understanding that the questions following any announcement revolve around one central theme: 'How does this affect me?' All stakeholders, the people who influence and are influenced by the actions of your company – employees, customers, managers, investors, suppliers, and even the community at large – quickly begin to speculate about the implications for them.*
>
> *Employees ordinarily speculate about job security, income opportunity, personal influence, and career opportunity.*
>
> *(Feldman and Spratt, 1999, p 71)*

Research conducted by Gilgeous and Chambers (1999, pp 44–58) found that certain initiatives were particularly successful in assisting change management:

1. Allow people to voice their fears, and where possible act on their views as a route to helping people feel more comfortable about the change.

2. Provide feedback through appraisals. By making people more aware of their skills they are more likely to feel valued and believe that change will not radically alter their job, with the result that they are less likely to resist change.

3. Involve people in the process of determining what to change and how, as this cultivates support for the change programme.

4. Ensure that people see change as a part of their job.

5. Make predictions of the outcome of the change, and communicate outcomes in terms of their impact on individuals rather than the company as a whole.

6. Ensure that everyone affected by the change knows its Why? What? And How? Again, these questions should be responded to in terms of their direct impact on individuals.

In conclusion, Gilgeous and Chambers state: 'In general, then, the most successful actions are those that result in the *involvement* of the people being affected by the change and the *communication* of how the change affects those people throughout the process'(1999, p 57).

The following case study illustrates how one organization attempted to manage change and communications from the creation of a vision to individual understanding.

Focus Central London – focusing on cultural change

Focus Central London contracted with the UK government to manage the promotion, delivery and quality-assurance of a range of government-subsidized training and development programmes in central London. Focus was formed from the merging of two similar organizations. The organization was a quasi-governmental body, though its targets and budgets were largely provided through government. It was intended to operate as a private sector commercial business, and generate substantial surpluses which could be reinvested in central London training and enterprise.

Following the merger it became evident that the organization was failing to perform to required standards. Financial and management control had broken down and the organization was losing money. It was also failing to meet many of its contractual targets and was therefore at risk of losing its contract with the government. The culture of the organization following the merger was highly politicized and driven by conflicting fiefdoms. Morale was low and Focus was not being directed along a specific strategic route.

At monthly briefings by the first Chief Executive, three strategic options were presented for the future based upon differing assumptions of events occurring in the external environment. Internal communication consisted of a monthly Chief Executive briefing and a staff newsletter that included work and employee social-related inform-ation. The briefings were expanded on occasion by non-executive directors giving pep talks in a style of 'let's-all-pull-together and keep a stiff upper-lip'. These talks did not provide employees with guidance on specific strategies or a vision for the future. As management had provided no strategic objectives, key decisions were simply not made and the organization became paralysed.

Various initiatives had been instigated within the organization, including the achievement of quality standards and a greater customer focus, but progress was poor. An inability to achieve adequate performance in some core contractual targets and fundamental business processes resulted in the organization being classified by government as high risk. Consequently, Focus was audited on a frequent basis creating regular disruption for employees and conflicting priorities.

A newly appointed Chief Executive, Alan Calder, recognized the need to achieve rapid change within the organization. Calder had extensive experience of acquisitions, turnarounds and organizational start-ups in the private and public sectors. Prior to joining Focus, Calder met with Focus's executive team and senior managers to evaluate their competencies and identify their key issues. On his first day, Calder made radical changes to his executive team, which sent a clear message throughout the organization that things would not remain as they were. Calder met with his staff to tell them what steps he had already taken, what steps he intended to take in the immediate future and warned that change would be continuous while the organization re-established itself. Within days, Calder led his team in developing a new vision for Focus. Calder presented the new vision in face-to-face meetings with all employees, followed by question and answer sessions. All employees were given the option of meeting with Calder personally and with their heads of department if they wished to discuss any aspects of the vision and its implications further.

The vision identified the need to change the organization's perspective. This new perspective required a 180° rotation in the organization's customer focus. The enduring view in Focus had been that government was the organization's customer. The new vision was to see government as a primary stakeholder and provider of funds. Focus's role was to add value to government funding and policy by promoting and delivering high-quality, valued services to intermediaries, partners and end consumers: organizations and individuals.

Each employee was given a written document that described this change in perspective and why it was needed. However, the route to achieving the vision was not presented in specific terms. The point was made to all employees that they would be actively involved in realizing the vision and that certain actions had to be taken immediately to ensure survival of the organization. This meant the restoration of financial and management control, the achievement of contractual targets and the development of quality standards that would ensure Focus retained its contract with government. In addition, Focus had to be turned from a loss-making organization to one that earned an annually increasing surplus. Calder also stated that people's value to the organization would not be based upon attendance at their desk. Performance would be evaluated upon the achievement of objectives and people would be given greater freedom in identifying how they would achieve those objectives. Also, salary levels were to be set in line with those of the private sector to encourage people with a performance-based mindset to stay with or join the organization. Any pay increases would no longer be related to an annual, Focus-wide raise linked to inflation, but solely on individual performance.

To meet immediate 'survival needs', small teams were created with singular objectives relating to the organization's difficult predicament. Each team successfully delivered its objectives. Financial incentives were provided to encourage contributions by all employees to the work of some of these teams, including the presentation of business cases for adding value to customer relationships through database development.

Following the presentation of the new Focus vision, a competition was announced to all employees asking them to suggest a mission statement for the organization. A financial reward was offered to the winning employee. Not only was this less expensive than hiring an external consultant (and reducing unnecessary expenditure was one of the subliminal messages being communicated), it ensured there was a widespread understanding and buy-in to the vision and eventual mission statement. The mission statement was agreed as: 'Developing the skills and competitiveness of the central London workforce'. Ambient media including mouse mats and posters were used to achieve awareness of the mission, and the statement was printed on promotional materials and stationery. As a part of evaluation processes, employee questionnaires completed at Calder's presentations included a question that asked people to write down the company's mission statement. Reviewing the responses provided an evaluation of how many employees had learned the mission statement over periods of time. By comparing the 'real' mission statement with incorrect responses it was possible to gain insights into how the mission statement was being misinterpreted and the type of language being used by employees to describe their view of what Focus was about. Responses to this question provided valuable information regarding areas of the organization where additional communication activity was required.

In parallel with the creation of the mission statement, an internal communication strategy was developed. This involved a coordinated, monthly cascade briefing that started with the executive team and fed information and views both up and down the organization. Responsibility for internal communication was placed with the marketing team. Marketing also acted as an internal resource to other teams in the development and communication of procedures and other documents, including HR policies, celebrations and project updates.

Following research that identified employees' preferred communications media and channels, a range of activities was introduced, and the staff newsletter eliminated. A team briefing process was implemented to complement the cascades and personal presentations were given every two months to small groups of employees by Calder. The presentations were used as a way of providing updates on performance and indicators of activity that were anticipated over the following two months. Celebrations became a regular event within the organization as key objectives were met.

A communications audit identified the primary information needs of employees, and an intranet/knowledge management portal was rapidly developed to improve information access and customer service. Copies of presentations and all questions and answers were placed on the intranet along with responses to questionnaires following Calder's presentations, including any criticisms. Questions and answers resulting from briefings were also provided.

As teams worked towards meeting the 'survival' objectives, a further range of initiatives was developed. The executive team spent two days in presentations by practitioners on a range of subjects, including business process re-engineering and quality, knowledge management, the radical restructuring of business markets following changes in government policy, information technology and the working environment and information systems. Following these presentations, the executive team agreed the broad terms of a range of projects that were considered critical if Focus was to further improve its performance. Teams were created to develop specific strategies for the projects. These projects included changes to the working environment to improve working conditions, an upgrading of information systems and the introduction of hot-desking. As a route to reinforcing a self-employed mindset, customer-facing employees were given mobile telephones and laptop computers with remote access to the organization's database and intranet. New quality procedures were developed and integrated within the intranet to provide common processes across the organization.

The development of the organization's mission statement ensured the identification of activities within Focus that were not aligned with the mission. As appropriate, projects were closed or outsourced, allowing a greater concentration upon core activities, whilst also producing substantial cost savings. In addition, the nature of the organization's relationships with key partners was changed to bring alignment with the mission, with Focus taking on a more supportive role with stakeholders.

Through the business planning process, a small number of key performance indicators (KPIs) were identified for the organization. These indicators included the achievement of specific government targets, quality standards, improvements in customer satisfaction and aspects of financial performance. The KPIs were supported by a large number of subsidiary targets and milestones that were cascaded to departmental, team and individual levels. Performance bonuses for all employees were linked to the achievement of these KPIs. Employees could identify performance against targets through a 'traffic light' page placed on the intranet. A green light against a target indicated performance was on track, amber that performance had slipped against plan but was likely to be brought back on track, and red that performance was unlikely to meet plan. Performance feedback was also provided through appraisals, cascade briefings and team meetings.

Through these initiatives Focus achieved significant, rapid improvements in its financial position, stakeholder and employee satisfaction levels and became a leading performer in its sector. Whilst Focus did go through radical change, this 'change' was at no point communicated as a strategic change programme. The vision was presented to all employees, and they had the option to either buy into it or work elsewhere. As the various projects that created change were launched, the aims of these projects were communicated to employees. Where projects were of major significance, their progress was communicated through the intranet, cascaded briefings, team meetings and Chief Executive briefings. Where projects were of lesser prominence, updates on progress were provided through appropriate channels and media to retain a focus for messages on the key drivers of performance.

Communication was therefore focused initially on providing a vision of the organization's direction to employees. This high-level vision was meant to provide a perspective of a high-performing organization where working life would be better and those that did well would be rewarded accordingly. The creation of the Focus mission allowed communications to 'chunk down' a level and for people to begin to consider whether what they did was contributing to the organization's mission.

As team-based projects were initiated to deliver outcomes that were aligned to the vision and mission, the emphasis of internal communication then changed to communicating project progress against objectives. In this respect, communication 'chunked down' a further level to a focus upon performance and achievement. Celebrating and rewarding people for performance achievements reinforced the benefits of meeting stretching targets at team and individual levels. Therefore, activity and communications were focused on the core drivers of improved performance rather than the process of change. Even for lengthy projects, communications and project plans were built upon the regular achievement of tangible outcomes and benefits.

───

Short, sharp and cumulative are words that could be used to describe Calder's approach to step change in the Focus case study. Gestalt principles of psychology are based upon a simple statement: the whole is more than the sum of its parts. There is also a saying that goes: 'by the yard it's hard, by the inch it's a cinch'. These sayings also in part describe Calder's approach. He often commented that the best way to eat an elephant is bite by bite. Rather than providing a highly detailed vision of a colossal hill to climb, attention was placed on the achievement of objectives relating to a series of speedily introduced initiatives. All of these initiatives were a part of a change that contributed to the

180° shift in the organization's perspective and a rapid improvement in organizational performance. Had a plan been developed detailing exactly what the 'new Focus' would have looked like (assuming that was even possible at the time the vision was presented), then this would have undermined the vision. As with the case study of the World Bank in Chapter 4, the use of storytelling provided a vision that people could commonly accept at a high level. Had the Focus vision also been attached to strategy and processes, people would have been able to chunk down and think of reasons why the step change could not be undertaken. The extent of the change would have been resisted and heels dug into existing behaviours. The gradual chunking down from vision to mission to team and individual objectives provided a space for communication and behaviour to change, which reinforced the benefits of that change. Calder believed that people needed to identify their personal progress and rewards in the context of contributing to successful change.

A further consideration is that the time required to develop a concrete plan for change that extended way out into the future would have taken a huge amount of time and resource to develop. Such a plan would have been full of assumptions and delayed the implementation of the immediate action that was required to improve Focus's performance. A conclusion from this is that the sum of a series of related projects provided a whole that was greater than any potential attempt at delivering and implementing a highly detailed change plan. In part, the plan emerged as projects were driven forward, and learning took place from each initiative.

In Focus, change was achieved through a concentration on changing behaviour, not through a concentration on the process of change. The heat within Focus was progressively turned up. The heat was in part fuelled by leadership and rewards and by the creation of a culture that became increasingly focused on delivering project-based and corporate targets on a regular basis. Calder provides this comment on organizational change and communication: 'All organisational change is culture change. If you try and change what people do, without changing the context within which they do it, you will fail. If you change the context, the business culture, all else will follow. And changing business culture is fundamentally about communication and requires the effective deployment of the whole range of overt, formal, informal and subliminal communication tools'.

This quotation provides insights to Calder's approach to change. His approach to cultural change is underpinned by a clear understanding of business drivers. The relationship between business drivers and change is illustrated well in the following quotation from Dickhout (1997): 'Recently, I have found that looking carefully at three types of levers has sharpened my vision. First, take aim at the direct economic levers: driving down costs and increasing revenues. Then, understand how levers that focus the organization – structures, processes, targets – affect performance indirectly. Finally, examine the performance context: levers such as vision, values, and power base'.

By comparing the levers identified by Dickhout with the approach to change adopted at Focus, it is possible to identify the relevance of these drivers to creating cultural change. What Calder provides is a further level of information by highlighting the importance of cultural change and communication in 'leveraging the levers'.

Bounty of the mutiny

Arguably, change and change management are perceived by the majority of people as things that happen to or are done to people. It's as if change is a large wave that smashes through an organization, with some people left to drown whilst others get dragged from the sea by the captain and officers. If change is closely related in many people's minds to restructuring and redundancies rather than expanding organizational and individual capacity, then drowning will be the enduring image. But to end this section on a more positive note, change can be a proactive force for the better. Change can be an opportunity to swim, not sink.

Gary Hamel was referred to in Chapter 2 on corporate strategy with regard to his work in developing considerations of core competencies. Hamel also writes extensively on innovation and the importance of innovation to the creation of competitive advantage. In an article published in the *Harvard Business Review* (July–August 2000), Hamel describes how the drive and skills of a member of IBM's workforce created great change within the company, leading to the development of the company's e-business capability. A key point from the case is that a huge change in the direction and fortune of the company was driven from below rather than from the top of the company. Creating this kind of change requires not only personal drive, but also strong communication and persuasive skills.

Hamel provides a list of seven steps for organizing a 'corporate insurrection', with communication being a river that runs through the steps:

1. Establish a point of view – stand out from the crowd with a point of view that is credible, coherent, compelling and commercial.

2. Write a manifesto – provide a vision that captures people's imaginations.

3. Create a coalition – build a group of colleagues who share your vision and passion and who speak in a coordinated way and fight to win.

4. Pick your targets – identify and target potential senior management targets who will support your ideas.

5. Co-opt and neutralize – win over people with win-win propositions rather than trying to embarrass or confront adversaries.

6. Find a translator – find someone who can act as a bridge between yourself and people with power.

7. Win small, win early, win often – win small battles that show your ideas work as a route to winning the war and to build confidence in those around you.

THEORIES, MODELS AND PERSPECTIVES

Synopsis – best practice model

Synopsis, the internal communications consultancy, has developed a best practice model for internal communications. Synopsis integrates the model with a published benchmarking study of internal communications practice titled _Talking Business_ (Bloomfield, Walters and Quirke, 2000). The Synopsis model identifies seven areas for consideration in relation to the implementation of internal communications:

1. Strategy – identifying the attitudes and behaviours that are required from people to deliver business strategy, with the subsequent focusing of communications on supporting people in meeting those requirements.

2. Leadership – where leaders inspire their people through communication and behaviour, including building commitment to shared goals and the promotion of good communications practice within the organization.

3. Planning and prioritization – the forward planning of communications activities and messages, including providing people with a clear view of the big picture and linkages between different initiatives.

4. Channel management – the planning and coordination of communications to target audiences and messages, and to avoid information overload and message conflict. Channel management should also include feedback processes and the training of managers who are effective communicators.

5. The internal communications function – the role of the function should be to create value for the organization. To achieve this the function should be staffed by professionals, manage the quality of the internal communications process and be aligned with organizational needs.

6. Face-to-face communication – helping people to improve the value of face-to-face communication through a greater understanding of the meaning and relevance of information and its communication.

7. Impact measurement – setting standards for communications and measuring their effectiveness, including return on investment.

Clutterbuck – communication competencies

David Clutterbuck is Chairman of ITEM Group, a communications consultancy. Clutterbuck has written extensively on a broad range of communication and management issues, and is recognized as a leading authority on mentoring. In a presentation delivered in 2001 he stated communication competence is really about clarity of purpose, effective interfaces, effective information sharing and leadership communication, and not about what communications professionals do. Clutterbuck identified components to each of the four key competence areas:

Clarity of purpose

▌ The business has a clear purpose that is shared by all of its leaders.

▌ Employees understand the purpose of the business and their role in achieving it.

Effective interfaces
Trusting face-to-face relationships between:

▌ leaders and employees;

▌ managers and direct reports;

▌ employees within working teams and supply chains;

▌ the business and its customers.

Effective information sharing
When systems and networks enable managers and employees to:

▌ have the right information at the right time to do their job;

▌ share opinions and discuss ideas;

▌ circulate best practice and learn from each other.

Leader's communication

▌ where a leader's behaviour is consistent with what he or she is saying, formally and informally;

▌ leaders are role models of good communication.

Clutterbuck states that business success is increased as an organization builds its competence in each of the four areas. Therefore, internal communication activity should not be considered as a series of tactical activities, but placed in a strategic context. From Clutterbuck's approach it is also possible to identify close links between internal communication and knowledge management.

Thomson – emotional capital

Kevin Thomson was referred to earlier in this chapter. Thomson has written extensively on the subject of internal marketing and internal communication. Thomson's book *Emotional Capital* (1998) has a secondary line to its title: *Capturing hearts and minds to create lasting business success*. Emotional is a word that appears with great frequency in Thomson's writing and in the promotional materials for his company. His approach to internal communication is closely related to aspects of emotional intelligence, knowledge management, the Balanced Scorecard and the Service-Profit Chain (and particularly the early links in the chain relating to internal service quality, employee satisfaction and employee loyalty).

Thomson makes a distinction between emotional capital and intellectual capital, and believes that both must be managed to achieve business success. Emotional capital is segmented as being internal or external. External capital relates to brand value and goodwill, internal capital includes the feelings, beliefs and values held by people in a business, and may be expressed by employees in emotive words such as passion. Emotional capital is the main focus of Thomson's attention. His belief is that emotional capital will be of increasing importance to organizations in developing loyalty, customer satisfaction and improved performance and that, as a result, it must be invested in. In the preface to *Emotional Capital*, Thomson writes:

> *I believe the blueprint for building businesses in the future will go well beyond the focus on traditional assets into new territory using two critical and interrelated assets, knowledge **and** emotions.*
>
> *Information and knowledge management will be vital. Yet even more importantly, the blueprint for the future will manage feelings, beliefs, perceptions and values – the asset of emotional capital – as the hidden resources that matter most.*
>
> *Managing emotions will be the essential core competence for organizations of the future, achieved by treating the old 'employee' as the new internal customer; the old divisions and functions as the new 'internal markets' and by applying what we call internal marketing, or marketing from within. I see a future in which organizations take an integrated approach to managing markets and emotions in businesses and around their stakeholders.*

Whilst emotional considerations are given great emphasis, Thomson also stresses the importance of intellectual buy-in (knowledge and understanding of organizational goals) as well as emotional buy-in (commitment to apply knowledge and abilities in support of goals).

Organizations developing 'employer branding programmes', and particularly service-based organizations, may find Thomson's thinking of value when considering experience marketing and 'living the brand'. His approach involves the integration of internal and external marketing and communication, with the aim of providing a strong emotional appeal to employees and other stakeholders. The anticipated outcome of the approach is greater loyalty from customers and employees.

Nelson and Coxhead – effective internal communication and change

In a paper published in *Strategic Change* (1997) the authors explore the importance of internal communication in relation to business process re-engineering (BPR) and cultural change programmes. The authors state that internal communication is one of the most overlooked activities within strategic change programmes. With the high levels of failure in BPR and culture change programmes due to employee resistance, a key role for internal communication is to achieve 'buy-in' at the beginning of the project. The authors also identify many of the challenges for communication during change projects due to message overload, distortion, ambiguity and the management of communication channels. In conclusion, the authors provide the following list of critical factors for developing a model for effective internal communication:

1. The creation of a common language through 'facilitated' workshops. Developing a common language is viewed as important for helping people understand and change other people's mental models, or viewpoints.

2. The development of positive and consistent behaviours by top management and facilitators.

3. Commitment from top-level executives, as evidenced by the development of a 'vision for change', support for the workshop approach, listening and contributing throughout the workshops, and providing feedback to raised issues during workshops that could not be answered during those sessions.

4. Raising self-esteem of all employees through sharing processes (facilitated workshops).

5. The development of specialist internal communications personnel to manage the internal and external communications processes, namely:

    – existing organizational vision;

    – consistent and supportive structure and policies;

    – side-to-side communication as well as top-down and bottom-up.

The authors also identify the importance of managing these critical factors concurrently rather than sequentially.

Feldman and Spratt – gut-wrenching change

As referred to earlier, Feldman and Spratt of PricewaterhouseCoopers have provided their views of managing change. Their book *Five Frogs On A Log* (1999) includes considerations, or critical points, when managing change that is as a result of mergers and acquisitions. They name their approach as The Accelerated Transition®, and the basic principles of the approach are:

1. base the transition strategy on the economic value drivers;

2. aggressively manage communication in order to secure stakeholder support and acceptance;

3. launch small, fast-paced, short-term transition teams that will accelerate implementation of the value drivers;

4. align organizational roles and responsibilities to ensure clarity of direction;

5. build a behaviour-based culture around defining events dictated by the value drivers;

6. select and deploy role models who support the desired culture;

7. link incentives directly to the creation of shareholder value.

KEY LEARNING POINTS

1. Internal communication is a core business process that should measurably contribute to the achievement of corporate purpose.

2. The aim of internal communication is to influence culture and behaviours that are aligned with an organization's purpose, strategy and objectives.

3. Communication channels, messages, frequency and content must be managed to ensure clarity of communication and to avoid clutter and interference.

4. Internal communication is not purely concerned with the content and tone of written and spoken communications, but also with behaviour and leadership.

5. Internal communication is not solely a top-down process, but must involve bottom-up and lateral communication to enable and encourage information and knowledge sharing and commitment.

6. Meaningful organizational change cannot be achieved without the implementation of an effective internal communication strategy that should take into account the negative impact that can occur through an inappropriate framing of change and an excessive focus on process.

7. Internal, interactive and external communications must be integrated to ensure consistency of messages and their delivery to all stakeholder audiences.

SOURCES

Beer, M and Nohria, N (2000) Cracking The Code of Change, _Harvard Business Review_ (May–June), pp 133–41

Bloomfield, R, Walters, D and Quirke, W (2000) *Talking Business II – Using communication to connect people and strategy*, Synopsis, London

Chestney, R (2001) *Better Use of Technology to Become More Agile, Swifter and Responsive in the New Economy*, BT, Conference presentation, February, Next Generation Communication Strategies, IQPC, London

Dammann, A (2001) *Global and Virtual Communities – 'Global communication – simply everyone's job'*, Shell Chemicals, Conference presentation, February, Next Generation Communication Strategies, IQPC, London

Farrant, J (2000) *Internal Communications*, Hawksmere, London

Feldman, M and Spratt, M (1999) *Five Frogs on a Log*, John Wiley and Sons, Chichester

Greener, A (2000) *Internal Communications*, Blackhall Publishing

Quirke, W (2000) *Making The Connections*, Gower Publishing, Aldershot

Strebel, P (1996) Why Do Employees Resist Change?, *Harvard Business Review* (May-June), pp 86–92

Thomson, K (1998) *Emotional Capital*, Capstone Publishing, Oxford

Welch, J and Byrne, A (2001) *Jack: Straight from the gut*, Warner Books

Web sites

http://www.item.co.uk [accessed 24 September 2001]

http://www.quicksight.co.uk [accessed 16 November 2001]

http://www.synopsis-communication.com [accessed 24 September 2001]

http://www.widelearning.com [accessed 16 November 2001]

REFERENCES

Abbey, G (2002) Staff Morale Tops The Agenda, *Human Resources*, January, p 9

Birkinshaw, J (1999) Acquiring Intellect: Managing the integration of knowledge-intensive acquisitions, *Business Horizons* (May–June), pp 33–40

Brown, A (2001) *Getting the Best Value from your Communications Research*, MORI, Conference presentation, February, Next Generation Communication Strategies, IQPC, London

Clutterbuck, D (2001) *Does Communication Competence Contribute to Business Success?*, ITEM, Conference presentation, February, Next Generation Communication Strategies, IQPC, London

Dawson, M (2000) Embedding Core Values at Pfizer, *Internal Communication*, **57** (July/August), pp 11–12

Dickhout, R (1997) All I Ever Needed to Know About Change Management, *The McKinsey Quarterly*, **2**, pp 115–21

Farrant, J (2000) *Internal Communications*, p 43, Hawksmere, London

Feldman, M and Spratt, M (1999) *Five Frogs on a Log*, pp 36, 69–71, 186, John Wiley & Sons, Chichester

Felix, E (2000) *Strategic Change in the BBC*, BBC, Conference presentation, May, Innovative HR Structures & Strategies, Linkage International, Hampton Hill, Middlesex

Gilgeous, V and Chambers, S (1999) Initiatives for Managing Resistance to Change, *Journal of General Management*, **25** (Winter), pp 44–58

Greener, A (2000) *Internal Communications*, pp 173–74, Blackhall Publishing

Greenhill, T (2000) *Communicating Corporate Vision and Values*, Basten Greenhill Andrews, Conference Presentation, October, Communicating Corporate Vision & Values, Conference Partnership, London

Hamel, G (2000) Waking Up IBM, *Harvard Business Review* (July–August), pp 137–46

Lee, T (1999) [accessed 9 March 2000] *The Twelve Dimensions of Strategic Internal Communication* [Online] http://www.melcrum.com/communication/articles/02.htm

Nelson, T and Coxhead, H (1997) Increasing the Probability of Re-engineering/culture Change Success Through Effective Internal Communication, *Strategic Change*, **6**, pp 29–48

Pfeffer, J and Sutton, R (1999) Knowing 'What' to Do is Not Enough: Turning knowledge into action, *California Management Review*, **42** (Fall), pp 98–99

Quirke, W (2000) *Making The Connections*, pp x, 162, Gower Publishing, Aldershot

Reardon, K and Enis, B (1990) Establishing a Companywide Customer Orientation Through Persuasive Internal Marketing, *Management Communication Quarterly*, **3** (February), pp 376–87

The Economist, anonymous (2000) [accessed 4 May 2001] An Inside Job, July 13 [Online] http://www.economist.com

The Economist, anonymous (2001) The Worst Car Factory in the World, March 31, p 34

The Economist, anonymous (2001) While Welch Waited, May 19, pp 93–94

Thomson, K (1990) *Corporate Internal Marketing*, Pitman

Thomson, K (1998) *Emotional Capital*, Capstone Publishing, Oxford

Thomson, K (2001) *Charting a Course for the Future: Building brands and business performance*, Conference presentation, February, Next Generation Communication Strategies, IQPC, London

Tiebout, J (2000) Thoughts on Culture, Organizational Change and Communication, *Internal Communication*, **57** (July/August), pp 8–9

Williams, A, Dobson, P and Walters, M (1996) *Changing Culture – New organizational approaches*, IPD, London

Wood, P (1995) Corporate Identity and Internal Communication, *Profile*, November, p 6

6

HR strategy

AIMS

1. To identify the importance of HR strategy and people to the successful implementation of internal marketing strategy;

2. to emphasize the importance of integrating HR strategy with corporate strategy.

INTRODUCTION

The previous chapters have identified the pivotal role of the right people in the successful implementation of IMS. People, and more specifically, the ways in which people cooperate, communicate and behave, are fundamental to the outcomes of IMS. And that includes an organization's leaders. An organization's people strategy must be aligned with its purpose, strategy and objectives, and this alignment will only have some chance of success if it is driven from the top of an organization.

However, with the change in the 'psychological contract' between employer and employee, the nature of workplace expectations and relationships have changed fundamentally. Gone is the 'job for life', replaced by a mindset for many people that is about maximizing their quality of life and career, followed in third place by considerations of the welfare of an individual company.

Companies too have played their part in this changed relationship. Downsizing and any other term used to mask the word 'redundancy' must create a backlash. Trying to encourage employees to cooperate and deliver an organization's strategy is therefore one of the greatest challenges facing organizations. In many companies the strategy for meeting this challenge will be led by the HR team. HR people have a pretty tough time of things, and they need cooperation to deliver the kinds of benefits that so many people expect, yet frequently fail to see materialize. There is little point in introducing family-friendly policies, for example, if they are not implemented across an organization. HR strategy must be an integral part of business strategy formulation and implementation rather than an afterthought or add-on.

The fundamental changes in the relationship between employer and employee must also be placed in the context of structural change. Increasingly organizations must focus on the development of their intellectual capital, and therefore their people, as sources of revenue generation and competitive advantage. Recruiting, developing and retaining the right people who can work in teams to deliver constant change, innovation and performance improvements are amongst the current issues faced by HR specialists. This challenge is made all the more difficult for HR people by changing attitudes to work. Not surprisingly, a lot of people do not find burning up at their desk and dying early from stress-related health problems an attractive way of leading their lives. Considerations of a work-life balance and family-friendly policies are therefore amongst the workplace changes that are being included within some strategic HR approaches.

A report published by the Institute of Management, regarding the quality of working life, provides these insights to the changes in the workplace and their impact on people:

The responses of public sector managers and managers in PLCs share a number of similarities: for example, they are least likely to agree that their organisation's commitment to them has increased and more likely to indicate that they are now more likely to work for the highest bidder.

Responses to change over the last three years have been most negative in organisations employing over 500 people: managers in organisations employing over 500 people are more strongly of the opinion that their organisation's commitment to them has declined and that their commitment to their organisation has decreased. Generally, people in larger organisations are most likely to feel more inclined to change jobs to pursue their career.

(Worrall and Cooper, 1999, p 48)

The findings show clearly that managing the home and work balance is very problematic for many managers, but that the pattern of responses has changed over the three years of the study. For all managerial levels, more people are now likely to indicate that home and work are of equal importance and the percentage thinking that work is more important than the home has declined.

Our analysis reveals that managers are very conscious of the adverse effects that working long hours has on their relationships with their partners and children and on their social lives. Managers are also concerned that working long hours may also be affecting their health, morale and their productivity.

The very strong relationship between hours worked and the levels of adverse effects that managers admit to – particularly on home-based relationships – remains a major issue for concern.

(Worrall and Cooper, 1999, p 63)

Arguably, what organizations need are superstar HR professionals who create cultures, structures, policies and systems that enable a reconciliation of potentially opposing individual and corporate demands and expectations. In turn, these structures, policies and systems should seamlessly connect the internal, interactive and external marketplaces. As a simplistic, rational deduction of what many companies need, this is probably the case. But actually doing it is probably the greatest challenge of IMS. Meeting this challenge effectively will also impact upon other areas that have been discussed in previous chapters, such as knowledge management, service quality standards, internal communication and change.

The HR question mark

If people are at the core of IMS, then this places HR professionals in a position of great influence in relation to business performance – or at least theoretically. Unfortunately, question marks are frequently placed over the heads of some HR Heads. The question might be – can they deliver? And this is often accompanied by a further question – are they strategic?

It seems impossible to pick up a copy of an HR-related magazine in the United Kingdom at the time of writing without there being an article in which someone thumps the table regarding just how strategic HR is – or should be. An example of this kind of article was published in May 2001 in *Human Resources* magazine. The title of the article was 'My name is Lynne Weedall and I want to blow up HR' (Weedall, 2001). Weedall wrote the article as HR director of David Lloyd Leisure – one of the leading health and fitness club networks in the United Kingdom. Weedall is presumably from the military wing of the HR profession, and the article presents a case for blowing up HR and rebuilding it in a new form. Under the heading of 'The people brand', she writes:

> *It's remarkable how little HR has to do with getting the best from people. Too much time is spent formulating policies, watching legal issues, recruiting, training, devising pay structures and the like. We shouldn't be afraid to devolve this responsibility down the line and focus on being the conscience of the people brand and the values that support it. HR should treat people in the same way that marketing departments approach customers – researching, listening and responding accordingly. These findings should then be analysed and the lessons learned used to create a 'people brand template' for the business. It's basic: it's about defining employees – who you want and why. And in turn, why should they want you as their employer?*

Later in the article, under the heading of 'Planning strategy' the author continues with: 'The HR role should not be tagged on to the overall business plan but needs to be placed so that it can help the CEO to define the overall direction and strategy. Each board member should be accountable for their own elements – HR: people plan; marketing: customer plan; finance: growth and returns and so on. HR can draw all of the above together and help the board look into the future and plan strategy'.

Weedall may be right, but finding someone of the required calibre to act as an HR catalyst for IMS may prove difficult. If this is the kind of role that interests you, then the author suggests you will require these skills and abilities: courage; vision; grit; commercial nous; intuition and focus. Weedall appears to be supporting Michael Porter's view that: 'You have to make sure HR practices are absolutely wired into the strategy of your organisation. That's not going to happen unless you get very business-orientated. Think of yourself as a business manager, not an HR person' (Crabb, 2000).

As an indication of Weedall's strategic skills and abilities, in the *Human Resources* HR Excellence Awards 2001, David Lloyd Leisure won the 'Best Contribution to HR Business Strategy' Award. At David Lloyd Leisure, Weedall practices what she preaches, focusing on developing the right people, tools, processes and structures, as opposed to policy and administration, with HR operating as a collective responsibility within the organization.

But there remain people who believe there are not enough HR professionals who are prepared to blow up existing HR practices and deliver strategic change through people. A further issue for many HR professionals to overcome is the demonstration of measurable results from HR activities so the return on investment of HR expenditure can be identified. Measuring the effectiveness of their strategies will increase their influence within a business. One of the reasons that HR is considered by some to be soft and fluffy is because it has not been driven as hard as some other disciplines in developing metrics that provide exact measures of the return on investment of HR spend.

HR in the boxing ring

A review of literature relating to the strategic positioning and value of HR provides doubts regarding the ability of some HR practitioners and the HR function to deliver successfully service quality, change and competitive advantage through people.

The March 2000 issue of The Strategic Planning Society's magazine *Strategy* included a reference to a report by CSA Management Consultants. Keith Hughes of CSA stated that HR departments: '. . . are not maximising their potential value, may be over-staffed, and yet have no time to add strategic value to the bottom line. If the HR department wants to add real value to a company, and be a true strategic function, this should be passed out within the organisation'.

This provides a key issue in the development and implementation of internal marketing strategy. People are key to the delivery of service quality, yet many HR practitioners are viewed as non-strategic, insular and ineffective. This raises a question as to how an organization can recruit, develop and retain good people if the HR function is viewed as lacking credibility.

Hughes suggests the response should be the 'outsourcing' of HR activity within an organization. This appears to be the approach adopted at David Lloyd Leisure. However this approach was presumably made possible at David Lloyd Leisure through the implementation of a strong HR strategy that was developed by a highly competent HR professional, and integrated with corporate strategy.

A further example of how HR can be 'pushed out within the organization' occurred with the transformation of HR functions following the merger of Lloyds Bank and the Trustee Savings Bank (TSB) to form Lloyds TSB (Mitchinson, 2000). The change adopted by Lloyds TSB to create higher levels of service, flexibility and value at lower cost from its HR function included appointing an HR business partner to report to each line director. The role of the business partner was to identify HR-based solutions to business issues and to ensure HR services met business needs, whilst also providing strategic input to the business planning process. The change in the structure of the HR function was supported by the introduction of an HR helpline and other HR support services. Increasingly HR functions are improving their efficiency and effectiveness through the implementation of HR helplines and e-HR systems. In turn, this frees up resource to concentrate on strategic HR issues. IBM implemented common processes supported by a multi-lingual response call centre and Web site to achieve substantial improvements in its Europe, Middle East and Africa HR operations (James, 2000).

These examples show how HR can be integrated at a strategic level within a business, and the influence that can be achieved by HR professionals. However, this would not appear to be a common occurrence.

Williams, Dobson and Walters (1996) carried out a study of culture change programmes in 12 large organizations, including Abbey National, Jaguar Cars, Rank Xerox UK and Royal Mail. Williams *et al* identified a broad range of techniques used to change company culture, including: recruitment and selection; induction; training and development; communications; payment and rewards; appraisals; employer relations and terms and conditions of employment. However, the issue as to whether the HR function is capable of delivering cultural change was raised again: 'The personnel function is not generally in a position to initiate or lead such changes. Change must be strategically driven and must be supported by the full commitment of the Chief Executive or equivalent' (Williams *et al*, 1996).

Even academics send out similar messages. The Human Resources Planning Society's 1999 State of the Art/Practice study concludes:

*Cutting through the complexity, the general tone is one of urgency eman-
ating from the intersection of several underlying themes: the increasing
fierceness of competition, the rapid and unrelenting pace of change, the
imperatives of marketplace and thus organizational agility, and the
corresponding need to buck prevailing trends by attracting and, especially,
retaining and capturing the commitment of world-class talent. While it
all adds up to a golden opportunity for human resource functions, there
is a clear need to get on with it – to get better, faster, and smarter – or
run the risk of being left in the proverbial dust. Execute or be executed.*

(Wright, Dyer and Takla, 1999, p 2)

So HR is fundamental to the successful development and implementation of IMS, but some critics express doubts as to the ability of some
members of the profession to deliver an effective people strategy. A
part of this problem rests with the 'brand image' of HR. Clutterbuck
and Dearlove (1993) identified the need for HR as a discipline to rebrand
and reposition itself through a marketing-oriented approach: 'Today,
the HR profession in the UK stands at a crossroads. It can remain isol-
ated, elitist and inward-looking, or it can assimilate itself within client
organizations as a driving force for change. The latter will only happen,
however, if senior HR professionals are prepared to listen more closely
to their customers and learn from each other, from other staff departments and from best practice globally'.

Now, close to a decade on from 1993, many people still hold an image
in their minds of HR as a pink and fluffy discipline that is removed
from the frontline of strategic thinking and action. Not only that, but
they will probably call it personnel and think of it as the office where
people go because they like clucking around people and filing papers
rather than producing outcomes. There is no doubt that HR still suffers
from poor 'brand image' because the HR function in many organizations
is disengaged from business strategy. An article published in *The
Economist* (December, 2001) on the subject of outsourcing illustrates
that eight years on from Clutterbuck and Dearlove's comments, things
appear to have changed very little. The article began with this para-
graph: 'The human resources department is rarely a good place to
work if you are an ambitious young grafter. Mocked as the "human
refuse" department, it is corporate Siberia. Companies see it as gobbling
resources that do nothing to improve sales or profits. No wonder some
wish it would disappear'.

This image is not assisted by chief executives who state 'people are our most important asset' and do little or nothing to integrate HR best practice with corporate strategy.

But change is occurring in some organizations through a greater recognition that success is closely related to organizational capabilities that can be influenced through HR strategy. Similarly, there are many HR professionals who are having meaningful impact upon the strategies and performances of companies. If success is increasingly about leveraging knowledge, innovation, learning, team-working and speed to market, then HR potentially has a key role to play in enhancing corporate performance through cultural and behavioural change.

The state of play

The National Human Resources Directors Survey, 1999, published by Development Dimensions International and the Institute of Directors, explored some of the key issues faced by HR directors in 1,000 of the United Kingdom's leading organizations. The results from the survey indicated that the most critical people issues were around hiring the right people and retaining and motivating employees. Of the firms responding to the survey, 10 per cent calculated that staff turnover costs for them were in excess of £5 million pounds per year. However, 69 per cent of respondents did not measure the cost of staff turnover.

Perhaps surprisingly, the survey results showed HR directors would rehire less than 60 per cent of their current employees, suggesting inappropriate recruitment and development processes in many organizations.

The survey also provided information relating to some of the issues mentioned above. The greatest opportunities for HR over the next five years were identified as:

I HR's understanding of business issues;

I HR's relevance to core business goals;

I HR becoming more of an internal consulting role;

I rapidly changing training needs.

The two greatest weaknesses of HR were identified as a lack of business/strategic focus and image within the organization. Regarding effective methods for retaining employees in the longer term, the four most important factors in order of importance were identified as:

▌ the fit between organizational culture and individual motivation;

▌ management effectiveness: good coaching and feedback;

▌ the clear communication of an organization's goals;

▌ empowering employees by providing the freedom to make decisions.

This survey highlights the strategic issues that must be addressed by HR professionals as a part of the development and implementation of IMS. They go beyond considerations of business strategy to the positioning of HR as a discipline. Whilst the preceding paragraphs cast a shadow over the positioning of HR as a discipline, some HR professionals are using a broad range of tools to address key IMS issues.

The Sunday Times Top 50 Best Companies to Work For – 2001

In 2001 *The Sunday Times*, London, published a listing of the United Kingdom's 50 best companies to work for. The listing was compiled in cooperation with Moskowitz and Levering who generate a list of the top 100 companies to work for in the United States.

Benefits, how employees felt they were treated, their pride in their work and pride in their company were all compared in arriving at the final list of companies. The study also compared the performance of a share portfolio of the best UK companies to work for with that of the FTSE All-Share Index, starting with an index of 100 in 1996. In early 2001 the FTSE index was slightly below 200 versus approximately 550 for the 'portfolio of best companies'. By reviewing the policies of these 'best companies' some common themes can be found regarding the types of benefits provided for employees and approaches to encouraging workforce performance, including family-friendly policies:

▌ time out – extended periods for job-protected maternity leave and career breaks as well as bonuses for mothers returning to work, with bonuses related to length of service, an onsite nursery, paternity leave;

▌ flexible working – flexible work programmes including flexitime, part-time working, job-sharing, hot-desking, shift-swapping and working from home, with the provision of IT systems and equipment to enable this kind of flexibility;

▌ rewards – share options, bonuses related to corporate, team and individual performance, bonuses for successfully referring new employees, interest-free loans, six-monthly bonuses for perfect attendance, paid sabbaticals for working in the community, prize-winning suggestions for business improvements;

▌ development – training and development for advancement including online training and personal development programmes that may not be strictly related to job responsibilities;

▌ benefits – pension contributions from the employer, private healthcare, dental insurance, insurance for critical illnesses, increasing holiday entitlement linked to length of service, confidential employee assistance programmes;

▌ flexibility and fun – 'banking' holidays to accumulate extended leave, home Internet access and a free computer to use at home, a day off on birthdays, free onsite therapies including reflexology, massage and aromatherapy, health centre, hairdresser, dry cleaner, personal concierge service, delivery of groceries to the workplace during work time, free or subsidized restaurant, free drinks and fresh fruit, a 'fun budget' or frequent social events so people can meet socially, holiday cottages for rent at highly subsidized rates, the selection of benefits from a combined salary and benefits package;

▌ environment – clean, airy, light;

▌ culture – flexibility, 'buzz', flat and open structure, pleasant people, trust, frequent appraisals and feedback, friendly, people show respect, participation in decision-making, annual staff attitude survey.

Two organizations that were amongst the 'Top 50' in the United Kingdom were legal firm DLA and food retailer Pret a Manger. These organizations meet the needs of very different customers and face very different challenges in their business and HR strategies. The following cases provide background on how they have addressed external and internal challenges through the integration of HR strategy with business strategy.

DLA – professional, services, firm

DLA is a law firm that has adopted an aggressive approach to business development whilst simultaneously expanding its internal resources. DLA is provided as a case because the firm has adopted a broad range of activities including the development of its people, processes and systems (and therefore implemented an internal marketing strategy) as part of a strategy to achieve substantial growth. The firm has also won a large number of awards. Consequently DLA provides an example of an organization that has adopted good HR practices as a part of a dynamic business strategy, and where HR strategy has been integrated with the firm's business strategy.

For the year 2000–2001, DLA was listed as the United Kingdom's tenth largest law firm (by fee income, by *Legal Week* magazine), with income during this period of £175 million, an increase of 25 per cent over the prior year, with an increase in profits of 36 per cent. Comparative performing regional legal firms achieved an average profit growth of 13.2 per cent in the same period.

DLA has achieved its size in part through mergers and acquisitions whilst also expanding its overseas activities through the development of relationships with European and Asian firms. The firm anticipates introducing a single European brand in 2003.

In 1998 DLA announced its objective of becoming a 'top 10' firm in the United Kingdom, an objective it has achieved. In mid-2001 the firm announced it would become a 'top 5' full-service European law firm. The firm's track record suggests it may well achieve this objective. Though some ex-partners and commentators believe the firm may be setting an unrealistic objective. These doubts are in part based upon views that cultural divides exist within the firm resulting from previous mergers and acquisitions, where a homogenous culture has not been created, leading to conflict. In addition, the partnership structure of professional service firms, where differing reward structures are adopted across a firm, may be a further cause of difficulty.

However, despite these criticisms of the firm, it achieved sixteenth place in *The Sunday Times*' list of the Top 50 Best Companies To Work For – 2001. Of the 50 companies, three were law firms.

Change within the legal sector

The legal sector in the United Kingdom is going through great change, with a large number of firms driving domestic and overseas mergers and acquisitions to provide increased domestic and global market share. Change is also occurring within law firms. The partnership structure of these firms has traditionally created an 'us and them' type of culture, where a gulf existed between partners and employees of the firm. Firms have therefore been forced, through changing market conditions and intense levels of competition, to adopt, with varying levels of success, new approaches to the recruitment and retention of non-partners. For example, one law firm addressed the 'omnipotence' of partners and poor attitude towards employees by withdrawing support teams from partners who refused to work in an appropriate manner.

Law firms have also been forced to adopt, and again to varying degrees, modern business practices and processes. Within the United Kingdom, for example, it is only within the last decade that firms have been able to advertise. Change has also had an impact upon the roles of solicitors in firms. The introduction of e-based legal services provides clients with some legal services electronically and at a lower cost than traditional methods. This places pressure on solicitors to develop more value-adding activities for developing revenue.

The roles of solicitors have also been influenced by developments in information systems and the processing of large numbers of transactions, including personal injury and other insurance claims. DLA and other firms compete for large, price-sensitive contracts that involve the processing of a significant number of transactions. In these situations, a solicitor may be managing large numbers of people in what is similar to a call centre environment. To do this effectively, a solicitor will require the development of significant people management and other business skills that go beyond the technical skills of a legal specialist.

This provides an indication of the changes occurring within the legal sector, where market competitiveness and turbulence have been further increased through United States-based law firms opening offices in London, causing salary spirals and great challenges in the recruitment and retention of top talent. For example, a recruitment advertisement in the 31 August 2001 issue of *Gazette*, the journal of The Law Society, included an opportunity for a partner in a London firm with a salary of up to £750,000.

Building on competencies

DLA has developed a portfolio of businesses as well as its core business, building upon its competencies in specific areas of law and relationships outside the United Kingdom. The firm is clearly determined to develop revenue streams from new services, including 'non-directly-legal' activities. At the time of writing, DLA was in merger talks with an HR consulting group, with the aim of building further the firm's HR division. The potential benefits of the merger to DLA would be access to specialist skills in benchmarking and structuring executive pay, auditing and pay and grading systems.

From the firm's expertise in employment law, DLA created DLA Advance, a provider of training to managers and executives regarding employment and related aspects of business law. To stimulate new client acquisition and corporate positioning, the company runs conferences on such issues as Handling Cross Border Differences In Employment Law, for HR professionals facing differing national employment legislation within European Union countries.

Related to this area of operations, the firm offers a 'rapid response team' to help organizations facing regulatory investigation. This support goes beyond legal issues to media relations in an attempt to manage individual and corporate reputations. The firm emphasizes the importance of its knowledge of European Union regulatory bodies through its links to practices in Brussels, Paris and Barcelona. Building on this network and knowledge, DLA has also launched DLA Upstream, a public affairs practice that integrates the firm's knowledge of European Union public affairs and regulatory practice.

There are parallels between DLA Upstream and the London Communications Agency (LCA), referred to in Chapter 2 on corporate strategy. LCA was built from knowledge that was specific to the London political arena, and a recognition that changes to the political structure within London would provide new business opportunities. For DLA Upstream, the firm recognized opportunities provided by the changing political structure in Scotland resulting from devolution. The firm also viewed the US political environment, noting that in Washington, public affairs are normally driven by legal rather than PR-based organizations. The DLA takeover of a Scottish law firm provided the opportunity to offer a specialist public affairs service to clients.

The firm's knowledge of HR-related issues and strong process-related competencies also enabled the firm to win a UK government contract to run a national telephone advice centre, providing businesses with confidential advice on equality issues.

DLA is also expanding its operations by building upon skills and necessities that are fundamental to legal practices. Risk management is a critical aspect of legal work and the firm has recognized that enhancing its own positioning in this area could also lead to further business opportunities and benefits. In late 2000 DLA hired a highly experienced specialist in risk management who had previously set up the United Kingdom risk management departments at KPMG and Andersen Consulting (now Accenture). Following the development and implementation of internal processes for risk management, DLA will extend its range of services to its corporate clients to include risk management.

This emphasizes the importance of hiring the right people with the right knowledge in developing new business opportunities where these competencies do not exist within an organization. In addition, it is possible to assume that DLA will accrue further benefits from this appointment. A potential threat for law firms is the development of legal practices by accountancy firms, with the creation of multidisciplinary practices. By hiring someone with experience of a 'Big 5' accountancy firm, DLA again develops knowledge that will be of benefit to its future competitive strategy.

HR strategy

The managing partner at DLA described the firm's working environment as 'nurturing'. Based upon the policies adopted by the firm, it appears that its approach is to combine commercial acumen with a strong recognition that developing and supporting the right people is fundamental to the organization's success.

DLA claims to have invested £6 million in its HR department, with substantial expenditure on training (including e-learning) and mentoring to develop competencies that support its people in addressing key success factors that are foundations to its strategy. As a result of its HR strategy, the firm won the *Human Resources* Excellence Award for Best Learning and Development Strategy in 2001. The firm's strategy recognized the importance of attracting, retaining and supporting the right people.

Following a major merger that formed DLA in 1997, a new vision, values and strategy were created for the firm. Focus groups were used to involve the firm's people in the development of these elements, with people being one of the firm's core values: 'We bring the best out of our people by encouraging mutual respect, responsibility and teamwork; we invest in the reputations and careers of all our people'. A similarly cooperative approach was taken in the development of the firm's HR strategy, with the aim of being an employer of choice, whilst integrating HR strategy with the firm's business goals. The senior partners of the firm were all actively involved in the development and delivery of DLA's HR strategy.

DLA is perceived in the legal sector as a highly aggressive player, yet it has introduced 'nurturing' approaches to its internal market. For example, the firm reduced the working week from 37.5 to 35 hours per week without reducing salaries. The compensation system for partners was changed so that shares of profits are recalculated every year and related to the contribution each partner had made to the firm. For 2000–2001, average profits per equity partner were £395,000, which compared favourably with Eversheds, a similarly 'national networked' firm (£301,000), but unfavourably with 'Magic Circle' firms that do not have the associated costs of local offices, and where profits per partner are between two and three times those of DLA.

To help its people focus on their work and manage their time more effectively, the firm introduced a concierge service and telephone helpline. The service can help staff with a broad range of activities, including booking theatre tickets, finding builders and making sure someone is at home to let in repairers of domestic appliances. The firm is also involved in promoting firmwide events to raise money for charities and sponsoring art awards, with the purchase of art works to decorate the firm's offices.

Complementary strategies

With the importance of developing and managing processes and systems to its transaction-based business, DLA has also created internal processes and systems to support the delivery of service quality. This includes an extranet that provides clients with the opportunity to drill down into financial information relating to DLA's work. This system also provides for consistent processes across the firm. The *Insider's Guide to Legal Services – Employment 2000* awarded Client Service Law Firm of the Year to DLA's employment law practice, making this comment about the firm: 'DLA is a good choice among the national firms. It has a more structured approach to service than any of the others, and a vigour somewhat lacking in some of its major competitors' (http://www.dla.com [accessed 4 September 2001]). In addition, the firm has invested in other IT systems to improve efficiency including workflow and case management systems.

IT is an area of strength for DLA 'outside' the organization, with its IT practice awarded 'IT law firm of the year' in 2000 by *The Insider Guide to IT and Telecoms*. The firm's strength in the IT sector has enabled it to set up a further operation – dla.net – to specialize in legal work relating to companies in IT-related sectors. Again, DLA has aligned its knowledge across the internal and external marketplaces.

Pret A Manger – passion's fruit

Pret A Manger, or Pret, provides an example of how internal marketing strategy can be a key contributor to business success, whilst also demonstrating how placing people and HR strategy at the centre of that strategy can be a critical factor in that success. Unlike DLA, which is a knowledge-based, professional services firm, Pret serves thousands of customers each day with coffee, sandwiches and other food items. Operating in an increasingly competitive environment, levels of product and service quality are key success factors. Not surprisingly therefore, Pret has adopted very different approaches to its HR strategy relative to DLA.

Pret has become ubiquitous in London and other UK cities, and recently started to open shops in the United States. In central London it seems impossible to walk for more than two minutes without coming across a Pret outlet.

Passion is a word that is frequently used in Pret's communications. The Pret mission states: 'We are passionate about food. Pret creates handmade, natural food, avoiding the obscure chemicals, additives and preservatives common to so much of the 'prepared' and 'fast' food on the market today'.

Walking into a Pret shop provides tangible evidence of that passion and commitment. Statements identifying the company's mission, values and 'food facts' are on the shop windows, walls, merchandising units, napkins and packaging. The company's commitment to customer satisfaction includes postcards that can be handed to employees to provide comments and a telephone number that can be called if you have further comments or are dissatisfied.

Pret has created a very distinctive corporate identity, which is carried through rigorously in its shop design, packaging and product selections. It's modern, it's fast, it's clean, it's friendly, it's premium priced. The friendliness comes from Pret's employees, many of who are young people from outside of the United Kingdom and not permanent residents of the country. Julian Metcalfe, one of Pret's founders, illustrates the centrality of people to the organization's success: 'I believe that Pret is successful because of the passion of our people who want to come to work and enjoy what they do. If we pay attention to what our people think, then Pret will continue to flourish' (Adams, 2000).

Pret's consideration of its people also extends to its suppliers, and it uses its focus on the word passion to lever even further its communications to its customers. The packaging to one of its sandwiches includes this 'Passion Fact No 92':

> *Pret PassionPots are made by a wonderful man called Tim in converted farm buildings on the edge of the Fens in East Anglia. Tim was born and raised there with his five Friesians, Penelope, Primrose, Patricia, Prudence*

*and Poppy. He had one Jersey called Janet. He is still crazy about all things
to do with cows and milk. PassionPots are made from milk which comes
from welfare accredited Friesian herds. We don't use gelatine, stabilizers
or any other strange factory stuff. The vanilla is real, the cream is fresh.*

The level of integration of the components of Pret's IMS is such that it
appears senseless to ask the question: is it marketing or is it HR or is it
operations? The answer is that it doesn't matter. To paraphrase an ex-
president of the United Sates of America – 'It's the customer, stupid!'
The internal processes of an organization should be invisible to a
customer. What counts are the moments of truth when customer and
organization interact. Pret appears to have adopted Peter Drucker's
assertion that marketing is about the way in which customers see an
organization as a whole. So behind the froth, steel and stars of Pret,
what goes on?

Recruitment

Pret has adopted highly selective practices that focus upon recruiting people that can
deliver the brand experience through a strong service orientation. People involved in
the recruitment of shop-based employees have experience of working in Pret shops
and can provide honest answers to questions from potential employees.

If a person passes the early phases of the recruitment process, they are paid to
spend a day working in a shop carrying out a variety of duties. The shop team will be
responsible for training and communications during that day, and will decide whether
the person should become a part of the shop team. Team members will evaluate the
candidate's performance across a range of agreed competencies.

In a sector where staff turnover is traditionally very high (around 300 per cent),
Pret has achieved a significant improvement versus the industry norm at below 100
per cent, and aims to take it lower still.

Rewards

Pay at Pret is slightly ahead of the sector norm, with opportunities for people to earn
bonuses and prizes following Mystery Shopper reports, or through customers naming
individuals when reporting favourable customer service incidents. Employees praised
by name by customers (people in Pret shops wear name badges on their caps) are
awarded a silver star from Tiffany's of New York. A Mystery Shopper can present an
instant reward of £50 cash for service excellence, with over £60,000 in total allocated
to this type of bonus in 2000.

Monthly team rewards related to performance are also provided, with 12 top
teams given £25 a head for a night out. Individual incentives include subsidized drinks
at bars every Friday night and two massive parties every year. This level of social
activity is particularly attractive to young people arriving in an unknown city, and
provides instant access to a social network.

Cash prizes of up to £1,000 are given for submitting good ideas for improving the business, with reply-paid cards included in the employee magazine. The first line in the return address reads: 'Your Ideas Are Vital!'. Less formal rewards include the opportunity to win prizes such as cinema tickets through the employee magazine.

Pret has also introduced maternity packages that go beyond the purely financial to items that reflect the company's passion and flair. Benefits include flowers when the child is born, a voucher for one month of nursery care and a contribution to a new pair of jeans. Fathers are given a pager during the last two weeks of their partner's pregnancy and a week off on full pay at the time of the birth. Parents that adopt children are allowed four weeks off at full pay and are given £100 in Baby Gap vouchers for buying clothing.

Managers can achieve performance-related bonuses of up to 30 per cent. Viewing the activities of a Pret manager in action shows they are highly flexible, service-oriented people who support their staff. Managers can be seen filling up fridges with food and serving customers to keep the shops moving during busy periods.

Training and development

Each operations region has a dedicated training manager, who will assist with training requirements related to specific competencies as part of a defined career ladder. In the 2000 Staff Survey, 72 per cent of respondents stated they wanted a long-term career with Pret. To encourage mentoring within teams, rewards are provided for developing colleagues. People who are promoted can receive £250 to give to colleagues that have helped them with their move up the company ladder.

Communications

Communications within Pret are both formal and informal. Informal communications include daily team briefings, weekly management meetings and an open-door policy. Once a quarter, all head office staff work for a day as a team member in a shop, including the founders of the business. Formal direct communication includes a quarterly briefing for all managers and head office staff.

An annual staff survey is carried out, and the results are made available to everyone in the company. The survey leads to actionable activities in response to key issues highlighted through the survey.

An award-winning monthly magazine (*The Pret Star*) is targeted at people working in Pret shops. The magazine combines social and work-related information. The style is youth-oriented (the majority of people working in shops are aged 21–26), and recognizes that many of Pret's teams include young people from overseas. For example, articles on best deals for international telephone calls and Internet access.

To demonstrate the openness of the company, the magazine is not seen by people at Head Office before it is distributed to the shops, and letters critical of the company are published. Articles in *The Pret Star* include admissions of where processes or activities have failed to meet expected standards, providing a sense of honesty and openness to the publication and the organization.

To reinforce the company's values, top performing people and teams are celebrated in the magazine, but the strong social side of working for Pret is also given substantial coverage. Messages reinforce individual, team and corporate achievements, including monthly sales figures and comparative performance versus prior year.

To give people knowledge of the marketplace, the magazine has included an article on the service quality and products of competitors, based upon mystery shopping by Pret shop staff. Pret was placed tenth in *The Sunday Times* 50 Best Companies to Work For – 2001.

Re-engineering the work environment

HR also has a role in supporting change in new ways of working that are made available through technological advances. Performance and cost improvements can be achieved through remote working, hot-desking and other approaches. However, even greater change can be achieved through the redesigning and re-engineering of the working environment to support new ways of working that support cultural change, knowledge sharing and the demands of continuous improvements in individual and market performance.

For example, British Airways (BA) created a new headquarters near London's Heathrow Airport. The headquarters was designed in such a way that it included a bank, shops, restaurants, a hairdresser, dry cleaner and supermarket, with six buildings linked to a covered boulevard. Working areas within the building include open spaces where people can meet. As a result, the overall environment is like walking into a community space that includes dedicated office areas. The BA Waterside complex challenges traditional notions of the work environment and the separation of work and 'non-work' life.

The new headquarters represented a major change in the working environment at BA and the way in which work was carried out. Recognizing these important changes, the company went through two years of consulting with employees and testing new working methods before they were introduced. This consulting process is critical to the successful adoption of changes in work and environment design. A study published by the Work In America Institute (2000) in *Business 2.0*, showed that changes in work-life policies and organizational culture are unlikely to be successful unless employees are involved in the work redesign process. The study also concluded that changes in these policies must be rooted in business strategy and be consistent with corporate culture to avoid incongruity between new policies and culture.

'Employer branding'

The DLA and Pret cases illustrate that key challenges for employers include the hiring and retaining of the right people who will work together in effective teams. Currently, a popular response to these issues from HR specialists is to develop and implement (so called) 'employer branding' programmes. Branding is a word traditionally linked to marketing activities, and aspects of employer branding can be related to other marketing activities such as customer relationship management (CRM), communication and brand identity.

In the introductory section of this book, reference was made to the application of marketing principles to the internal marketplace through the segmentation of communications, as well as the creation of job 'products' that people would wish to consume. Employer branding is, at a basic level, the application of these marketing principles to the internal market. In an article by Bernard Stamler published in *The New York Times* in 2001, the author provided these comments on why companies are adopting employer branding:

> *Times are tough these days in the employment market. But it does not mean that companies are not hiring. Despite cutbacks and layoffs, many firms are still searching for top-rate talent. And to lure and keep these employees they are using advertising to find them – and not just plain old classified advertising.*
>
> *Instead, many companies are undertaking large-scale campaigns to identify their corporate culture and to impress it upon the minds of those who work – or might one day work – for them. Their efforts are aimed at creating a brand message for employees; not surprisingly, the phenomenon has come to be known among many as employer branding.*

Within the article Stamler refers to an internal branding project undertaken by Southwest Airlines. The airline's corporate brand message targeted at consumers is: 'A symbol of freedom'. From this, a linked internal brand message was created: 'Freedom begins with me'. This message is incorporated within communications to the airline's employees, including a freedom planner that provides details of employee rights, duties and benefits. In addition, the planner informs employees of their eight freedoms that include financial security, learning and growth and making a positive difference. These freedoms relate in turn to the impact individual employees can have on company culture and performance.

Employer branding is founded on the simple realization that people are critical to profitability, and that developing an environment in which good people are recruited, retained and encouraged to perform at their best is one route to improving business performance. The role of strategic HR is therefore largely concerned with the recruitment, development and retention of people that as individuals and as part of teams can contribute to the creation of competitive advantage. Meeting objectives related to this core activity involves the integration of activities with other departments, and will include considerations of training and development, organizational culture, communications, knowledge sharing, the work environment and delivering the brand experience.

If 70 per cent of perceptions of a brand result from interactions with an organization's people, then you might conclude that the role of HR is absolutely critical to business success. How many times have you decided not to buy from a company because of the poor attitude or service delivered by its people?

Being able to deliver high levels of service quality again and again is assisted through staff retention (or at least the retention of good people). The costs of employee churn are enormous, and if a good member of staff leaves for one of your competitors, how many of your clients might that person take with them?

HRM/CRM

If employer branding is in part about attracting and retaining people, then we can assume that a part of HR strategy must address issues resulting from the lifecycle of the relationship between employee and employer. Sales, IT and marketing people speak frequently about CRM or customer relationship management, where the aim is to provide an integrated approach (or experience) to individual customers across the organization. CRM is the current Holy Grail for many marketers. In an increasingly competitive environment, identifying and retaining your most profitable and potentially profitable customers is key to business growth and survival. It sounds easy, but it's very difficult to do. The majority of CRM projects do not deliver the benefits assumed at project inception and costs will frequently exceed budgeted levels, in part because they rely heavily on substantial IT investments, process change, and of course, people working together.

Many companies will find the same with employer branding programmes if they do not approach them with realism. A part of that realism is that brands are not built overnight or without the concentration of resources and aggression in a competitive environment. A further consideration involves considering exactly what it is that you wish to build through an employer branding programme, which is effectively about developing a particular type of culture that will in turn deliver success in the marketplace. This in turn impacts an organization's architecture, messages, policies, processes and systems. If the aim of CRM is 'marketing of one', then this implies developing HR-based approaches to retention and development that are similarly focused. This may also mean saying farewell to those that do not fit with the brand identity: you cannot be all things to all people all of the time. A part of the trick therefore is to focus on the areas where activity can have the greatest impact in relation to internal value drivers.

There are many figures that get quoted at seminars on CRM, such as: it costs five times as much to find a new customer as it does to retain an existing one. But whatever the economics of CRM might be for a particular organization, the basic assumption is that you need to identify and retain your most profitable customers to protect and leverage lifetime customer value. Typically, the Pareto rule is considered to apply: 80 per cent of revenue will be driven by 20 per cent of customers.

For HR people, they will often speak about HRM, or human resource management. If HRM stood for human relationship management, then this might provide a greater focus upon the kinds of issues that marketers and others try to manage through the principles of CRM, for the internal marketplace.

In a time where human and customer capital are key aspects of organizational value, HR professionals need to focus upon the strategic levers that develop the internal customers who produce and retain the greatest contributions to competitive advantage. Human relationship management (or employee relationship management [ERM], as it is normally referred to) is no easier to manage than customer relationship management. But fundamental to considerations of CRM are strategies and measures that are focused upon obtaining the greatest possible value from the target market.

Taking the lessons from CRM, HR specialists should not necessarily take as an overall goal the reduction of overall staff turnover, but instead focus retention on key areas of the business that generate the greatest impact on performance drivers, with differing strategies for different segments of employees. This in turn suggests the need for a segmented approach to retention, with different individuals and groups being offered packages that reflect the importance of those individuals and groups to the organization. This is not to say that recruiting the right people is not a priority. As with CRM, there is a constant need to prospect for and develop new customers of the right kind.

A key aspect of CRM is the development and maintenance of trust, flexibility and respect between a buyer and a seller, and the enhancement of the relationship by encouraging the buyer to contribute to the development of new, better products and services. For HRM similar issues exist regarding flexibility and profitability. We are at an early stage in the creation and evaluation of employer branding strategies. A key question is how far organizations will be prepared to go in creating flexible approaches to relationships with employees, and how this flexibility can be balanced with demand for short-term financial returns and fluctuations in the economic cycle. If employer branding programmes are amongst the strategies and budgets that are substantially reduced or eliminated when the stock market or revenue figures go into decline, then such programmes may be tarred with the familiar 'management fad' brush of so many other initiatives.

A further consideration for ERM or HRM is that creating a CRM structure requires the integration of activities across an organization and resource in terms of people and technology. Just as loyalty cards have failed to deliver the anticipated financial returns for many retailers, approaches to HRM/ERM will no doubt meet similar challenges of costs and benefits. Will employees wish to be 'marketed to' in the way that external marketing communications operate? Or will they become increasingly permissive in their purchasing behaviour?

Confusion marketing

Also of note in considering the challenges of employer branding and employee loyalty are criticisms of marketers. In the early part of this chapter the mirror was held up to the HR profession. Marketers are also finding that their image does not always reflect well on their profession. Both practitioners and academics have identified fundamental flaws in brand marketing resulting from marketing education and the career progression process that many brand marketers follow. With the drive to advance through brand hierarchies, some brand marketers are being criticized for taking a short-term view on brand values, preferring to take decisions that provide career progression, recognizing that they will not be in the job long enough to have to mop up any adverse impacts of their decisions. A similar approach for employer brands would lead to similar difficulties.

Marketers are also criticized for adopting 'confusion marketing'. Confusion marketing exists where marketers make decisions based on the comparison of similar products deliberately difficult for consumers. Is this the kind of behaviour that will generate loyalty with employees if adopted within organizations?

In considering the impact of confusion marketing within the financial services sector, Newman (2001) concludes:

One serious consequence of the practice of 'confusion' marketing has been a sharp decline in consumer trust. Trust in the service-reliability of banks fell from the already low proportion of 31 per cent to a quite unacceptable low of 26 per cent in the last year of the millennium. Yet, consumer trust is an essential component in a service which is largely intangible and which consumers already find difficult to understand or evaluate. For banks, above all, consumer trust is the foundation stone on which their income and profits ultimately repose. To jeopardize the traditional stability of their service reputation with this novel, fancy-footwork of confusion marketing may yet be seen for the short-term and misguided strategy which, I think, it is.

Consequently, the term 'employer branding' is a poor description of what most employers probably wish to achieve through their HR strategy. There may be aspects of branding that are appealing to HR professionals, such as providing 'consumers' with trust, quality, reliability, assurance, a promise, a dream – but just as marketing/branding are being forced to change in relation to social attitudes, then so must 'employer brands' if they are to be integrated with 'external brands'. The two must move in tandem, in fact, they must be the same thing. HR professionals developing 'employer branding' campaigns should ensure they do not create a 'virtual positioning' that fails to reflect corporate and brand strategy. Employer branding is really an inappropriate term for good HR practice. There should be no such thing as an employer brand, because it suggests a separation between the internal and external brand marketplaces. This is rather like the false separation that used to exist in the marketing services sector between 'above the line' and 'below the line' advertising. Eventually people realized that this false line was just that: false. What was really needed was an integrated approach to branding and communications to effectively meet client needs.

If organizations continue to express a separation between 'external' and 'internal' brands it might be an indication that the marketing and HR teams within those organizations have failed to erase another false line and been unable to deliver an integrated approach to the brand experience. Living the brand is not about a schizophrenic identity or dysfunctional marketing and HR teams. To return to Drucker, it is about how the entire organization is seen by the consumer. Or perhaps to clarify that further, how the consumer experiences that organization as a whole, whether that consumer be an employee, a supplier or an end purchaser, or any combination of the three.

Marketing mixed

A further consideration regarding the creation of an integrated approach to branding must be the evolution of branding in the external market-place and the potential resulting impact on HR strategy. Gone are the days when pushing new, one-size-fits-all, mass-market products and communications at consumers was a route to brand success. This is paralleled by an increasing cynicism regarding marketing activities and communications from consumers, and some marketers also. (Visit www.cluetrain.com and www.nologo.org for insights to the views of some non-traditional marketers.) Not surprisingly, consumers of all ages are displaying less loyalty to global brands.

Marketers have set running an ever-escalating game of cat-and-mouse with buyers and non-buyers of their products and services. This game gets more and more expensive and increasingly relies on gaining insights to human psychology and behaviour as marketers try to gain share of mind in increasingly cluttered, cynical and competitive market-places.

In over-crowded markets it becomes evermore important to attach emotional values to encourage target consumers to buy, with products increasingly promoted and purchased in relation to self-image and lifestyle rather than for what they actually do. As noted in the earlier chapter on strategy, social issues will increasingly impact the future of branding at product/service and corporate levels. These changes in the nature of branding have implications for IMS. People are not stupid, and blatant attempts to spin 'an employer brand' using the techniques that create cynicism in the external market may lead to similar levels of cynicism within an organization. If people are drawn through communications to try a product or service, and the experience does not meet their expectations, they may never buy again and ask for a refund. They will probably also tell their friends not to buy. Similarly, inappropriate communications will not encourage people to 'buy' in the first place.

In an article discussing the state of branding, Mitchell (2001) provides these comments on the challenges for branding in relation to the internal marketplace:

Word from the front line of those involved in change management and corporate rebranding is that brand overload has set in. Being told what your company's brand values are, and what sort of behaviours and attitudes are 'on brand' or 'off brand' is hardly new anymore. Initiative-weary employees are completely 'branded out', complains Lynn Hall, consultant director at identity consultants Enterprise IG. The B-word is almost off limits, agrees Hall's colleague Hans Arnold. No matter how enthusiastic a company's marketers may be, among engineers, account-ants and production line workers, the B-word is still associated with smoke and mirrors and flim-flam. The challenge now, says Hall, is to 'make people live and breathe the brand, without using the word "brand"'.

Arguably, the emotional aspects of HR strategy will become of increas-ing importance, as will the relationships between an organization's activities and social issues. As noted in the previous chapter on internal communications, Kevin Thomson of MCA has stressed the importance of emotional attachment to work and the workplace as a key driver to improving business performance.

A report published by the Industrial Society, London (Draper, 2000) identifies the importance of corporate social responsibility in relation to employee attitudes (based upon 255 responses to a questionnaire). The findings published in the study include:

▌ Eighty-two per cent of UK professionals would not work for an organization whose values they did not believe in.

▌ Fifty-nine per cent chose the company they work for because they believe in what it does and what it stands for.

▌ Ninety-nine per cent care if the organization they work for acts responsibly or not.

▌ Sixty-two per cent stated employees were likely to influence them to be more socially active.

Again, communications and HR strategy must be integrated to avoid significant clashes between the value structures of consumers and employees. For some organizations these values are being increasingly focused on corporate social responsibility. If those values become part of a core proposition to prospective employees, but are not demonstrated through corporate behaviour, then it is possible to imagine challenges for the retention of people who have 'bought the brand' as a result of the influence of an emotional attachment to those values on their decision-making.

The economics of retention

Marcus Evans, Chairman of the Carlson Marketing Group, a company specializing in relationship marketing, commented on research undertaken by the company over five years to identify customer reaction to loyalty programmes (Evans, 2001). For research published in 2001, 'good staff' was identified as the key factor influencing loyalty. Evans also stated that the real cost of replacing key staff as being at least 150 per cent of their salary, taking into account lost knowledge, training, recruitment, inconvenience and customer goodwill.

These kinds of real costs have been identified by some employers and have resulted in changes to HR strategy. For example, the Business Development Director of one of the United Kingdom's leading trade magazine publishers identified that the cost of losing a key member of staff was approximately £60,000, considering recruitment, induction and training costs and lost revenue. This person had also identified that staff churn was greatest after approximately one year of employment, with leading people leaving to work for competitors as the company was not providing employees with adequate career development. The response to this situation was to create a 'best practice' management development programme to encourage the best people to remain with the company for at least three further years.

To return to Marcus Evans, Evans is a strong believer in the importance of people in the delivery of a brand experience and, in turn, that customer relationship management should be practised with customers and staff:

> The reality is that we think of them as 'staff' when we should be thinking of them as 'customers'. They are the most frequent purchasers of our brand – they buy it every day when they decide to throw off their duvet, leap into the shower and turn up for work.
>
> We know we want our customers to feel recognised, valued, appreciated and trusting, so how must our people feel in order to deliver this? The same. We must invest the same effort in understanding and nurturing them to harmonise their needs with the needs of the business.

One of the tougher aspects of CRM is recognizing that not all customers are equal or profitable, and then developing differing strategies to manage relationships with these unprofitable customers. This might include changing terms and conditions of sale, or simply not supplying them with goods and services. Managing 'unprofitable' employees requires considerations in terms of action and communications, as identified in the previous chapter. Just as a dissatisfied external customer may tell 13 other people of his or her discontent, angry employees can communicate their dissatisfaction to others also, including other employees.

Headcount reductions are an early manifestation of an economic downturn, and trying to protect an employer's otherwise good reputation when redundancies are taking place may be an impossible short-term task. Similarly, trying to maintain the morale of those that remain provides further challenges. Some organizations attempt to reduce the blow of redundancy through outplacement support. Fortunately, there are organizations that have developed more creative ways of responding to difficult situations, and where positive relationships with ex-employees can be maintained.

Accenture has introduced a scheme that provides employees with 20 per cent of their salary and their other employment benefits if they take a 6–12-month sabbatical. This type of scheme provides the company with reduced costs during an economic downturn, with the assumption that during an economic revival it will be able to once again draw upon the skills of important and retained staff.

Some organizations have developed highly effective strategies for the management of employees they do not wish to retain. Many professional services firms have adopted 'up or out' approaches to retention where people who, following a number of years service, will not reach partner status are not retained by the firm. Management consulting firm McKinsey uses an approach to 'up or out' that serves both the organization and the employee. Exit strategies are managed to maintain a positive relationship by trying to place the outgoing employee in a senior position within a large (and probably client) organization. In this way the firm retains positive links with a growing number of large organizations, with those links expanding as people move to new jobs. The network of ex-McKinsey employees is therefore a growing group of individuals that have the potential to refer increasing amounts of business to McKinsey. An article published in *The Economist* (July 2001) provides this insight to the McKinsey network:

> *McKinsey's old-boy network is the envy of all. Its roll call of chief exec-*
> *utives includes Lou Gerstner, the boss of IBM; Harvey Golub of American*
> *Express; Lukas Muhlemann of Credit Suisse; Jeffrey Skilling of Enron;*
> *and Anton van Rossum of Fortis, to name but a few. It extends into*
> *other areas too: in Britain, for example, Howard Davies, the head of the*
> *FSA, the country's financial super-regulator, and Adair Turner, the*
> *former head of the Confederation of British Industry (CBI), both once*
> *worked for McKinsey.*

Developing new relationships with employees does not always occur as a result of 'unfortunate' circumstances. Toni&Guy, a fashionable network of hair stylists, took a very positive approach to the development of its relationships with some of its employees.

Toni&Guy

A 'glass ceiling' is often used as a term to indicate the restrictions placed upon the career advancement of women through sexual discrimination. But the term might be equally applied to certain professions where the opportunities for advancement 'dry up' for the majority of people, unless they are able to strike out on their own and start their own business.

One profession where this situation could occur is hair styling. Whilst there may be a hierarchy for hair cutters within a salon or organization, there comes a point where a high achiever's only future option is to start his or her own outlet.

Toni&Guy addressed this issue for some of its people when it implemented a growth strategy based upon opening franchised outlets in Europe. The opportunity to own a franchise was given to some of the organization's best people. To support the transition from employee to business owner, Toni&Guy developed support packages and infrastructure, including finance deals and training.

This strategy not only allowed Toni&Guy to expand rapidly, it also meant the investment it had made in its people was a source of further, ongoing advantage. Franchisees already knew the company's processes and culture and were amongst its top hair stylists.

Operating in a fashion sector and with a strong brand image to maintain, the company also developed and implemented extensive training programmes. To train people working in franchised outlets with knowledge of the 'latest cuts', stylists toured these shops, showing staff how to carry out the latest styles.

Training and development

Training and development has traditionally been a core area of HR activity. Whilst classroom-based training remains an important contributor to learning activity, increasingly, learning through doing and e-learning are taking a 'share' of the learning marketplace (though the approaches should not be seen as mutually exclusive).

Learning through doing recognizes the importance of people participating in activities as a route to learning. With the increasing need to implement emergent strategic approaches, it is through doing that learning occurs. This in turn builds knowledge.

The costs of face-to-face learning, including travelling and the opportunity costs of people being away from the workplace have contributed to the rising popularity of e-learning. For large organizations, e-learning programmes allow people to access common course materials at times that fit with their work and lifestyle. The value of the corporate e-learning sector is estimated by the consultancy IDC to rise from $1.7 billion in 1999 to $23 billion by 2004 (Murphy, 2001). Unilever is one of many organizations that is exploiting the benefits provided by developments in e-learning.

Unilever – Uni leverage

Unilever is an organization that has built a strong reputation for its approach to branding and marketing in general. Unilever's brand portfolio includes Signal toothpaste, Ragu sauces, Calvin Klein fragrances and Magnum ice cream. With the fundamental importance of marketing as a core competence of the company and the global nature of its operations, the organization set about improving the skills of its marketers on a global basis.

One of the learning points from the approach adopted by Unilever is that its strategy for training and development was driven by a marketing-based approach, re-enforcing a point made in Chapter 2 regarding decision-making in relation to an organization's core competencies. Training and development might traditionally be viewed as an area of responsibility for HR teams. The Unilever approach might therefore act as a shot across the bows of HR departments in organizations where professional competencies drive strategy, rather than 'delegating' training and development to an HR team. With the increasing adoption of e-learning within organizations, HR professionals will have to work hard to demonstrate how they can add value to training that is focused upon specific rather than general development skills.

In 1999 Unilever set up a Marketing Academy, with a group of highly experienced Unilever marketers from around the world driving the project (Miles, 2001). The Academy identifies good practice within and outside the company. This knowledge is then used for developing new ideas and as a part of the creation of learning strategies for marketers that are delivered through workshops, intranet and e-learning media.

Advantages delivered through the Academy include a lengthy induction for all marketers providing a global standard, and the ability to distribute new learning and best practice to people working at different levels within the company. As appropriate, learning materials and case studies can be changed to meet the needs of people working in particular countries. Local-orientation and support is provided through the development of department heads that are encouraged to coach their teams.

The approach adopted by the Academy also recognizes that learning is not something that is limited to classroom situations or standardized learning materials. Learning through doing is an important part of learning, and therefore people will work on real life issues as part of their training and development. The work of the Academy has been expanded to the delivery of training for the company's agencies, to communicate key aspects of corporate strategy.

Delivering the brand experience

A part of the responsibility of HR specialists is training people to deliver a brand experience to internal and external customers. With the growing importance of experience marketing, the need to train people to deliver the required experience increases. Disney, for example, goes to great lengths to recruit and train people to provide customers with the 'Disney experience' at locations such as Euro Disney and Disney World, as well as in their retail outlets. The Disney vision is 'To make people happy' and Disney is a world-class practitioner of experience marketing. The UK-based Tussaud's Group are also marketers of experiences through such attractions as Madame Tussaud's waxworks and Warwick Castle in England.

Warwick Castle

Warwick Castle is in the Top 10 of the most visited historic houses and monuments in the United Kingdom and one of the best performing units in the Tussaud's Group. The vision for people working at Warwick castle is: 'Bringing 1,000 years to life'.

Similarly to many other tourist attractions where interaction is a key aspect of the experience for tourists, Warwick Castle is interesting from an internal marketing perspective because the Castle is an 'experience'. Delivering that experience requires the seamless delivery of entertainment and knowledge to visitors. This means that people, processes and the physical environment (an historic location) must be brought together to repeatedly deliver a memorable experience for first-time and repeat visitors.

To encourage participation by visitors in the experience, specially recruited, trained, knowledgeable staff dressed in period costume mix with customers to provide information and encourage an extended stay. There are clear economic benefits in trying to retain customers within the Castle: the longer they stay, the greater the amount of money they are likely to spend.

Internal communication activities adopted by Warwick Castle are typical of many organizations and include a weekly newsletter, monthly departmental meetings and an annual address regarding prior year performance and future business plans. Staff inductions include a treasure hunt around the Castle to provide a feel for its history and culture. The induction is therefore in part an experience of an experience.

To gain a broad view of the roles and responsibilities of colleagues, people have the opportunity to go on job swaps and product knowledge tours when a new part of the Castle is developed. To understand issues faced by internal and external customers, senior managers work on a regular basis on the frontline.

Individual objectives are set, which are in turn related to team objectives that are in turn linked to external service quality standards, as monitored through visitor questionnaire responses and Mystery Shopping. Therefore, Warwick Castle links internal and external service quality, whilst emphasizing the core foundation of its proposition: the delivery of a memorable experience.

Conclusions

With the increasing complexity and challenges of branding and the need to repeatedly deliver high quality brand experiences, it is predictable that for service-based organizations or companies with a significant service element to their products, a gradual blurring will occur between the roles of HR and marketing professionals. As the current distinction between 'employer' and 'external' branding becomes viewed as yet another false line, so HR and marketing will be increasingly centred on the same issues: culture, communication, relationship management and measures of effectiveness.

Arguably there is a case for proposing that in these 'people centred' organizations, marketing and HR directors be replaced by a single 'brand experience' director whose responsibility is the delivery of the required brand experience. And will that brand experience director be from a marketing or HR background? The general lack of representation of these disciplines on the boards of many companies would suggest that a brand experience director is beyond the structural horizons of most companies. In the short term, both disciplines generally have to provide a greater accountability and stronger business case for their 'brand images' to be improved, and for their influences to be exerted credibly on general managers and accountants. The following quotations from Lannon (2001) and Stern (2002) identify the struggle faced by marketing and HR people in achieving influence upon the direction of companies. Whilst marketing and HR are perceived within many organizations as 'support functions', the opportunities for developing and implementing internal marketing strategies will be very limited:

I recall a survey many years ago examining national cultural differences in business practices. The analysis that took my eye was the amount of time that the boards of directors of large companies in different countries spent on three subjects: profits, products and people. Not surprisingly, the financially dominated British spent most time on profits and the engineering dominated Germans spent most time on products. The point the survey could have made (but didn't) was that nobody spent much time on people – either consumers or staff (unless as overheads to be cut, then this fell into the category of profits). A recent survey in The Director *showed that only a handful of CEOs of major UK companies come from marketing backgrounds, suggesting that the situation has probably not changed, and it's likely to be the same in other countries too.*

(Lannon, 2001)

According to research from the Cranfield Institute of Management, by the end of the 1990s there were 20 per cent fewer HR directors on company boards than there were at the start of the decade. Today only one in five FTSE-100 companies has an HR director on the board. (Human Resources' *own survey of the FTSE-100 as at 19 June 2001 put the figure at 18.) Bizarrely, this could be explained by the lack of priority some service companies have given to HR – the manufacturing companies they have displaced had better established HR structures.*

(Stern, 2002)

HR and marketing professionals might slog it out in political battles in an attempt to gain 'brand leadership', but this might be through an ignorance of the kinds of things these people should be anticipating every day: change. The annual conference for the Marketing Society, London, in 2002 includes a presentation regarding whether the future for marketing might increasingly look like the future of HR: outsourced.

If the future of marketing and HR for service-based organizations is not marketing or HR, but knowledge management techniques applied to stakeholder segments, then many marketing and HR professionals need to take account of this in their career development and act swiftly, gaining perspectives and experience outside of their functional disciplines.

Earlier in this chapter an article by Lynne Weedall was referred to. Weedall was suggesting that HR should be blown up and reassembled. Marketing as a discipline might benefit from the same approach. Traditional marketing theory is largely derived from the application of techniques and models in fast moving consumer goods markets. Many components of this theory are proving to be inappropriate, and potentially harmful, if applied in service-based organizations and markets. Just as Weedall has called for HR to be blown up in the hope that the reassembly of what falls to the ground might lead to a vastly improved discipline, there is a similar case for marketing theory and practice. If a simultaneous combustion of HR and marketing were to take place, then the reassembled pieces might lead to an integrated HR and marketing strategy that was focused on delivering a holistic experience of an organization to its stakeholders – something many organizations and functions are failing to do.

THEORIES, MODELS AND PERSPECTIVES

The PZB Gaps Model

In Chapter 3 on processes, service standards and measures, the importance of Gaps theory and in particular the PZB Gaps Model was identified. Within the four gaps of the PZB Model, Gap Three relates specifically to people, hence why it is often referred to as 'The People Gap'. This gap recognizes that people are core to service marketing.

Zeithaml and Bitner (2000) present the following HR strategies for closing Gap Three through an emphasis upon customer-oriented service delivery:

Hire the right people

▊ compete for the best people;

▊ hire for service competencies and service inclination;

▊ be the preferred employer.

Develop people to deliver service quality

▊ train for technical and interactive skills;

▊ empower employees;

▊ promote teamwork.

Provide needed support systems

▌ measure internal service quality;

▌ provide supportive technology and equipment;

▌ develop service-oriented internal processes.

Retain the best people

▌ include employees in the company's vision;

▌ treat employees as customers;

▌ measure and reward strong service performers.

A review of these strategies and their components identifies that HR professionals will need to work closely with other managers if they are to implement such approaches. For example, providing supportive technology and equipment would require the application of another identified approach: promoting teamwork through cooperation with IT and operations staff.

The Centre For Advanced Human Resource Studies (CAHIR)

CAHIR is based at Cornell University, Ithaca, New York. The Society's paper titled 'Execution: the critical "what's next?" in strategic human resource management' was published in November 1999 (Wright, Dyer and Takla, 1999). The paper looked three to five years ahead to identify some of the key issues that were anticipated to impact Human Resource Management. The conclusions in the paper were based upon global perspectives of HR professionals and academics. The key findings in the report identified several important issues for HR professionals:

▌ Globalization and increased competition in the external market-place, including the impacts of rapid technological advances, an increasing number of mergers and acquisitions and the general challenge of rapid and unrelenting change. The implication of this is that an organization and its people must be able to adapt to changing marketplaces through agility and the ability to develop and implement emergent rather than prescriptive strategies.

▌ Increased competition for talent due to a shortage of skilled employees, as well as the impact of companies no longer providing a 'job for life' and the consequent attitudes and behaviour of 'free agent' employees.

▌ The need to focus on effective management of people, supported by business processes (including the sharing of information and knowledge), IT and supportive leadership, with the aim of increasing organizational agility. Supportive leadership was identified as communicating corporate vision, setting broad strategic direction, championing an agile approach, instilling a sense of urgency, as well as coaching, mentoring and communicating to encourage a flexible, results-oriented approach from employees.

▌ The need to improve attracting, selecting and retaining talent.

▌ Aligning behaviour with goals, including employer branding and an in-depth understanding of an organization's critical success factors, the related personal attributes for employees, with the related communication of a culture that appeals to people possessing those attributes, including the ability to adapt to constant change and a competitive marketplace. Supporting employees through training and development and communication relating to the competition and encouraging empowerment.

▌ The need to wire the HR function into the business and demonstrate the value of the HR function with speed.

The report findings illustrate the need for HR professionals to be fully involved in strategic decision-making. The kinds of issues identified in the report could equally apply to senior marketers and leaders of other departments. This reinforces that responses to external drivers require action from within an organization through the strategic development and management of the organization's internal resources.

KEY LEARNING POINTS

1. For organizations that recognize their people are the source of current and future wealth, HR strategy should be integrated with business strategy to ensure that HR strategy is aligned with organizational purpose.

2. HR strategy should be focused upon creating a high-performance culture through recruiting, developing and retaining the people with the right skills, attitudes, competencies and communication abilities to work effectively in teams.

3. The changing nature of the relationship between employer and employee means that more flexible relationships between employer and employee are required for people to be attracted to work in organizations and to perform at their best.

4. In response to this change and shortages in skilled workers, some employers have created 'employer branding' programmes to attract and retain talent. These programmes are better described as good HR practice than 'employer branding'. Creating a separation between an external brand and an internal brand acts against delivering a consistent, integrated experience to customers.

5. HR as a function within many organizations has suffered from an image of being removed from strategic importance and measurable outcomes. Addressing these issues requires a business-like approach that clearly demonstrates the direct links between effective investments in human capital and business performance.

6. In some organizations, HR is performing a consulting role to support the needs of business units, teams and departments or being outsourced. This change is frequently enabled by electronic systems and new approaches to support and learning that provide greater efficiency and effectiveness versus traditional methods of delivery.

7. The involvement of employees in the development of new HR policies and working practices is more likely to pave the way for successful implementation than if an autocratic approach is taken.

SOURCES

Allen, S (2000) [accessed 4 September 2001] Baker and McKenzie Shades it to Take Employment Prize, The Law Society *Gazette*, 15 September [Online] http://www.lawgazette.co.uk

Allen, S (2001) [accessed 4 September 2001] DLA Named as IT Law Firm of the Year in New Guide, The Law Society *Gazette*, 28 July [Online] http://www.lawgazette.co.uk

Bartram, P (2000) Space: The final frontier, *The Director* (July), pp 30–34 IoD, London

Baxter, J (2001) Results 2001: A tale of two cities, *Legal Week*, 2 August, p 2

Budhwar, P (2000) A Reappraisal of HRM Models In Britain, *Journal of General Management*, **26** (Winter), pp 72–91

Cappelli, Peter (2000) A Market-driven Approach to Retaining Talent, *Harvard Business Review* (January–February), pp 103–11

Chambers, E, *et al* (1998) The War for Talent, *The McKinsey Quarterly*, **3**, pp 44–57

Clutterbuck, D (2000) [accessed 23 September 2001] *Time to Apply Customer Relationship Management to the Internal Market*, The ITEM Group, October [Online] http://www.item.co.uk

Crowe, R (2001) Sense and Responsibility, *Business Voice*, February, pp 30–36

Fitzgerald, N (2001) Life and Death in the World of Brands, *Market Leader*, **14** (Autumn), pp 17–22, The Marketing Society

Fleming, J (2001) [accessed 4 September 2001] Wragges, DLA and Simmons Among Top 50 Places to Work, Says Company Survey, The Law Society *Gazette*, 12 February [Online] http://www.lawgazette.co.uk

Gazette, anonymous (2001) [accessed 4 September 2001] Landlords have Time on their Side, 9 March [Online] http://www.lawgazette.co.uk

Gazette, anonymous (2001) [accessed 4 September 2001] DLA Talks Equality, 9 March [Online] http://www.lawgazette.co.uk

Golzen, G (2000) The Trouble with Letting Go, *The Director*, July, p 27, IoD, London

Harvey, J (2001) [accessed 4 September 2001] DLA Launches Staff Concierge Service, *Legal Week*, 5 July [Online] http://www.legalweek.net

Harvey, J (2001) [accessed 4 September 2001] DLA in Merger Bid with HR Firm, *Legal Week*, 9 August [Online] http://www.legalweek.net

Human Resources magazine, anonymous (2001) Human Resources Excellence Awards 2001

Legal Week, anonymous (2001) [accessed 4 September 2001] DLA to Reveal All in Transparency Move, 14 June [Online] http://www.legalweek.net

Lumley, J (2001) [accessed 4 September 2001] DLA Moves Upstream North of the Border, *Legal Week*, 31 May [Online] http://www.legalweek.net

MacCallum, V (2001) [accessed 4 September 2001] Firms Add to Perks, The Law Society *Gazette*, 8 June [Online] http://www.lawgazette.co.uk

Mitchell, S and Hayes, M (1999) Internal Marketing: The ultimate relationship?, *Journal of Targeting, Measurement and Analysis*, **7** (3), pp 245–60

Newman, K (2001) *The Sorcerer's Apprentice? Alchemy, seduction and confusion in modern marketing*, Marketing and Service Quality Research Centre, Middlesex University Business School

Salomone, W (2001) [accessed 4 September 2001] DLA To Be 'Top Five' In Europe, In Just Five Years, *Commercial Lawyer*, July [Online] http://www.chambersandpartners.com

Syrett, M (2000) Check Before you Balance, *People Management*, 9 November, p 61

The Economist, anonymous (2000) [accessed 14 August 2001] The Battle Of The Atlantic, 24 February [Online] http://www.economist.com

The Economist, anonymous (2001) An Alternative to Cocker Spaniels, 25 August, p 57

The Economist, anonymous (2001) Inside Out, 25 August, p 58

The Economist, anonymous (2001) The Case for Brands, 8 September, p 9

The Economist, anonymous (2001) Who's Wearing the Trousers?, 8 September, pp 27–29

The Sunday Times, anonymous (2001) 50 Best Companies to Work For – 2001, February

Thomson, K (1998) *Emotional Capital*, Capstone Publishing, Oxford

Towler, A (2001) [accessed 4 September 2001] DLA Tops Human League as £6m Investment Pays Off, The Law Society *Gazette*, 20 July [Online] http://www.lawgazette.co.uk

Tromans, R (2001) [accessed 4 September 2001] DLA Outlines Plans for Financial Integration with Alliance Members, *Legal Week*, 24 May [Online] http://www.legalweek.net

Zeithaml, V and Bitner, M J (2000) Services Marketing – Integrating customer focus across the firm, McGraw-Hill, p 295

Web sites

http://ww.dla.com [accessed 4 September 2001]
http://www.dla.net [accessed 4 September 2001]
http://www.indsoc.co.uk [accessed 7 August 2001]
http://www.unilever.com [accessed 7 September 2001]

REFERENCES

Adams, N (2000) Making the Company's Vision and Values 'Live' for its People, Pret a Manger, Conference presentation, October, Communicating Corporate Vision & Values, Conference Partnership, London

Business 2.0, anonymous (2001) Design for Work-life, February, p 39

Clutterbuck, D and Dearlove, D (1993) *Raising the Profile – Marketing the HR function*, IPD, London

Crabb, S (2000) Handy and Porter Rally the Faithful, *People Management*, 9 November, p 9

Draper, Stephanie (2000) *Corporate Nirvana: Is the future socially responsible?*, The Industrial Society, London

Evans, M (2001) The Best Brand Customers are your Employees, *Marketing*, 19 April, p 22

James, M (2000) Increasing The Contribution Of HR Through the Introduction of an HR Service Centre, IBM, Conference presentation, May, Innovative HR Structures & Strategies, Linkage International, Hampton Hill, Middlesex

Lannon, J (2001) The Compleat Marketer, *Market Leader*, **15** (Winter), p 5, The Marketing Society

Miles, L (2001) Passionate About Learning, *Marketing Business* (December–January), pp 24–26, The Chartered Institute of Marketing

Mitchell, A (2001) The Emperor's New Clothes – A backlash against branding?, *Market Leader*, **15** (winter), p 29, The Marketing Society

Mitchinson, N (2000) Innovating New Models and Structures to Transform the HR Function, Lloyds TSB, Conference presentation, May, Innovative HR Structures & Strategies, Linkage International, Hampton Hill, Middlesex

Murphy, D (2001) The Lure of e-learning, *Marketing Business*, *Professional Development* (September), p XIII, The Chartered Institute of Marketing

Newman, K (2001) *The Sorcerer's Apprentice? Alchemy, seduction and confusion in modern marketing*, p 19, Marketing and Service Quality Research Centre, Middlesex University Business School

Stamler, B (2001) [accessed 15 July 2001] Advertising: Developing brand loyalty among employees, *The New York Times*, July 5 [Online] http://www.nytimes.com/2001/07/05/business/05ADCO.html

Stern, S (2002) The Future of Visionary HR, *Human Resources,* January, p 27

Strategy (2000) The Strategic Planning Society, March, p 3

The Economist, anonymous (2001) Spoilt for Choice, 7 July, p 89

The Economist, anonymous (2001) Outsourcing – Out of the back room, 1 December, p 75

The National Human Resources Directors Survey (1999) Development Dimensions International/Institute of Directors

The Sunday Times, anonymous (2001) The 50 Best Companies to Work For – 2001, February, London

Weedall, L (2001) My Name is Lynne Weedall and I Want to Blow Up HR, *Human Resources*, May, pp 62–63

Williams, A, Dobson, P and Walters, M (1996) *Changing Culture – New organisational approaches*, IPD, London

Worrall, L and Cooper, C (1999) *The Quality of Working Life – 1999 survey of managers' changing experiences*, The Institute of Management, London, p48, 63

Wright, P, Dyer, L and Takla, M (1999) *Execution: The critical "what's next?" in strategic human resource management*, Center for Advanced Human Resource Studies, School of Industrial and Labor Relations, Cornell University

Zeithaml, V and Bitner, M J (2000) *Services Marketing – Integrating customer focus across the firm*, McGraw-Hill, p 295

7

Integrating internal, interactive and external marketing

AIMS

1. To illustrate the importance of integrating internal, interactive and external marketing;

2. to identify some of the issues associated with integrating internal, interactive and external communications.

INTRODUCTION

The key reason for integrating internal, interactive and external communications is to provide a platform for the delivery of a consistent, integrated brand image and experience to different stakeholders. This coordination enables the integration of the key components of internal marketing strategy, providing a link between high-level considerations of corporate vision and purpose, and individual action in support of business strategy.

This chapter is largely comprised of a single case study that is presented as a way of trying to bring together the various components of internal marketing that have been discussed in the previous chapters. In this chapter the processes adopted by a company as it developed its business and marketing strategies, including its internal marketing strategy, will be explored.

This case study draws heavily upon a real example, but aspects of the development of the company have been changed, including its name. For the purposes of this chapter, the company will be called LearnFlow. At the time of writing, no reference to a company of this name could be discovered through Internet searches. However, if such a company has been registered, it does not have any relationship with the contents of this chapter. But before exploring LearnFlow, a case study of a different organization is presented as an illustration of what can happen when external, interactive and internal marketing are not integrated. This organization is Benetton.

Benetton – the colour of money

Benetton has an international reputation as a retailer of clothing, particularly woollen products, through a global network of over 6,000 outlets (mostly franchised) in 120 countries. Its corporate reputation has been largely driven through its high profile external communications, which have been controversial, and for some people, deeply offensive.

By looking at the company's external communications and linking them to its strategy, operational processes and internal marketing, it is possible to identify how a global leader was significantly damaged by its communication strategy. Benetton provides an extreme case of how strategic decision-making, regarding communication strategy, that fails to integrate core aspects of internal, interactive and external marketing can have a negative impact on corporate reputation and performance.

Benetton has created a highly sophisticated value chain through a combination of innovative production processes, technology and communications. Colour is a key theme for Benetton. Production processes are so sophisticated that much of its materials are held in a single colour, and then dyed to meet changing fashion requirements. This provides the company with remarkable flexibility in meeting changes in fashion and differences in requirements for local markets, and in turn reduces its investment in inventory.

Colour is also a theme for the company's external communications. Benetton's advertising and communications have included a very simple strapline: United Colours of Benetton. This simple statement unifies the organization's promotion of a variety of social causes including racism, sexism, human rights, animal rights and the environment. This statement also relates to the importance of colour and fashion to its products and the diverse, global nature of its marketplace. The strapline also provides a very positive statement regarding internal policies on diversity and equal opportunities. Therefore, such a simple yet effective statement provides links between the organization's core competencies, communications, employee practices and target market.

The photographer Oliviero Toscani has masterminded Benetton's most well-known communications campaigns. Toscani held a strong and remarkable relationship with the company's founder, Luciano Benetton. Luciano Benetton allowed Toscani to develop the company's external communications without his interference, and in doing so delegated (or perhaps abdicated) responsibility for one of his company's greatest strengths: its brand reputation.

Toscani's images are highly memorable, and in viewing them chronologically they display a progression from images with a direct and obvious message related to Benetton's products, to images where the product is not shown, but where social messages come to the fore. These memorable images include nuns kissing, one horse mounting another, a black woman suckling a white child and prisoners from death row in jails in the United States. The images relate to issues including racism, discrimination, HIV, war and human rights.

Benetton's description of its communication campaigns is: 'International, homogenous, and characterized by universal themes, Benetton Group's advertising campaigns have been, since 1984, not only a means of communication but an expression of our time'.

The campaigns deliberately courted controversy and therefore media impact that went beyond the costs of posters and related promotional activities. These controversies undoubtedly alienated some potential customers, but created awareness and discussion amongst many others. In 1995 a court ordered the company to pay damages to French citizens infected with the HIV virus, as Benetton was considered to have exploited human suffering. Benetton had used an image of the naked buttocks of an AIDS carrier that were tattooed with the words 'HIV Positive'.

Benetton appears to enjoy this controversy. For example, a comment from one (presumed) customer is provided on the company's Web site (http://www.benetton. com [accessed 28 April 2001]) in response to an image of coupled black and white horses: '. . . ANIMAL PORNOGRAPHY!. . . What the hell are you thinking?. . . All I want is a shirt'.

In 1999 Benetton achieved a major coup in the United States, a country where it had experienced challenges in achieving meaningful market penetration. The company entered a contract with Sears, Roebuck that provided Benetton with distribution through all 400 Sears stores. Benetton's management in the United States were elated, but not for long.

In early 2000 Benetton launched an advertising campaign that showed images of 26 convicted murderers in jails in the United States. These people had been convicted of murdering a total of 45 victims. The public backlash against the campaign caused Sears to terminate its contract with Benetton. Benetton US Executive Vice President Carlo Tunioli provided a statement that gives a damning perspective on the relationship between marketing, communications and people in relation to Benetton's activities: '. . . the campaign has little to do with the morality of capital punishment. It's all about marketing', he explained. 'There's no correlation between these guys' he said, gesturing to 5-feet-high portraits of David Leroy Skaggs (two counts of first-degree murder) and Bobby Lee Harris (first-degree murder) 'and our sweaters. In terms of advertising strategy, what we are really doing is building brand awareness'. (http://www. prodeathpenalty.com/Benetton.htm [accessed 28 April 2001])

Sears was not prepared to have its corporate reputation damaged through its relationship with Benetton. A company spokesman stated: 'The advertising campaign was inconsistent with what Sears has come to stand for and is inconsistent with the customer base we serve. We have a high level of customer trust and loyalty, and there has been some strong emotional reaction to (Benetton's) campaign' (http://www.prodeathpenalty.com/Sears.htm [accessed 28 April 2001]).

Sadly, within Benetton's senior management there appeared to be a lack of understanding and integration of strategies regarding brand awareness and brand reputation. It is also worthwhile considering the impact of this campaign on Benetton's employees and Benetton's internal communications.

Luciano Benetton's reaction was to end his company's relationship with Toscani in April 2000. But ultimately, the impact of this decision must rest with Luciano Benetton through his strategy of non-interference with the campaigns developed by Toscani. Having invested in and developed such sophistication, it is remarkable that Benetton was prepared to risk the company's corporate reputation through such a strategy. Things would no doubt have been very different if they had stuck to their knitting.

Background to LearnFlow

LearnFlow is a business unit of a company that provides payroll and remuneration-related consulting services to large-sized organizations. The Group has relationships with HR departments in over 1,000 companies and public sector organizations, and has a core competence in the processing and management of data.

The Group board wished to leverage further its relationships with HR departments and develop revenue opportunities through the creation of new services. A team of people was seconded from within the Group to create the business strategy for what became LearnFlow.

The initial stage in the development of the LearnFlow business strategy was the commissioning of research that provided an overview of the HR services marketplace. The research identified areas of growth and decline, major users and players in each segment of the overall marketplace, and key market drivers by segment. The research also pointed to a potential gap in the marketplace that management decided to explore further. Technological change was predicted to create great turbulence in the market for the delivery of training and development to organizations. The traditional approach to training involved people travelling to a central location or attending a group session at a company's offices, where a trainer would deliver a training programme.

Research predicted rapid growth in e-learning, both in terms of content and management systems. Management systems provide managers with information regarding training undertaken, training plans, training outcomes, and so forth. The research also predicted a growth in the online delivery of learning over the Internet or via an intranet, and further into the future, via interactive TV and PDAs. It was anticipated that e-learning would account for 60 per cent of the training market by value by 2004. A further trend identified through research was the likelihood of rapid growth in the outsourcing of HR-related services.

The United States was the lead market for e-learning solutions and it was anticipated that leaders in this market would also dominate the United Kingdom and other European markets. LearnFlow would therefore need to act quickly to establish itself in the United Kingdom and achieve sustainable competitive advantage through its own e-learning technology.

The Group decided it wished to take advantage of the growth in e-learning, but recognized the market for training and development provision was largely polarized between online and offline training providers. It therefore aimed to integrate these two approaches to offer customized training solutions that would provide the optimum combination of both types of delivery. To support this combined approach, the Group acquired a company that had developed a new form of authoring software that facilitated the speedy creation of e-learning content, and at much lower cost than through traditional programming methods.

Learnflow also developed a diagnostic tool and business model that could be used to measure the return on investment of training and development activity at corporate, team and individual levels. By relating key performance measures to training and development activity, LearnFlow aimed to assist HR directors develop value-adding training and development strategies with measurable benefits that were linked to business strategy. One of these strategic options was the outsourcing of training and development activities to LearnFlow.

Proposition development

To return to the early stages in the development of LearnFlow, based upon the HR services market research, the Group board agreed that a small team of people from within the organization should develop and test a business proposition and strategy that was built around the key conclusions from the research. Qualitative research amongst a sample of the Group's customers showed that HR directors found the proposition of developing integrated training and development solutions linked to business strategy and improved performance to be very attractive. This research also identified that prospective clients wished for providers of training and development services to deliver savings in costs and time, whilst reassuring the client by demonstrating that training and development activities were quality-assured.

Quantitative research amongst potential customers identified what these HR directors valued most from HR consulting organizations, seen here in Table 7.1:

Table 7.1 *What customers value most from HR consulting organizations*

Average score for importance	Criteria
9.0	competence of staff (experts in their field, understanding of the customer's business, knowledgeable, informed)
8.8	meeting of objectives
8.4	quality of deliverables (process management, training, documentation, reports, presentations)
7.8	attitude of staff (customer-focused, helpful, friendly, 'can do' attitude, fun to work with)
7.7	ease of doing business (understanding the customer's organization and processes, getting in touch, knowing who to talk to)
7.5	responsiveness (responding to questions/queries, messages, problems, complaints)
7.4	meeting time scales
7.3	adding value (going beyond the brief, exceeding customer expectations)
7.0	value for money
6.8	flexibility (in meeting customer needs)
6.5	keeping you informed

Critical factors for success

Through the results of the research into the market for HR services and research with prospective customers, the following critical factors for success were identified in the overall marketplace for the delivery of training and development to businesses:

▮ an integrated approach to online and offline training delivery;

▮ speedy development of a brand name and brand position;

▮ provision of an end-to-end, one-stop solution through the integrated delivery of content, technology, services and tutor support;

▮ the ability to develop partnerships or joint ventures with suppliers of IT systems;

▮ training content must be developed and delivered with speed, and customized to corporate requirements, including branding.

Marketing

The management team at LearnFlow recognized that it would need to adopt a sector-based strategy for launching its services if it was to meet the key customer value of expertise and understanding of the client's business. This approach would also provide additional benefits through the creation of sector-specific benchmarking indices. Through a combination of secondary research analysis and further discussions with Group customers, four business sectors for initial targeting were identified. These decisions were then carried through to considerations regarding recruitment, team development and information system requirements. The management team also identified the core training and development portfolio it would anticipate delivering to clients in these sectors, and which providers it would wish to 'recruit' to operate under its own brand.

However, the company needed to fully test its services, processes and standards as a route to developing several reference sites that could be used to provide evidence of the quantitative benefits of its services. If the LearnFlow core proposition could not be delivered, the project would need to be stopped. It was decided that current Group customers within the four business sectors would be contacted in an attempt to recruit two sites within each sector for testing the LearnFlow proposition and services. These customers would be provided with preferential terms for LearnFlow's services, with the aim of achieving reference site status from each test site. To support the test site sales process, the Group became a 'guinea pig' for an initial testing of the LearnFlow approach, with results that supported the core proposition.

In the assumption that reference sites would be secured, marketing communications planning continued with the aim of generating brand awareness, positioning and lead generation with speed. The tactical activities to be adopted included PR, the sponsoring of research, sector-related advertising, events and shows, Internet-driven communication, seminars, case studies and direct marketing. Communications messages were developed in parallel with the creation of the corporate vision and supporting statements.

Targets were also identified for the development of relationships with suppliers of IT systems as well as providers of complementary consulting services, where a symbiotic relationship might be developed.

Structure

LearnFlow was to operate as a flexible organization, outsourcing its IT, HR and finance support services to Group companies. In this way, LearnFlow could concentrate on marketing, selling, delivering training, developing learning content and managing relationships with third party providers of training.

At its launch, LearnFlow had a chief executive (who also filled the role of Sales Director), a marketing director and an operations director. The senior management team was supported by a total of 100 sales, marketing, customer service and operations people, and a network of quality-assured, associate training providers who were managed through the operations team. The sales and operations teams operated largely in the field, but had remote access to the company's IT systems.

The longer-term aim of the company was to recruit its own dedicated trainers, but it would commence with associates who were trained to appear as if they were employees of LearnFlow.

Developing the vision

Prior to the launch of LearnFlow, the chief executive wished to involve all existing employees in the process of developing the company's vision, mission and values. All employees were invited to participate in half-day workshops involving groups of 10 people from different teams. The chief executive led the workshops, beginning with an explanation of why the workshops were being organized, an overview of the company's anticipated market positioning and the key results of market and prospective customer research. Participants were then invited to describe their vision of LearnFlow across eight components of the business environment:

1.   systems and procedures;

2.   management style/structure/communication;

3.   finances/business viability/performance and results;

4.   external relationships;

5.   internal relationships;

6.   house rules/norms/values;

7.   physical environment/infrastructure;

8.   individual development.

Each component of the business environment was taken in turn, with participants giving their ideas in respect of each component, either as single words or phrases. At the end of each workshop, comments and words relating to each component were noted, and this routine was repeated for each workshop. After the final workshop, all the comments were aggregated and the most common responses under each component identified.

   A review of comments provided in the workshops yielded a consistent set of core views and attitudes on the key components of the business environment. The following common views were presented in the workshops:

Systems and procedures

▌ customer-focused, non bureaucratic, flexible, simple to use;

▌ maximum automation;

▌ fit for purpose, robust and reliable;

▌ continuously reviewed and improved;

▌ must be understood by all.

Management style/structure/communications

▌ must reflect and champion company values;

▌ openness to risk, no blame;

▌ manage by results, not office attendance;

▌ encourage innovation and ideas;

▌ encourage team working;

▌ empowering with accountability;

▌ humour;

▌ two-way communication, build trust;

▌ entrepreneurial.

Finances/business viability/performance and results

▌ company must be profitable;

▌ finance team must be a part of the customer process;

▌ both corporate and individual bonuses must be in line with customer needs;

▌ share options for staff;

▌ everybody involved in team-level financial planning to achieve ownership and buy-in;

▌ need for access to updates on company performance;

▌ tight cost control.

External relationships

▌ always courteous;

▌ professional;

▌ always available for contact by customers;

▌ punctual;

▌ excellent service to customers;

▌ measure the value of our services to customers;

▌ concentrate on growing long-term relationships.

Internal relationships

▌ individual respect for all employees, regardless of role;

▌ supportive and positive, finding proactive ways of improving;

▌ always courteous;

▌ excellent communication between departments;

▌ social events to mix people from different teams;

▌ use voicemail and e-mail effectively.

House rules/norms/values

▌ dress code is smart, authoritative;

▌ we do what we commit to – individually and as teams;

▌ punctuality;

▌ trust.

Physical environment/infrastructure

▌ access to Web;

▌ enabled information systems 24/7;

▌ 24-hour support;

▌ the right kit – laptop, mobiles, PDAs, printer, scanner, etc;

▌ meeting space for teams and customers;

▌ comfortable temperature;

▌ hot-desking;

▌ tidy offices, clean desk policy;

▌ no food smells or eating at desks.

Individual development

▌ desire for success should be intrinsic;

▌ loyalty – commitment to the goals and values of the organization;

▌ recruit giants not pygmies whose values are in line with the company values;

▌ clarity about the skill sets and competencies of staff;

▌ encourage and develop healthy lifestyles.

The marketing director then took the outcomes of the workshops, and in combination with key aspects of the previously conducted market research, developed draft vision and supporting statements for Learn-Flow, which were as follows:

▌ *The LearnFlow vision* – 'To change the way organizations think about their people'.

▋ *The LearnFlow mission* – 'To become the European leader and authority in the benchmarking, design and delivery of integrated, measurable, business-oriented, training and development solutions for organizations'.

▋ *The LearnFlow values* – 'Our corporate values are: Insight, Innovation and Authority':

- Insight – 'We are insightful by gaining a thorough understanding of each client's business and its environment. Insight means providing new visions and solutions that are relevant, measurable, tailored and value-adding'.

- Innovation – 'To achieve and sustain market leadership we must create a sustainable competitive advantage. Through the continuous development and delivery of innovative solutions we will drive the marketplace'.

- Authority – 'Through innovation, insight and rigorous implementation we achieve authority. Leaders have authority and this is embedded in their communications and actions. People seek out leaders for insight and innovation'.

Positioning

Our Comprehensive Positioning Statement is: 'To knowledge-driven organizations with above average expenditure on training and development, LearnFlow is a pioneer brand delivering improvements in organizational performance through integrated online and offline solutions that link training and development to strategy and results.

LearnFlow clients will benefit from increased efficiency through measurable reductions in costs and savings in time, plus measurable improvements in organizational performance that are supported by the reassurance that training and development investment has been quality-assured.

The advertising and communications for Learnflow should emphasize cost and time saving and must mention Learnflow's expertise in the delivery of flexible, results-based, quality-assured training and development solutions linked to an organization's strategy'.

Our Concise Positioning Statement is: 'Measurably improving training and development linked to strategy and results'.

The LearnFlow brand personality

The key traits for describing the LearnFlow corporate personality are: Competitive; Value-adding; Technologically advanced; Nimble and Trustworthy.

LearnFlow's personality is:	*LearnFlow's personality is not*:
competitive	taking second place, giving up
value-adding	being the cheapest, cutting corners
technologically advanced	last year's model
nimble	glitzy, reactive, stumbling, shallow
trustworthy	indulgent, over-familiar

▌ Competitive – being competitive means being confident of our ability to deliver superior value and results versus our competitors. We must be constantly vigilant regarding our competitors. We can only achieve market leadership by taking from our competitors what they want for their own.

▌ Value-adding – we provide value for money at premium prices because of our core values of Innovation and Insight. Premium prices are charged by organizations that deliver superior value versus competitors.

▌ Technologically advanced – we will use advances in IT to improve our service quality and communications. We will not 'sell' technology itself to clients, as this is not the benefit sought by them.

▌ Nimble – speed of response and implementation are key to high performance in service quality. Customer expectations and a competitive marketplace demand we are fast in anticipating and responding to customer needs.

▌ Trustworthy – we will build long-term relationships with profitable clients by being better than our competitors. In doing this we will build trust and greater opportunity for the future.

The LearnFlow workplace

The LearnFlow brand values and personality are things we live in our relationships with colleagues, suppliers, partners and clients. As members of a team we will work together to deliver Insightful and

Innovative solutions to business issues. By respecting and showing consideration for each other we learn of our individual strengths and how these build great teams.

Through developing and sharing knowledge, and learning and development that is focused on delivering real value, we will hold Authority as individuals and as an organization.

The vision and supporting statements were discussed in workshops and agreement achieved on its elements. The key aspects of the document were then used for the development of a document titled 'The LearnFlow Experience' and for the development of LearnFlow's external communications materials.

The 'LearnFlow Experience'

From the research that had identified key customer values, service blueprints were developed that identified behaviour and communications for every moment of truth across each component of service quality. The blueprints were developed in parallel with process flows covering all aspects of lead generation, customer relationship management, service delivery and research. Research processes included customer satisfaction questionnaires to identify levels of service quality and to source information regarding competitor activity, market drivers, process improvements and referrals. Customer impact research was planned as a route to monitoring the quantifiable impact of LearnFlow's work with its clients. Further research processes included employee, customer, supplier and channel partner panels to gain information on LearnFlow performance, competitors and input to the development of new products and services.

The LearnFlow Experience therefore served as a document that provided guidelines to team structures and responsibilities, processes, standards, best practices, competitive positioning, service blueprints, behaviour (including dress codes, and tone of voice for communications). The guidelines were to be adopted by both employees and third party suppliers of training to provide a consistent brand experience. Input to the LearnFlow Experience included the results from the workshops where employees provided their views on how LearnFlow should operate in relation to aspects of the business environment. The LearnFlow Experience was also linked to the LearnFlow corporate visual identity. Templates were created for all forms of written communication, proposals and presentations. The templates were to be made available through an intranet. The corporate identity and supporting elements were created as an online induction tool for all suppliers, providers and employees.

Internal and interactive communications

A communication strategy was created recognizing that LearnFlow had to be perceived by its employees, suppliers and providers as a new company where a particular culture needed to be developed that was based on living the company's values and personality. The business environment workshops had provided a route for employees to contribute directly to creation of the 'culture framework', but it was necessary for all employees, providers and suppliers to behave in ways that represented the company's values, personality and positioning.

Workshops were planned for employees, providers and suppliers, with the aim of exploring 'The LearnFlow Experience' through role-playing how the company's values would influence behaviour and communications with customers and colleagues. All employees and suppliers participated in induction workshops and were required to 'sign-up' to 'The LearnFlow Experience'.

Following the launch of LearnFlow, the communication of company performance was to be carried out through chief executive briefings for publication on the intranet and extranet, and through quarterly events that would provide opportunities for networking and transferring information. These meetings were also to be used as opportunities for sharing best practice, reviewing LearnFlow performance, market and customer activities and brain storming new solutions to problems encountered. In addition, an annual employee, partner and supplier conference and awards were planned to enhance communication between teams, and to reinforce a key message regarding the need for teams to work together to provide value-adding solutions to clients.

All employees were required to make frequent visitors to customers' sites, to ensure that non-customer-facing employees had an understanding of client issues and the usage and impact of the company's products and services.

In addition to communications that were facilitated through the extranet to enhance communications with customers, suppliers and channel partners, quarterly advisory panel meetings were planned. These panel meetings were to be used for encouraging insights and comments regarding marketplace change and as a part of processes for improving service quality and new service development.

Systems

To support a workforce that was largely comprised of remote employees and suppliers, creating systems that would support communication and information transfer was of fundamental importance. To facilitate communication, an intranet was planned for employees and an extranet for training providers and other suppliers. Prior to the development of the intranet, in-depth interviews were held with key managers and members of the sales team to identify their information requirements. From this research, the structure of the intranet was created.

Intranet

The aim of the intranet was for it to act as a knowledge hub and search engine, linking CRM and project management systems, diaries for making sales appointments, quality and document management systems as well as other sources of business-critical information that could be accessed over the Internet through laptop computers and PDAs. The system was specified to provide access to information that could be segmented through the following areas:

Home page

▌ LearnFlow news items;

▌ system search.

Performance

▌ business plan and milestones;

▌ updates on corporate performance and bonuses;

▌ customer satisfaction measures and results;

▌ employee satisfaction measures and results;

▌ internal service quality measures and results;

▌ benchmarking results.

Internal communication

▌ organagram;

▌ team/department overviews;

▌ induction materials;

▌ employee calendars and contact information for making appointments;

▌ Chief Executive briefings and online discussions;

▌ job vacancies;

▌ calendar of employee social activities;

▌ details of pan-LearnFlow projects;

▌ employee chat room;

▌ links to Web sites to help organize work travel, etc;

▌ links to Web sites to help staff organize their domestic lives.

Competitors

▌ details of competitors and links to competitor Web sites;

▌ market overview;

▌ sector overviews.

Products and services

▌ calendar of events;

▌ product/service descriptors;

▌ sales presentations;

▌ FAQs;

▌ 'test drives' of products in development;

▌ LearnFlow training content;

▌ press releases and media coverage;

▌ case studies, promotional materials.

Quality system

▌ process documentation;

▌ employee suggestion scheme;

▌ document management;

▌ corporate library.

Extranet

Suppliers needed access to some of the information held on the Learn-Flow intranet, but for reasons of security, an extranet was specified for suppliers. The extranet was designed to provide critical information related to their activities, and feedback on their performance. The extranet was, in effect, a cut-down version of the intranet to support interactive communication.

A further extranet was specified for clients, to provide direct communication with client organizations and individual trainees, and to support the delivery of Web-based learning materials and management systems.

Internet

The corporate Web site was specified to include many of the areas within the intranet that related to external communications. In addition, diagnostic tools were identified to provide immediate feedback to prospects on how LearnFlow could bring benefits to the prospect's organization, and to act as lead generation tool.

Content and content design for the corporate Web site, extranet and intranet were all to be managed by the marketing department of

LearnFlow to provide consistency of messages across all media and channels. The marketing team was also to be responsible for monitoring usage of the systems.

Knowledge network

Combined, these systems served as an extensive marketing information system. In an attempt to avoid information overload, employees could set up procedures for 'pulling' particular information they required as it was updated. Training was also required to allow some employees to post specific types of information to the systems.

Overall, the system provided access to information that could be used by employees to drive the company in pursuit of its purpose, once LearnFlow had accumulated sufficient information to populate a large number of information depositories that were linked through the knowledge network. The vision for the knowledge network was that it would provide information that could be segmented as follows:

CRM database

▌ customer/prospect information;

▌ customer/prospect metrics;

▌ product/service metrics;

▌ marketing campaign measures;

▌ channel information/metrics;

▌ reference sites and case studies;

▌ customer communications;

▌ accounting data.

Employee panels

▌ customer analysis;

▌ sector analysis;

▌ environmental analysis;

▌ competitor analysis;

▌ new product/service input;

▌ debriefs from shows, events, etc.

Customer panels

▌ sector analysis;

▌ environmental analysis;

▌ competitor analysis;

▌ new product/service input;

▌ input to improving service delivery.

Employee suggestion scheme

▌ process improvements;

▌ new product/service input.

Internal service quality

▌ internal service quality questionnaire results;

▌ employee satisfaction questionnaire results;

▌ HR metrics;

▌ training and development records.

LearnFlow performance metrics

▌ corporate measures;

▌ team measures;

▌ individual measures.

Customer questionnaires

▮ experience of service quality;

▮ brand positioning mapping;

▮ repeat buying likelihood;

▮ referrals;

▮ competitors identified;

▮ qualitative input to improving service delivery and new product development.

Benchmarking and impact analysis

▮ customer analysis;

▮ sector analysis;

▮ segmentation analysis;

▮ country analysis;

▮ new product development input;

▮ sector-driven lead generation.

Environmental analysis

▮ competitor analysis;

▮ macro trend analysis;

▮ segmentation analysis;

▮ input to new product/service development;

▮ government procurement opportunities;

▮ communications/networking mappings;

▌ Web database searches, e-newsletters;

▌ printed publications.

Channel partner panels

▌ sector analysis;

▌ environmental analysis;

▌ competitor analysis;

▌ new product/service development input.

Market research

▌ prospect 'door opening' reports;

▌ sector analysis;

▌ segmentation, gap analysis;

▌ competitor analysis;

▌ macro forecasting;

▌ new product/service development input.

Customer complaints

▌ experience of service quality;

▌ recovery outcome;

▌ service improvement potential.

Supplier panels

▌ sector analysis;

▌ environmental analysis;

■ competitor analysis;

■ new product development input.

Document management system

■ archived documents.

Measures

Performance measures were developed at corporate, team and individual levels to support the objectives in the LearnFlow business plan. Targets were also related to the LearnFlow values and personality, by encouraging concentration on not just revenue growth, but customer satisfaction, relationship development, new service development, continuous improvement and teamworking. Bonus payments were related to the achievement of key corporate targets. Team and individual targets were in turn linked to the key corporate targets. The structure of performance measures was developed as follows.

Corporate level

Corporate level measures were linked directly to strategic targets and key measures of customer satisfaction, as identified through customer satisfaction and impact questionnaires:

■ average gross profit margin;

■ total revenue;

■ total revenue developed from new service introductions;

■ total savings from new process improvements;

■ average length of time between first contact and first sale;

■ average length of time taken between go-ahead to implement solution and actual implementation;

■ overall evaluation of satisfaction from customer satisfaction measurement questionnaires;

▌ overall evaluation of satisfaction from customer impact measurement questionnaires;

▌ percentage of customers completing customer satisfaction measurement questionnaires that would recommend LearnFlow;

▌ percentage of customers completing customer satisfaction measurement questionnaires that provide referrals;

▌ percentage of customers completing customer satisfaction measurement questionnaires that would purchase again;

▌ number of reference sites achieved as a percentage of new clients;

▌ number of defecting clients.

Team level

Team level targets were developed as follows:

Sector sales teams

▌ overall sales objective;

▌ overall sales objectives by product/service;

▌ sales objectives by customer;

▌ average margin per customer;

▌ success ratio for bids submitted;

▌ average share of overall training and development budget of clients;

▌ average length of relationships with customers;

▌ average length of relationships with channel partners;

▌ problems resolved on first contact.

Marketing

▮ ratio of leads generated of sufficiently high quality for conversion;

▮ volume and quality of PR coverage in relevant media;

▮ number of speaking engagements to target audiences;

▮ customer evaluation of communication materials and content;

▮ ROI on marketing budget;

▮ number of case studies achieved as a percentage of projects completed;

▮ problems resolved on first contact.

Operations

▮ delivery of services to agreed budgets;

▮ delivery of services to meet or exceed client objectives;

▮ satisfaction level for trainers used in the delivery of training;

▮ satisfaction level for training content and materials;

▮ meeting all health and safety requirements;

▮ problems solved on first contact.

For support functions that were outsourced to other companies within the Group, service level agreements were created, which included the following measures, where monthly monitoring took place:

HR

▮ staff retention rate;

▮ days lost through sickness;

▋ exit interviews completed with departing employees;

▋ average time for hiring gap;

▋ frequency of salary errors;

▋ frequency of employee contracting errors;

▋ staff evaluation of induction programme;

▋ ROI on training and development budget;

▋ number of tribunals;

▋ problems solved on first contact.

Finance

▋ frequency of billing errors;

▋ frequency of payment errors;

▋ timeliness of invoice payments;

▋ timeliness of expenses payments;

▋ timeliness of debt collection;

▋ value of any bad debts;

▋ problems resolved on first contact.

IT

▋ provision of network services and support 24/7;

▋ access to network by all staff;

▋ desktop strategy to meet communication and computing needs of all employees;

- provision of proven, technologically advanced systems for meeting internal and external customer satisfaction;

- problems solved on first contact.

Individual level

Individual level targets would be developed following discussion between managers and team members, and be consistent with corporate and team targets.

Internal service quality

Internal service quality and people satisfaction measures were linked through the development of two questionnaires: an internal service quality satisfaction questionnaire and a people satisfaction questionnaire.

People satisfaction questionnaire

This questionnaire was segmented to take into account the values and drivers of the business, as well as the views expressed during the employee workshops regarding components of the business environment. The questionnaire was to be completed by employees, suppliers and training providers.

Questions were developed across a range of areas, with people able to evaluate a number of statements and the relative importance of those statements. This provided information on perceptions of company performance and, over time, changes in evaluations of the perceived importance of the areas of the questionnaire.

Following the launch of LearnFlow, quarterly employee and provider focus groups were planned to develop an understanding of perceptions of the development of the company culture, and for appropriate action to be taken as required. Findings from the focus groups were to be supplemented by the completion of the people questionnaires on two occasions during the first year of operations. Areas of the questionnaire included:

Resources

▊ provision of and adequacy of systems and equipment in relation to meeting customer needs and delivering more efficient and effective solutions than competitors;

▊ comfort of the work environment and whether it conforms to company values;

▊ resource sharing.

Quality

▊ understanding of internal and external service standards that must be delivered;

▊ actual levels of internal and external service quality delivered;

▊ service orientation;

▊ robustness of procedures and systems;

▊ delivery of promises.

Corporate vision and values

▊ understanding of the vision, values, personality and strategy;

▊ communication of the vision and values;

▊ individual contribution to strategic planning;

▊ living the values.

Communications

▊ quality;

▊ clarity, timeliness and relevance;

▊ understanding of the marketplace;

■ understanding of customers;

■ understanding of competitors.

Rewards and performance

■ perceptions;

■ relationship between performance and rewards;

■ encouragement of teamworking;

■ relationship to meeting customer needs.

Training and development

■ quality;

■ feedback;

■ appraisals;

■ preparation for performing job role.

Continuous improvement

■ feedback from stakeholders;

■ contributions to new product/service development;

■ innovation.

Market positioning

■ evaluation of corporate values in relation to market position;

■ understanding of core positioning proposition;

■ understanding of job role in relation to the positioning proposition.

Trust

▌ relationships with colleagues, suppliers, partners and customers.

Management

▌ leadership;

▌ commitment;

▌ living the values.

Company culture

▌ evaluation of corporate values in relation to culture and recruitment;

▌ living the brand.

Internal service quality satisfaction questionnaire

To evaluate employee perceptions of the quality of services provided by other companies in the Group, an internal service quality questionnaire was developed for the evaluation of IT, finance and HR services. During the first year of operation, the questionnaire was to be completed every quarter by all employees. The results of the questionnaire were combined with other measures that were identified above as part of the team performance measures to evaluate the quality of services provided.

For this questionnaire, respondents were able to evaluate performance across 13 areas of questioning, as well as the perceived importance of each area of questioning. Space was also provided for respondents to identify the most important thing a supplier could do to improve its service, plus any further comments. The questions were related to the components of service quality as well as key LearnFlow values and drivers. Attributes evaluated through the questionnaire included:

▌ the overall quality of the service provided;

▌ the overall value of the service;

▌ overall satisfaction;

▌ accessibility;

▌ responsiveness;

▌ effectiveness of solutions provided to problems;

▌ delivery of solutions within the required time frame;

▌ level of courtesy provided;

▌ ability to work within a team towards a common goal;

▌ reliability;

▌ ability to deliver continuous improvements and keep up with changing technologies;

▌ ability to understand needs and provide value-adding solutions;

▌ trust.

HR policies to support internal and external service quality

The following key HR policies were adopted to support LearnFlow's purpose and values:

▌ candidates evaluated against a range of competencies that relate to key customer criteria, including expertise within their field, service orientation and drive to achieve required outcomes;

▌ psychometric testing of individuals included as a part of the recruitment process to gauge their 'fit' with the LearnFlow culture and business objectives;

▌ rewards related to performance, with corporate bonuses that are in turn related to key performance metrics, including service quality;

▌ stock options to be offered to staff to encourage retention of high performers;

▌ annual awards ceremony for high performers as part of an annual supplier and employee conference;

▌ clear paths for progression identified for high performers to encourage retention, with all new or vacant roles advertised within LearnFlow;

▌ quarterly focus groups to provide an indicator of the internal service climate and actionable information for improving internal and external service quality;

▌ quarterly 'fast appraisals' and annual 360° appraisals, including input from colleagues, customers and suppliers to provide a strong market orientation to appraisals;

▌ training and development geared to improving levels of customer satisfaction;

▌ induction procedures to assist employees in performing a full role in the organization with speed;

▌ encouragement of face-to-face communication at all levels to encourage direct, clear communication;

▌ encouragement of 'visible management' and 'living the brand' for all employees;

▌ the provision of support facilities to help people balance work and non-work lives;

▌ exit interviews conducted with all staff leaving LearnFlow.

LearnFlow – conclusions

As identified earlier, an aim of this chapter has been to illustrate how the components of internal marketing strategy were adopted within the planning for the launch of a new business. Underpinning the chapter has been an emphasis upon identifying how communication was co-ordinated. The vision and supporting statements (and particularly the comprehensive positioning statement) and The LearnFlow Experience all provided LearnFlow's employees, suppliers, partners and providers with a clear understanding of the values and drivers for the business.

The planning for the commencement of LearnFlow involved a great concentration upon issues relating to internal and external service quality. This was driven by the understanding that to rapidly increase market share in what was anticipated to be an increasingly competitive market, LearnFlow would need to recruit and retain customers, and that these customers would be critical to the future development of the business through referrals, reference sites and case studies.

The need to deliver high levels of service quality was directly related to customer needs, as identified through research. With the structure of LearnFlow being a combination of employees, third party suppliers and related companies, a critical success factor for LearnFlow would be its ability to provide a consistent identity and experience to its operations, regardless of who was representing the company with clients and channel partners. Therefore, integrating internal, interactive and external communications was about encouraging communication and behaviour that supported the LearnFlow positioning statement, values and personality, with the aim of providing a brand experience that was of a consistently high standard. This could only be achieved through people working in a team-based manner to meet customer needs.

The great deal of attention given to customer, supplier, provider, partner and employee satisfaction and service quality was to ensure the perceived LearnFlow experience was consistent with required service levels and customer expectations. The planning of communications and the knowledge network was to provide people with access to the information that would allow them to carry out their roles better through an understanding of key business drivers. Face-to-face contact was to be used for people to discuss and pass on information that was of value to sector teams and more broadly across the company, including suppliers and providers. As appropriate, this information would be formalized through the posting of information to the intranet and extranet.

Outsourcing the brand experience

In the example of LearnFlow, the company was in effect outsourcing parts of its service delivery through the use of third party training providers. With the growth of 'virtual organizations' it is increasingly common for companies to develop relationships with other organizations that are able to provide a part of the value chain, but under the brand of the 'hiring' company. For example, in the United Kingdom, Virgin provides a mobile telephone service. However, One 2 One provides the 'back end' of the service through its relationship with Virgin, but all communications are provided under the Virgin brand. As with LearnFlow, this presents key issues that must be addressed regarding the delivery of the brand experience of the 'hiring' company. For example, the low-price airline Go has outsourced its non-UK reservation and customer care calls to Sitel UK (Gray, 2000). To manage the 'call centre experience' Go provides training programmes for call centre staff. These people are also encouraged to fly with the airline through discounted and free flights, with the belief that experiencing the airline will provide them with a greater understanding of the airline and their role in the overall service provided. Ian McNuff, the managing director of Sitel UK states:

> *To underestimate the value and importance of how a brand is represented by a contact centre is to fail to recognize one of its core offerings.*
>
> *With a brand such as Go, for example, our people must reflect the style of a fun, cost-effective and reliable airline. In this instance, simple management of information between the call centre team and Go ensures that all the people are up to date on Go's internal issues and special offers. This enables them to offer the level of customer service that reflects Go's corporate values.*

With growth in the market for business process outsourcing and an increasing reliance on partnerships, issues surrounding training, development and communication in relation to a brand experience delivered by non-employees will be of increasing importance to companies.

THEORIES, MODELS AND PERSPECTIVES

Lynch – the Four Links Model

Lynch's model provides a link between internal and external environments and considers the importance of an organization's external relationships as a consideration in strategy development. This in turn has implications for the internal capabilities of an organization in exploiting and managing relationships.

The Four Links Model (Lynch, 2000) proposes four main elements relating to relationships that should be considered as a part of strategic analysis:

1. Informal cooperative links and networks – these occur where organizations are linked together for a mutual or common purpose without the relationship being formalized through a legally binding contract.

2. Formal cooperative links – examples of these links would include formal alliances, joint ventures and joint shareholdings in an organization, where a contractual link exists.

3. Complementors – where the products from a different organization add more value than would be derived from the product by itself. For example, whilst manufacturers of video machines produce a product with a level of value, consumers may perceive that a pre-recorded video of their favourite film provides a higher level of value, as this is what helps them to draw real value from the use of the video machine. A similar relationship may be perceived to exist regarding computer hardware and software.

4. Government links and networks – for manufacturers of products and services purchased by government agencies and departments, relationships with governments will be of critical importance.

An article by Richard Koch published in *Business Voice* (Koch, 2000) refers to the importance of relationships to organizations. Koch refers to a 1999 study by Coopers and Lybrand that showed that firms involved in alliances with other firms had 20 per cent higher growth rates than comparable firms without alliances.

The importance of relationships to an organization's value is further reinforced in this quotation from Jim Maxmim, Chairman of Global Brand Development: 'In the new world, it's not the assets that you own, it's the partnerships you have. Accenture (previously Arthur Andersen) forecasts that by 2003, 40 per cent of all evaluations will come from partnerships' (Thatcher, 2001).

Through the Four Links Model, Lynch brings to the fore the importance of relationships to corporate wealth, and from this it is possible to identify the importance of an organization's internal, interactive and external marketing (and their integration) to the exploitation of these relationships.

Wood – integrating internal and external communications

Wood (1995), proposed a model to integrate internal and external communications, whilst providing a direct link between vision and values and corporate or brand reputation. The model included considerations of vision and mission, values, competencies, identity, internal marketing, behaviour and customer experiences.

Wood stated that the components of the model must be in place before a corporate vision is realized as an enduring reputation. Also, Wood emphasizes the importance of not just communications, but other policies and activities that are required if values are to be translated into desired behaviour:

> . . . *leaders of that organization must not only communicate a set of values to guide behaviour within the organization, but must actually be seen to live by them. The required values must be communicated clearly and expressed in terms relevant to specific jobholders. Examples of success based on them must be communicated and rewarded. The performance management and promotion system must demonstrate that they really matter. Support mechanisms must be installed to assist everyone on the difficult journey of making them second nature: workshops, skills training, career development plans, customer service feedback and problem-solving teams.*

Wood's model makes plain the importance of integrating internal and external marketing in delivering customer experiences and creating corporate reputation (and therefore supports the underpinning to Gap 4 – The Communications Gap – in the PZB Gaps Model): 'This framework reinforces the need to ensure that the expectations created by external marketing and PR are supported by the reality that customers, suppliers, job-seekers and others experience when they come into contact with the organization'. The Wood model also identifies the central role of internal marketing in influencing behaviour and service standards.

Hatch and Schultz – organization studies

In a paper published in 1997, Hatch and Schultz provided their perspectives upon the implications of the breakdown between the internal and external boundaries of an organization. Their paper provides several important considerations regarding the linking of an organization's corporate (external) identity or image, and the (internal) identity or culture as experienced by employees. The paper not only contributes thoughts regarding HR-related aspects of behaviour and communications, but the importance of linking internal and external marketing through management vision and behaviour. The writers identify a number of points that are relevant to IMS, including:

▪ People who are 'insiders' (employees) can also be 'outsiders' (consumers, community member and/or a member of special interest groups). This can clearly lead to conflict. For example, an employee of an oil company may express critical views regarding the company's environmental practices if they conflict with the values of an environmental interest group where he or she is a member.

▪ It is important to provide a consistent approach to organizational identity that integrates an external perspective (visual identity/image) with an internal organizational perspective (culture and how people perceive, think and feel about the organization). This means that the way an organizational image is projected needs to be consistent with the way the organization is experienced by internal and external audiences.

Hatch and Schultz place corporate culture central to the effective alignment of organizational identity and image, framing this part of their argument as follows:

In general, we believe that the intertwined relations between culture, identity and image suggest the forming of a new interdisciplinary field of study combining organization theory, design and corporate identity, strategy and marketing in promoting understanding of the symbolic processes that flow around the organization and cross the boundary between the organization and the environment. Interdisciplinary study of the relationships between culture, identity and image will begin to challenge and work toward erasing these arbitrary and outworn distinctions.

Kunde – brand heaven

Jesper Kunde has also proposed a model that links internal, interactive and external marketing. Kunde's approach has been presented in his book *Corporate Religion* (1999), and this approach is adopted by the agency that takes Kunde's name, in relation to strategic marketing and advertising services.

Underpinning Kunde's approach is the belief that a company's culture, market position and mission must be integrated to provide a 'consistent corporate concept'. This concept requires research, development and communication so that employees, intermediaries and consumers receive a consistent and authentic message that encourages involvement and delivers value.

Kunde's approach is demonstrated in promotional materials through nine sequential steps where 'slides' 8 and 9 in the Kunde system include the following commentary: '8. Management takes charge and communicates the new message clearly so that everybody – from the factory floor, through dealers and in the external market – understands the direction in which the company wants to go. 9. Customers receive a consistent and authentic message'.

The pinnacle of all this activity is identified as 'brand heaven'. Kunde's concepts make perfect sense. His approach can be deconstructed through nine succinct visuals that provide a progressive distillation of the value of integrating internal, interactive and external marketing. The logic is undeniable, the potential benefits indisputable. But as with all things that relate to the implementation of IMS, the problem is in the doing. Nine visuals cannot fully describe the challenges of implementing change that has the aim of creating 'a consistent and clearly defined connection between product, vision, mission, profile, organization and communication'. This is not just the stuff of marketers or their agency suppliers. This is the stuff of entire organizations. And to repeat a point made at the beginning of this book, the tough stuff in organizations is with people. The preceding chapters in this book have attempted to draw attention to some of the issues that may stand in the way of achieving 'brand heaven', and how some of them might be addressed.

KEY LEARNING POINTS

1. Coordinating internal, interactive and external marketing brings together many of the key aspects of each of the components of IMS. Whilst the seven components of internal marketing have been viewed individually within this book, they are not mutually exclusive, but closely interrelated.

2. There are key themes that run through each of the components of IMS, including business strategy development and implementation, information and knowledge management, internal communication, service marketing theory and HR strategy. For service-oriented organizations, the effective coordination of internal, interactive and external marketing is a critical success factor in the delivery of the desired brand experience through the integration of the components of IMS.

3. As identified at the end of the earlier chapter on internal communications: internal, interactive and external communications must be integrated to ensure consistency of messages and their delivery to different stakeholder audiences.

4. Failing to integrate internal, interactive and external communication may lead to conflicting and confusing messages being communicated to differing audiences, which in turn may undermine attempts to deliver a particular brand experience to audiences.

5. The integration of internal, interactive and external marketing provides a relationship between high-level considerations of corporate vision, purpose and competencies, and individual behaviour that is linked to business strategy.

6. The integration of communications requires the development and communication of clearly defined standards and messages that can be translated into specific behaviours. These standards and behaviours should be related to customer needs and expectations.

7. Ongoing measures of behaviour and communication are required to ensure required levels of service quality are being provided to target audiences, and to generate action points for gap closure, where appropriate.

SOURCES

Clarke, R (1996) [accessed 28 April 2001] *Benetton's use of networks in its industry value-chain*, Xamax Consultancy Pty Limited [Online] http://www.anu.edu.au/people/Roger.Clarke/EC/Benetton.html

Kunde and Co (2001) Advertisement – What's your point? *Marketing*, 17 May

Zeithaml, V and Bitner, M J (2000) *Services Marketing – Integrating customer focus across the firm*, McGraw Hill

Web sites

http://www.benetton.com [accessed 28 April 2001]

http://www.corex.net/visitors/benetton.htm [accessed 28 April 2001]

http://www.kunde.co.uk [accessed 24 September 2001]

http://www.prodeathpenalty.com/Benetton.htm [accessed 28 April 2001]

http://www.prodeathpenalty.com/Sears.htm [accessed 28 April 2001]

REFERENCES

Gray, R (2000) Listen to the Brand, *Marketing Direct*, December, pp 37–38

Hatch, M and Schultz, M (1997) Relations Between Organizational Culture, Identity and Image, *European Journal of Marketing*, **31** (5/6), pp 356–65

Koch, R (2000) To Have and Have Not, *Business Voice* (October), pp 43–46, CBI

Kunde, J and Cunningham, B (1999) *Corporate Religion*, Financial Times, Prentice Hall

Lynch, R (2000) *Corporate Strategy*, p 132–36, Prentice Hall, Harlow

Thatcher, M (2001) Defining Strategy in a Digital Age, *Marketing Business*, (March), p 13, Chartered Institute of Marketing

Wood, P (1995) Corporate Identity and Internal Communication, *Profile*, November, pp 4–6

Index